"When reality is mixed with faith, it brings a true picture of the great love of God. Another word for faith is faithfulness. Fern Willner's life speaks of faithfulness to her God. This is a beautiful book. It mirrors the beauty of the life of Christ in Fern."

REV. ROBERT AND BRENDA SMITH
Senior Pastor of London Gospel Temple
London, Ontario

"In a day when people are unsure of what to trust, these stories of great faith in a great God will thrill your heart and encourage you in your journey of faith. Fern Willner is a living example of a godly woman whose life is directed to believing that 'nothing is impossible with God.'"

PASTOR ROY COWISON
Shallow Lake Community Church
Shallow Lake, Ontario

"This book has inspired, illuminated, and challenged me to expand my own beliefs. Fern Willner sheds fascinating light on the subject of faith with a depth of revelation that is Biblical, practical, workable, humorous, and God-honoring. There are a thousand sermons in this volume, and the Body of Christ will be richer."

MRS. ANNA MAE MCPHAIL
Associate Pastor, Chatham Christian Centre
Chatham, Ontario
Editor, "Canadian Mantle," I.A.O.G.I.(Canada)

"We found this book exciting and honestly written with a sense of humor. It encourages us to trust the Lord for the 'impossible.' We whole-heartedly recommend it. Thanks, Fern, for your obedience in writing this book."

DR. JAMES & GEISLA JONES
Retired Professor of Physics, Emeritus
University of Western Ontario
London, Ontario

When FAITH is enough

When FAiTH is enough

A SAFARI OF DESTINY THAT REVEALS PRINCIPLES TO LIVE BY

Fern C. Willner

BELIEVE BOOKS
Life Stories That Inspire
WASHINGTON, DC

WHEN FAITH IS ENOUGH
By Fern C. Willner

All Scripture quotations, unless otherwise indicated, are from the *King James Version* of the Bible.

Author's note: "Thou Hast Enough to Pay thy Fare," which appears in Chapter 3, and "Beloved Should the Brook Run Dry," which appears in Chapter 6, were taken from *Gold Cord* by Amy Carmichael (published by the Christian Literature Crusade, Fort Washington. PA. USA, © 1932. Used by permission). "The devil may wall you round" by Annie Johnson Flint, which appears in Chapter 19, and "Is Thy God Able?" M.E.B., which appears in Chapter 37, were taken from *Springs in the Valley* by Mrs. Charles E. Cowman. The song "Anywhere With Jesus," composed by Jessie B. Pounds, which appears in Chapter 10, was taken from *Hymns of the Christian Life*.

ISBN: 0-9787428-7-7
Library of Congress Control Number: 2006933288

Cover design: *Jack Kotowicz, Washington, DC, VelocityDesignGroup.com*
Layout design: *Annie Kotowicz and Jen Anderson*
Editing: *Vivian Otteman and Elizabeth Stalcup*

Believe Books publishes the inspirational life stories of extraordinary believers in God from around the world. Requests for information should be addressed to Believe Books at www.believebooks.com. **Believe Books** is a registered trade name of **Believe Books, LLC** of Washington, DC.

Printed in the United States of America

CONTENTS

This book is lovingly dedicated to my parents
SIDNEY AND BLANCHE CROUCH

The Fourth of July church picnic was a yearly, and sometimes memorable, highlight for members and relatives of the Quaker-town church in Quakertown, Connecticut. It was July 5th, 1937 when Sidney Crouch and Blanche Phillips, with their attendants and pastor, took their places amongst the surprised picnickers and conducted their unannounced wedding.

Dad was proud of the woman he had won. Mom was born in Fullerton, California in 1912, the daughter of pioneer evange-lists who travelled from Connecticut to California in their "gospel truck." While in southern California, they received the Pentecostal experience. As a little girl, Mom learned to play the tambourine and joined her parents in leading singing during their revival meet-ings. Their life of faith was not an easy one, but one remarkable ex-perience held Mom's faith steadfast during her challenges of life.

Mom loved the sunshine, and she had learned a repertoire of songs like, "Heavenly Sunshine, Heavenly Sunshine," "Sunshine, Sunshine in my Soul Today," "Jesus Wants Me for a Sunbeam," and "Let the Blessed Sunshine In." One morning as she lay in her little bed singing, she was startled to see a beautiful, glowing hand appear. It was like nothing she had ever seen before, but when she raised up to see it better, it faded quietly away. The experience was so remarkable, nothing in her life would ever convince her that God wasn't real.

I never heard Mom preach, except to me and my siblings, but she was a quiet force to be reckoned with. Her confidence in God ran deep, and she knew that if she could instill faith in God in her children, they would be safe. To that end, she taught us in family devotions, she disciplined us with determination, she prayed for us without ceasing, and she loved us unconditionally. She never sacrificed her convictions or her morals as we challenged her faith while ours emerged. She was an anchor for us during the testing, teenage years of self-discovery, and a haven of stability as our own homes and ministries developed.

Dad loved his seven children. I remember the days he took me for coffee at the diner. We walked into the men's unofficial meeting place, and I watched Dad's eyes twinkle as he proudly introduced me to his friends. I was a little embarrassed but honored by Dad's pride. How I missed the gentle wisdom and that vote of approval when Dad died in 1973 while I was in Africa.

Mom continued to strengthen us by her faith. Then, on December 9, 1998, she slipped quietly away, leaving us with a legacy of faithfulness, a shelter of love, a spirit of joy, and a bedrock foundation of faith in God. This book is not only my story, but it is also a reflection of my father and mother's guidance and my heritage of faith. Thanks Dad and Mom!

ACKNOWLEDGMENTS

First of all, I want to thank my God for His faithful goodness and mercy. He is truly the author and the finisher of our faith, and without Him I could do nothing.

I thank my husband Charles for his life of faithful service to God, for his love and patience, for his God-given wisdom, and for our beautiful children.

I thank our children for their endearing love and support: our daughter Deborah and our son-in-law Erik, with their children, Samuel and Racquel; our son Jeffrey and our daughter-in-law Stacey with their children Maximilian and Jackson; our son William and his son Victor; our daughter Ruth, and our son-in-law Andrew, with their three sons, Michael, Christopher, and Richard; and our lovely daughters, Mina and our son-in-law Zoran, and Bethanie, and Christine.

And, I want to thank the myriad of friends who have ministered to us through the years. I could not possibly mention the names of all those who have made significant investments into our lives, but I thank each one of you and pray that God will bless you abundantly.

INTRODUCTION

Our heart's desire is to educate our children so that they can make their own way through the maze of life, gaining at least a degree of prosperity and social success. Deep in our hearts, we want only the best for them. And so, as we work and plan and arrange our lives, our society engages or attempts to create whatever assistance possible to achieve its goals.

What happens when God interrupts our lives and superimposes an unknown plan on the scheduled activities of one's life? Often it is the beginning of a dynamic struggle. Fear of the unknown wrestles with faith in God. Fleshly doubt in our own ability to actually hear from God grapples with the inward man of the Spirit, which has an ear to hear. Security challenges uncertainty. Self-made success protests vigorously at the absurdity of obedience to any voice outside of its own well-thought plan—the indignity of it all, the pride-crumbling, ego-shattering, flesh-killing, self-annihilating horror of total faith in a sovereign God.

Our generation is not the first that has scorned such a God-invasion of self. The Bible tells in detail of the ridicule borne by ancient prophets. Jeremiah was thrown into a dungeon and wallowed in mire up to his armpits for prophesying a word from God which was contrary to the plans of the local government. Elijah, a man who saw angels and raised the dead, fled in lonely exile by the brook Cherith after giving the word of the Lord to the wicked house of Ahab.

Even lovely Mary bore the shame of her encounter with God's angelic messenger. Why did God organize the arrival of the Saviour of the World so that His coming was cloaked in the shame of a virgin girl? Could God not have orchestrated a more ethical arrival than the scandals that greeted baby Jesus? It was a brilliant plan, an amazing event that would forever affect the destiny of mankind; yet it was masked by sordid stories, ridicule and rejection. Man would not have planned Jesus' birth in such a way.

Eve, the first violator of God's instructions, did so in order to gain personal wisdom. "You will not surely die," the devil said. "For God doth know that in the day ye eat thereof, then your eyes shall be opened, and ye shall be as gods, knowing good and evil." Man's original downfall is man's continuing downfall: the belief that "I can do it myself."

There are few who wish to risk the uncertainty of absolute obedience to almighty God. Jesus did. "I can of mine own self do nothing," Jesus said, ". . . because I seek not mine own will, but the will of the Father which hath sent me" (John 5:30). Daily, He met with His Father to receive instructions and strength. His only desire was to glorify His Father, even though it ultimately meant His death on the cross.

We do not wish to do what we cannot understand. We do not wish to participate in something which we cannot measure in terms of success or failure. We would really rather be seen in situations which exhibit accomplishment and predict success. We yearn to be masters of our fate in a well-ordered world. How can faith possibly be enough?

We hear God's cry in the book of Ezekiel, "And I sought for a man among them, that should make up the hedge, and stand in the gap before me for the land, that I should not destroy it: but I found none" (Ezekiel 22:30). What was God looking for? What quality was God seeking in the man that He could not find?

Could it be that He could not find anyone in that self-seeking land who would stand and say, "Not my will but Thine be done?"

The result of God's futile search was a "pouring out of His indignation upon the people of the land. He consumed them with the fire of His wrath: their own way did He recompense upon their heads" (Ezekiel 30:31).

For the Christian, faith is to invade and dominate every area of our life. There is to be no area which is reserved for the reign of self. Jesus said, "I know thy works, that thou art neither cold nor hot: I would thou wert cold or hot. So then because thou art lukewarm, and neither cold nor hot, I will spue thee out of my mouth" (Revelation 3:16,18).

When we attempt to mix disobedience with obedience, God views our spiritual condition as neither cold nor hot. Such confusion, such lack of integrity, God cannot tolerate. Eventually, the Holy Spirit will no longer strive with our stubbornness. Our hearts will be hardened by our own unbelief, and we will be locked into our own self-made destruction. If we do not understand God's ways and if we devise paths for our feet according to our own understanding, God is dethroned. Self is exalted! Failure is a sure result, either sooner or later, because faith fails where self reigns.

Is it true that as the years have gone by, "every day in every way we're getting better and better?" Interstate highways crisscross our nation, cars with air conditioners, regulated heaters, CD stereos, heated seats and even satellite directional devices, line our driveways and fill expensive garages. Computers are an everyday item in many households. More of our population holds doctorate degrees than ever before.

Churches now hold thousands instead of hundreds. Nationally computerized link-ups make it possible to hold nationwide prayer rallies. Bibles are a number-one bestseller, and seminaries and Bible schools are busy training people to work for God.

Yet, Jesus says, "Straight is the gate, and narrow is the way, which leadeth unto life, and few there be that find it." Why? Jesus goes on to say in Matthew 7:21, "Not everyone that saith unto me, Lord, Lord, shall enter into the kingdom of heaven; but He that doeth the will of my Father which is in heaven."

God did not call us just to assent to His will—He called us to do it. There is a big difference between the faith of admission and the faith of obedience. That is where the power of the Holy Spirit makes a difference in our lives. In ourselves, we cannot concede to the unknowns found in the will of God. It is only when we live in the Spirit, hear by the Spirit, and walk in the Spirit, that we begin to do the will of God. Hearing mixed with faith produces a walk of obedience.

Obedient faith in God scorns man's meager mentality. It places God in His rightful place as Master and Lord. It denies man's efforts at headship and enthrones Christ as King. Obedient faith is a righteous act which unites us with God and gives us the power to overcome the world.

Faith Overcomes the World

"And this is the victory
that overcometh
the world, even our faith."
1 John 5:4b

*Faith is believing who Jesus really is
and what He did for us.*

1

From Rats to Revelation

A piercing pain stabbed my left hand. I stirred in the darkness and heard a thump as if something fell off the end of my bed. Still groggy with sleep, I struggled to reach the source of the pain. I felt my hand. It was warm, wet and sticky. *Why?* Sleep fled and my senses were alert to danger as I crept out of bed and turned on the light. Blood stained my nightgown and dripped onto the floor. I grabbed my hand to stop the bleeding and saw the four sharp tooth marks of a rat. Cold, quiet fear made me shake involuntarily. *Would I die of rabies?* I was only ten years old. *How do you feel when you die? How long does it take?* I stumbled downstairs to my parents' room and woke them up.

"Mom, Dad, a rat bit me."

Dad cleaned and bandaged my wound and let me spend the rest of the night close to them, but I didn't sleep much. I kept waiting to die. I didn't want to. Morning came and I was still alive, but Dad let me stay home from school that day.

The house in which this trauma occurred was an old nine-bedroom house Dad and Mom had been fixing up in Quakertown, Connecticut, after Mom was healed of tuberculosis. A few years earlier, when I was only four, she had been diagnosed with the terrible disease. I was taken away and sent to live first with my aunt and then with my grandmother. When doctors decided to put Mom in a sanitarium, Dad was certain she would never come out alive. He packed a few belongings in the car and collected us four children from relatives. I remember the day he came to Grandma's and got me. He held my little hand in his big strong one as we walked across the road to the waiting car. In my other hand I clutched a paper sack containing my clothes.

We fled to the moderate climate of southern California where Dad built us a new home. Then, during a church service, Mom was miraculously healed by prayer. We moved to Houston, Texas where Mom's brother Palmer and his wife, Virginia lived. Dad bought a gas station and Mom's mother came to live with us so Mom could rest and be with Dad. The station in the sun became her clinic as she regained her strength. Prayer, fresh air, and the hot Texas sun worked wonders. Finally, with Mom cured, they decided to move back home to Connecticut.

Quakertown was one of those "blink-your-eye-and-you'll-pass-me-by" kind of little towns. We didn't have a grocery store, a school, or even a gas station, but right in the center of town was a little white church. It was pastored by Fred Watrous, one of the local men, and it was here that the foundations of my faith were strengthened.

Fred had a large family who all pitched in to help him run the small garden shop and nursery they owned. He worked hard to make a living, like the rest of the men in Quakertown, but on Sundays, kindhearted Pastor Fred faithfully shepherded his little flock.

When the church service was in progress, some of the local residents who didn't attend the church meetings were often seen sitting outside on their front steps listening to the singing. Our little church was blessed with an abundance of naturally-gifted musicians. A row of accordionists sat across the front of the church just below the platform. To the right of them was the piano, and to the left was the organ. Then on the platform, just behind them, was a surround-sound orchestra. A distant cousin played a violin and another a trumpet, Uncle John played the trombone, and Aunt Alice blew a hearty sax. There were even drums and guitars which added rhythm to the enthusiastic ensemble.

Leading the accordions was Roger Watrous, nephew of the pastor. He not only played the accordion with the strength and vibrancy of one who is divinely anointed, but he sang with the same fervor. We watched in awe as he stretched the accordion a full arm's length while he sang, "When He reached down His hand for me." It was heartwarming to join in with friends and relatives as they sang, played, and ministered because of their love for God and their faith in Him. Later, when Roger imported a lovely young wife from another town, everyone thought it was tremendously appropriate when he sang one of the congregational favorites at his wedding reception, "I won't have to cross Jordan alone."

As Roger and the musicians continued to lead the church in songs like, "Anywhere, anywhere, fear I cannot know, anywhere with Jesus I can safely go," "No never alone," and "Who will go?" I am sure they never guessed that one of the little girls who sang along with them would one day preach in Africa. They never knew that the words she learned from them would give her the faith to continue an amazing journey which sometimes seemed destined for death.

Pastor Fred never claimed to be an orator. There were some Sundays when we found it difficult to stay awake, especially the Sunday that he read the whole 119th Psalm and carefully gave an original exposition on each one of the 176 verses.

Then there was the beautiful, sunny Sunday that the bees came out. Pastor Fred was preaching, and I was trying to pay attention, when we heard a buzzing sound. I sat up to see where it came from. Someone in the front seat was respectfully trying to make a bee go away. The sound grew louder as more bees emerged from the platform area and sought landing rights on members of the congregation.

A couple of mothers with babies tiptoed quietly out of the sanctuary. Pastor Fred continued to minister. I noticed a few worried glances and flushed faces as the believers tried to maintain their composure and show respect in the house of the Lord. But as the bees continued to swarm, those sitting in the front row cautiously rose, one by one, tiptoed down the aisle, and exited out the back door.

Pastor Fred was dedicated. He ignored the intrusion and continued his sermon. Those in the second row squirmed uncomfortably. Then, with bowed heads, they sneaked down the aisle.

Oh, goodie, I thought, *this is great fun.* I knew I wasn't being very spiritual, but it was a wonderful diversion from the usual service routine.

People rolled their eyes in silent communication and respectfully smothered grins as they cautiously continued to exit. Finally, it was my turn, and I happily joined the church family on the front steps.

Pastor Fred was to be commended. He stayed faithful to his post until all the members had left and the swarm of bees made it impossible to preach. He made me think of stories I had read about sea captains always being last to leave a sinking ship.

His boys were not as spiritually-minded that morning. They hurried off to find a ladder and a large metal wash tub. With the help of some of the other male church members, they smoked the rest of the bees out from under the eaves, collected the honey, and shared it with all of us. It was a different type of communion that we enjoyed that warm Sunday in spring as we broke honeycomb together on the front steps of the church.

Another Sunday I remember well was the morning we had a guest speaker, a missionary from Africa. He told frightening stories. Once, he was mangled by a lion. He was rescued, but on the way to the hospital, he had a near-death experience. We were a captive audience as he described the event in vivid detail. He lost blood profusely. It sloshed back and forth on the floor of the car as they drove over the rutted jungle roads toward help. The devil talked to him, he said, and taunted him as he drifted in and out of consciousness, but God saved him. It was scary. At the conclusion of his story, he challenged us to commit ourselves to serve God with all our hearts. There in my seat I prayed, "Lord, I'll go anywhere you want me to go, and I'll do anything you want me to do, but please don't send me to Africa!"

Suddenly, I recalled hearing that God often calls us to do the very thing that we don't want to do. Hurriedly I changed my prayer, so that God would change His mind.

"God, I'll even go to Africa," I offered hopefully, not knowing that God would take me at my word.

When I was eighteen years old, tragedy struck. My brother Sidney died in an attempt to climb the Old Man of the Mountains, a mountain in the White Mountain National Forest of New Hampshire. Fred Whipple, a cousin and former captain of the football team at our alma mater, the Norwich Free Academy, died with him. It was a shocking and tragic event, later described in an issue of the *Reader's Digest*. After the terrible loss, Dad decided to give me the college education that my brother had longed for.

My time at Evangel College in Springfield, Missouri, was akin to being in seventh heaven. I made lifetime friends, honed talents, and developed skills. Intertwined with the fun were the disciplines of study and submission to school rules. It all combined to help train me for life and future ministry.

When I returned to Evangel for my third year, I noticed a large tent set up on an empty parking lot in the town. The most amazing organ music I had ever heard caught my attention and drew me inside where an afternoon service was in progress. As I watched the young evangelist pray for the sick, I was astounded to see some remarkable healings take place.

It must be wonderful to be used of God like that, I thought.

After more observation, I approached the evangelist and asked to join the team. He needed a secretary, and I was hired. As we traveled through the South holding healing meetings, I saw daring examples of faith. But it wasn't long before I realized that our young team needed a much more solid foundation from which to launch acts of faith. In innocence, I had evaluated the character of the team by the miracles that I saw. I didn't know then that, according to the Word, you will know a tree by its fruits—love, joy, peace, and long-suffering—not by its gifts—tongues, interpretation, word of knowledge, gifts of miracles. The fruit of a tree or a Christian is exhibited in direct relationship to the quality of its life and nature. Gifts are freely given by God and are not the standard used to qualify personal character. The gifts of God are not necessarily the endorsement of God.

But there was one amazing incident that took place while I was with them that I will never forget. The evangelist had decided to print a magazine with testimonies of healing and asked if I would do the interviews and help write the articles. I agreed.

We were in a southern city holding a healing crusade in an auditorium, and I was watching the healing line. I saw a child brought forward for prayer who was wearing a leg brace. One of his legs was four inches shorter than the other. This miracle, if it happened, would be very obvious, and I determined not to miss any part of the anticipated healing. When the child finally stood in front of the evangelist, I found a good vantage point, fixed my eyes on the child's leg, and made sure I did not blink or allow my attention to get diverted in any way.

The evangelist had the brace removed, knelt, placed the child's heels in the palms of his hands, and prayed. I watched. The leg grew. But strangely, as both legs slowly became the same length, I didn't see any jerking or any movement of any kind. Although I watched carefully as faith produced a miracle, I never really saw it happen. God performed a divine act of creativity, but He hid its process from the human eye. Afterward, the child ran, the family laughed and cried, and the audience was ecstatic. I pondered what I had just seen.

Are most miracles like that? Does God often hide His miracle-working process in secret and reveal His results unannounced? If no obvious change takes place at the outset, human perception may lead one to believe that prayer is not making a difference. Therefore, it is entirely possible for us to walk away from a test too soon and ignorantly leave behind a miracle in progress. And sometimes, unless we stop to compare the original condition with later results, the completed miracle even may go unnoticed.

Hebrews 11:13 says, "These all died in faith, not having received the promises . . ." Did those Hebrew believers understand that realm? Were they so convinced that their answers were coming, it didn't matter to them when the results of their faith were revealed? Stepping across the time-line of death into eternal life didn't mean their faith was a failure. It simply meant their answer was revealed in another dimension.

One of the choruses we sang in Quakertown was, "Faith is the victory, faith is the victory, O glorious victory that overcomes the world."

God knows the impatience produced by our shortsightedness, so the book of Hebrews lets us know that faith will keep us steadfast while God is preparing His answers in secret. There are many areas of life where we need overcoming faith, and this is one of them: to continue having faith when we don't see any response to our prayers. 1 John 5:4 says, "For whatsoever is born of God overcometh the world: and this is the victory that overcometh the world, even our faith." Faith is vital to overcoming and Revelation declares that overcoming is vital for every Christian. We are not called to be passive, to coexist with evil, or to learn to tolerate sickness and sin. By faith we rise up, live in agreement with God's Word, and enter into a state of victory. When we are tempted to be weak or give up, we are told to "gird up the loins of our mind" (1 Peter 1:13) by strengthening our minds with the truth (Ephesians 6:14).

There are many promises to the overcomer. Revelation says:

To him that overcometh will I give to eat of the tree of life, which is in the midst of the paradise of God (Revelation 2:7). This promises us eternal life.

He that overcometh shall not be hurt of the second death (Revelation 2:11). We do not need to fear judgment and hell if we are overcomers.

To him that overcometh will I give to eat of the hidden manna, and will give him a white stone, and in the stone a new name written, which no man knoweth saving he that receiveth it (Revelation 2:17). God will sustain us by revealing His secret truths to us. A new name speaks of a change of character which is written in solid purity.

And he that overcometh, and keepeth my works unto the end, to him will I give power over the nations (Revelation 2:26). God promises us a share of His power and authority.

He that overcometh, the same shall be clothed in white raiment; and I will not blot his name out of the book of life, but I will confess his name before my Father, and before his angels (Revelation 3:5). We will be clothed in righteousness, assured of eternal life, and recognized before God and the angels.

Him that overcometh will I make a pillar in the temple of my God, and he shall go no more out: and I will write upon him the name of my God, and the name of the city of my God, which is new Jerusalem, which cometh down out of heaven from my God: and I will write upon him my new name (Revelation 3:12). We will never be separated from the presence of God again, and we will have God's signature or character forever imprinted upon us.

To him that overcometh will I grant to sit with me in my throne, even as I also overcame, and am set down with my Father in his throne (Revelation 3:21). Jesus will share His position, as divine royalty, with us.

He that overcometh shall inherit all things; and I will be his God, and he shall be my son (Revelation 21:7). We are given a divine inheritance of everything God has and we are accepted in a loving relationship as sons of God forever.

Most of these promises to the overcomer are prefaced with a very important instruction, "He that hath an ear, let him hear what the Spirit saith unto the churches" (Revelation 2:7,11,17,29, 3:6,13,22). The instructions of the Holy Spirit give us faith to believe in God's promises, faith to continue walking in His instructions, and faith to implement His instructions in the nature and character of an overcomer.

I finally realized that my place was no longer with the evangelistic team and returned home to Quakertown to sort out my life and find God's direction. One night after reading my Bible and praying as usual, I fell asleep and dreamed an unusual dream. I saw myself standing on a platform, preaching to hundreds of people. The anointing of God was strong on me, and I preached with tremendous power. Interestingly, I didn't only dream the dream, I physically participated in it. As the power of it grew, it became so strong that it shook me awake, still preaching and still shaking under the anointing.

Faith Gives Us the Courage
to Follow Uncharted Paths

"By faith they
passed through the Red sea
as by dry land:
which the Egyptians assaying
to do were drowned."
Hebrews 11:29

*Faith in the known
is greater than
fear of the unknown.*

2

The Lord Build the House

For my thoughts are not your thoughts,
neither are your ways my ways, saith the LORD.
–Isaiah 55:8

The little Vauxhall flew over Connecticut's hilly, curving roads as I drove toward Rhode Island and Zion Bible Institute. The car was an economic wonder. A dollar's worth of gas would last for days. My Dad, a lover of cars, found it, bought it for an excellent price, and gave it to me for school.

After I left the evangelistic team, it was too late in the year to go back to Evangel College. I hadn't found a job yet, so with time on my hands, I decided to visit my sister Emily, who was studying at Zion Bible Institute in East Providence, Rhode Island. When I arrived, Em introduced me to some of her dorm-mates. Somewhere amidst the happy banter of new friendship, the girls decided I must stay.

"Go down and talk with Dr. Heroo, the president," they urged, "and ask him if you can become a student here."

"It isn't normal procedure to just walk in and ask to become a student," I reminded them. "The application process takes months, and what about uniforms?"

The school required female students to dress in navy blue dresses with white collars and cuffs.

"No problem. You go talk with Dr. Heroo. We are going to stay right here and have a prayer meeting," they declared. They were convinced that it was God's will for me to attend Zion.

Since I didn't have any immediate personal obligations, and this would be a positive step toward my goal to serve God, it occurred to me that maybe this visit was no accident. I set out to see if it was possible to speak with Dr. Heroo. Finding the newly built administrative offices, I went in. The secretary greeted me and yes, Dr. Heroo was in. She went into his office, spoke with him briefly, then escorted me inside. Dr. Heroo stood behind his big desk and greeted me as I entered and sat down. He was a large black man, built like a football player, with kindly features and a twinkle in his eye.

"What can I do for you?" he asked.

"I would like to transfer my two years of credits at Evangel College and enroll in Zion as a third-year student," I explained. He listened to my proposal with an interested smile, asked a few more questions, and accepted me on the spot.

A little stunned, I returned to the girl's dorm to report to the prayer meeting. The girls had gone to class, but on the bed were several uniforms, collars and cuffs, and a note of congratulations. "We knew you would be accepted," they declared. "Welcome to Zion. Here are some uniforms we want to share with you until you can get your own."

Zion was a "faith" school in those days, and there was no charge for room, board, or tuition. Sister Gibson, the founder, left a legacy of integrity and faith, and the faculty and staff continued to pass those principles on to the students of Zion. Dedicated Zionians by then ministered around the world, and here I was, the newest addition to the "faith school."

Because there were no charges, every student was assigned a duty. Mine was ironing boys' pants and handkerchiefs. My work site was in the laundry room, conveniently located on one side of the basement of our dorm.

It was refreshing to be alone in the basement, to think and pray while I did my duty. Like my Mom, I was a timid person and I found the crush of students in the dining hall so intimidating. So I often skipped meals and used the time to iron.

The other half of the basement housed the school's radio studio, where its daily radio program was aired. One day, I discovered I wasn't alone. The student disc jockey had also found his studio workplace a perfect spot to study and pray. I tried to discreetly ignore him when he passed by the laundry room door, but he noticed me and stopped in to chat. His name was Charles. Eventually he discovered that I was skipping meals and decided to make it his personal mission to supply me with food.

Charles and I were both active seniors. I wrote a play that our prayer group presented to the school. The student actors performed well, and the chapel altar was filled with praying students when the play concluded. Then Charles wrote a play that was filled with drama, challenge, and creativity. The students came forward and prayed even harder after his production.

One evening, as I was ironing, Charles invited me over to take a tour of his studio. As we sat and talked afterward, he slipped a recording of Hawaiian music onto one of the turntables. On the second turntable he placed a sound effects recording of ocean waves breaking gently onto a sandy beach. Then he dimmed the overhead lights, and the little studio glowed in the colorful, twinkling lights of the studio console. To complete the evening in our tropical oasis, he served dessert. This food ministry certainly was getting interesting.

We talked until curfew, and then I watched him close the studio down and lock the door. Together we walked through the basement hallway toward the outside door, but halfway there he suddenly stopped, drew me close to him, and gently kissed me. Students at

Zion were not encouraged to kiss in the basement—ummm, that's an understatement. We didn't linger long, but something special happened in our hearts in those few memorable moments.

Charles was the only child of an elderly German couple from southern Ontario. Life had not been easy for him, but he didn't expect it to be. His father was ill, and his mother supported the little family by selling handicrafts and cleaning the homes of the wealthy. Hard work and perseverance were his heritage.

When Charles felt led to go to Bible school, he applied by faith. He had gone to Vancouver hoping to find work in the logging camps when news of his acceptance reached him. He didn't have a car or enough money to buy a bus ticket to Rhode Island, but he was determined to go. He set out hitchhiking, believing that God would help him, and God did, all the way across Canada. He only spent one cold night in a ditch sleeping on top of his suitcase, wearing most of the clothes he had put in it to try and keep warm.

After our graduation from Zion, I returned to Evangel. Charles remained at Zion as a staff member and during that time served as the class advisor for Missionary Prayers. God spoke to him as they prayed and gave him some definite directions. He was to serve God as a missionary in Africa, marry me, and complete a Bachelor's degree. With typical perseverance, he set out to accomplish those goals.

Charles went to Moody Bible Institute to attend summer school and then followed me to Evangel. Now free to date, we began to discover a myriad of differences between us. But, the strong love that he had in his heart for me must have been planted by God, because he refused to waver in his affections.

Time passed. Charles returned to Canada, and I accepted an invitation to go to Pennsylvania to help out in a new church. Then one night I had a dream. Charles came to me, looked at me tenderly and asked, "Will you marry me?"

"No," I gently replied.

This wasn't the type of dream one has as a result of eating pickles and cheese; I awoke with a deep spiritual conviction that I had made a serious mistake. Was God using this method to bypass my brain and speak directly to my spirit in the quiet of the night? Apparently, He did not want me to make a decision for my future based on immature idealism, but on divinely imparted truth. By now, I had discovered in my young life that I certainly did not always know what was best. It comforted me to discover that even the mighty prophet Samuel would have passed over young David in his search for Israel's next king, had he followed his own observations (1 Samuel 16:6).

Now I faced a crucial decision. Was this dream of God or not? Dare I disobey the unusual prompting I felt? No. I loved God and valued the work of the Holy Spirit in my life too much to treat it lightly. If God was orchestrating a divinely arranged marriage, would faith be enough to carry me through? If this dream was of God, then surely I could trust God to help Charles and me overcome our differences, nurture our love, and mold us into a valuable team. Earnestly I prayed about it, and then decided that if Charles asked me again to marry him, I would say yes.

One night, Charles called. He was coming to Pennsylvania for a visit and would arrive about 10:00 P.M. I teased my hair and arranged it in the popular "beehive" style. I donned a chic yellow wool suit, selected some matching shoes, and waited for him to arrive. He didn't come. Finally, he called. "Fern, I'm really sorry," he said, "but I'm just too tired to drive any farther. I'm going to have to stop and get some sleep. You go ahead and go to bed. I'll see you in the morning."

Reluctantly, I took off my clothes, put on my flannel nightgown, and crawled into bed. At 3:00 A.M. I suddenly awoke, got out of bed, walked downstairs, and opened the front door. At that very moment Charles' car turned the corner and pulled up to the curb. Imagine his surprise when he looked up and saw me standing in the doorway. He ran up the sidewalk, picked me up in his arms, and kissed me.

"I wondered what I was going to do when I got here," he said. "Put your coat on. I have something to show you."

Quietly, we wended our way through the sleeping city and up the side of Mt. Penn, which overlooks Reading, Pennsylvania. Charles parked beneath the colored lights of the Chinese pagoda and took me in his arms.

"Look in the glove compartment, Fern," he said.

Inside I found a little velvet box. I opened it, and as the brilliant diamond sparkled in the multicolored lights of the pagoda, Charles asked softly, "Fern, will you marry me?"

"Yes, Charlie," I said.

Before we had a chance to even plan our wedding, Charles received a draft notice. His Permanent Resident Visa made him subject to the United States draft. *Now what?*

"If I go home, I might lose Fern," he reasoned. He decided to stay and serve the two years required of a draftee. He completed basic training, and while on leave, we were married in a beautiful ceremony that committed us to each other and to the work of the Lord.

We didn't have our initials engraved in our rings, but we instructed the jeweler to inscribe the letters TLBTH on the inside of them instead. The letters stand for "The Lord Build The House," taken from Psalm 127. It represented our prayer, "Lord, in this union, we commit ourselves to you and ask you to build us into a house for your glory. May we and our household serve you and honor you all of the days of our lives."

> *Except the LORD build the house, they labor in vain that build it: except the LORD keep the city, the watchman waketh but in vain. It is vain for you to rise up early, to sit up late, to eat the bread of sorrows: for so he giveth his beloved sleep. Lo, children are an heritage of the LORD: and the fruit of the womb is his reward. As arrows are in the hand of a mighty man; so are children of the youth. Happy is the man that hath his quiver full of*

*them: they shall not be ashamed, but they shall speak with the
enemies in the gate.*
—Psalm 127

Our first home was in Jersey City, New Jersey, about two hours
away from Fort Dix where Charles was stationed. We found an
apartment, and I took the first available job—cashiering in a nearby
grocery store. Because Charles was still in training, he was required
to live on the base; but his excellent work habits and discipline
earned him frequent weekend passes to see his new bride. After
each weekend rendezvous, he returned to the base and I lived alone
in the strange and sometimes dangerous city. It didn't take long to
discover that it often takes as much determination to stay in the
will of God as it does to choose it.

We had not received marriage counseling or manuals with information on such things as self-esteem, communication, forgiveness, dialoguing, or understanding the differences between the
male and female temperaments. The Bible was our only guidebook
and the Holy Spirit our only counselor.

As we attempted to balance a serviceman's budget and live in
conditions that were a far cry from the prophetic pronouncements
that we had received from anointed men of God, confusion and
discontent sometimes surfaced. The devil would then take such
opportunities to add a few thoughts of his own.

"Is this what you deserve in marriage? You have every reason to
leave. Look at those friends of yours, they didn't make it and neither will you." Sadly, even some senior church members didn't provide a badly needed example to follow either. They justified broken
vows and unfaithfulness, and eventually jumped ship themselves in
favor of calmer matrimonial seas and marital bliss.

"Lord have mercy. What do we do? Help Lord! Please build
our house."

When misunderstandings piled up and emotional dividing
walls came between us, the Lord showed Charles the principle of

forgiveness. "But if ye forgive not men their trespasses, neither will your Father forgive your trespasses" (Matthew 6:15). According to this Scripture, forgiveness isn't an option. If we want forgiveness from God, we must forgive. Little by little we were learning to exchange the storybook ideal of "living happily ever after" for the realistic commitment of "living faithfully ever after."

Once, when I was having a difficult day, I "happened" to hear someone on the radio telling the story of her marriage. It was over, she decided. She did not love her husband anymore. But as a new Christian, she decided that she should pray about what to do next.

She prayed, and God said, "Love him. This is my commandment, That ye love one another, as I have loved you" (John 15:12).

"I can't do that. I don't love my husband anymore," she said.

God answered back, "Then love him as a friend, A friend loveth at all times" (Proverbs 17:17).

"God, I'm sorry, but I can't do that either. I don't even love him as a friend," she exclaimed.

"Well then," God replied, "love him as an enemy! Love your enemies, do good to them . . . which despitefully use you and persecute you" (Matthew 5:44).

"Okay, Fern," I heard God say to my heart, "time to knuckle down, learn what you need to know, and work it out." As I prayed and studied the Word in my personal devotions, the Lord began to unlock more of His principles. For instance, Hebrews 10:36 declares, "For ye have need of patience, that, after ye have done the will of God, ye might receive the promise."

Oh. So the promises of blessing don't just follow the act of obedience! According to this Hebrews account, there is generally a period of testing between the time we act in obedience and the time we receive the promise. During that interval, patience is imperative. And it is often this test of patience that determines whether or not our acts of obedience will apprehend the promised blessings.

The attributes that encompass patience are often qualities that we prefer to do without. It is difficult to let down our barriers of personal pride and patiently identify with each other's weaknesses. In our society, we spend a great deal of effort trying to upgrade, to progress, to acquire a better standing with our fellow man and with God. But Jesus refutes our pride in self-achievement by telling us that it is more important for us to please and edify each other than it is for us to please ourselves.

This type of humble relationship does not result in one being greater and another less, because it acknowledges that without Christ, none of us would be anything. Because it is His power that is at work in us, not one of us has a right to spiritual pride or dominance. Even as Christ identified with us through a very humbling process, He requests that we do the same thing and learn to identify with each other.

> We then that are strong ought to bear the infirmities of the weak, and not to please ourselves. Let every one of us please his neighbor for his good to edification. For even Christ pleased not himself; but, as it is written, The reproaches of them that reproached thee fell on me. For whatsoever things were written aforetime were written for our learning, that we through patience and comfort of the scriptures might have hope. Now the God of patience and consolation grant you to be likeminded one toward another according to Christ Jesus: That ye may with one mind and one mouth glorify God, even the Father of our Lord Jesus Christ. Wherefore receive ye one another, as Christ also received us to the glory of God."
> –Romans 15:1–7

As one of two singles attempting to combine things like our philosophies of life, spiritual convictions, acquired habits, priorities in doing tasks, and pride in personal intelligence, I felt I had a fair share to offer this marriage. When we were driving, I almost always knew the shortest or best route. But strangely, when I convinced Charles to go my way, we encountered an unexpected roadblock or some other unusual problem. My tried and true proven methods suddenly didn't work anymore. What was happening? It finally dawned on me that God was helping me learn respect for my new "head." Charles had God working on his side until I learned to get my priorities straight.

Then, after several months, Charles came home from work one day and said, "Fern, God spoke to me today and told me that I need to learn to listen to you too." I was humbled. Now that I had learned my lesson, God was ready to make us a team. I would be very careful about what I said!

It was several years later, while reading in Hosea 2:19,20, that the Holy Spirit revealed an exciting discovery, the five basic ingredients of relationship:

> And I will betroth thee unto me for ever; yea, I will betroth thee unto me in righteousness, and in judgment, and in lovingkindness, and in mercies. I will even betroth thee unto me in faithfulness: and thou shalt know the LORD.

Each one of those ingredients produces important attributes in a relationship to make it lasting and balanced. The following are some of the ways they enrich a relationship:

1. Righteousness: In following God's Word to live righteously, we build a threefold confidence between God and one another, and bring divine blessing on our seed.

2. Judgment: In being humble enough to receive correction, to say "I'm sorry," and to submit our own ways to the agreement of our spouse, we bring upon ourselves safety and unity.

3. Lovingkindness: In showing lovingkindness, we gain romance and a gracious home.

4. Mercies: In giving mercy, we receive understanding and forgiveness in return.

5. Faithfulness: In remaining faithful, we avoid the snare of overreacting to an immediate problem and losing all we have gained. We don't fall prey to the pitfalls of temptation, and we reap the abundant blessings of heaven, promised only to the faithful.

The day we said our vows, we were probably about as confident as the children of Israel were when they walked in frightened awe across the sandy path between two great heaps of walled water. Just like them, we also experienced times to dance and shout, and just like them, when the dance was over, we discovered that today's victory will not protect us from tomorrow's battle.

Faith Must be Tried to Produce Patience

"The trying of your
faith worketh patience."
James 1:3

*Many a vision has been lost
simply for a lack of patience.*

3

Out of God's Will in the Basement

For the vision is yet for an appointed time,
but at the end it shall speak, and not lie: though it tarry,
wait for it; because it will surely come, it will not tarry.
—Habakkuk 2:3

Charles' two-year tour of duty with Uncle Sam was finally completed. The Army paid for our move back to Springfield, Missouri, and provided grants that made it possible for Charles to complete his college education. He earned a lifetime teachers certificate in math and physics and was accepted for a teaching position.

Several more years passed, and the call to Africa still burned in his heart. We now had three children, and I was pregnant with our fourth. Would God still open a door to the mission field? Charles had already renewed his contract to teach mathematics in an elementary school, when a missionary from Africa came to our church to speak. She needed helpers on her mission compound and invited us to move to Africa and work with her. Charles decided to accept. Some unknown factor made me hesitant, but I understood Charles' vision for Africa and his need to respond to this call, so I helped him prepare.

Since the missionary's time in North America was short and we didn't have much time to get ready, we novices decided to hold an auction at our home to sell our goods as quickly as possible. It was a busy time sorting, packing, and parenting, but the day of the sale finally came. Freezing temperatures and bone-chilling winds blew angry blasts of stinging snow against anyone who dared to venture outside.

The auctioneer and a few people arrived. They strode through our home examining our personal treasures with little thought of the young pregnant mother and innocent children who watched apprehensively. The size of the crowd made it obvious that this sale would end quickly. The auctioneer was unconcerned for our affairs and dispatched our treasures to ridiculously low bidding. In spite of too-good-to-be-true finds, many people still insisted that other items be included for the same price. Fifteen quarts of fresh jam, made from strawberries that I had picked and preserved for my family, sold for fifty cents. My paintings from art school days and other family mementos went for a similar pittance.

I determined to be a gracious hostess, but it wasn't easy as people with knowing, masked smiles walked away with our hard-earned possessions, the dining room suite, our living room suite, the coffee table stereo. When they started taking apart our French provincial bedroom suite, I broke. Silently, I escaped into the children's empty room, hid in a corner, and cried. Charles found me there, unable to face the pillage of our personal possessions any longer. He held me as I sobbed out my grief.

The missionary was scheduled to meet with a mission's board in Washington State. We were to rendezvous at a designated date and then travel on together. The plan continued to disturb me, but still I had no known reason to object. Charles' call to Africa, once seemingly so imminent, had now stretched into seven years. It was a long time to carry an unfulfilled dream, and, in spite of our losses, he was still excited with this open invitation. We put the house up for sale. Charles made arrangements with the school board to give his teaching contract to another applicant; we packed the car, said our good-byes, and were off.

It wasn't long before the expenses of the trip used up most of the funds we had carefully saved. Our deadline drew closer. If something didn't happen soon, we would miss our contact because now we didn't even have enough gas money to reach Washington state. Then we met a Christian lady who offered us money to take her to her destination. It would take us off-course and make it difficult to reach Washington on time, but the money she offered would pay for our gas.

We completed the drop-off and drove on toward Washington, but the sense of foreboding grew in my spirit. I wanted desperately to put what I felt into words, but I couldn't. Since I still had no explanation for my feelings, and because Charles is a man of his word, he decided to keep the appointment. We continued traveling. I attempted to quell my growing apprehension by reading the Word. Suddenly, the following passage came alive:

> But there came a man of God to him, saying, O king, let not the army of Israel go with thee; for the LORD is not with Israel, to wit, with all the children of Ephraim. But if thou wilt go, do it; be strong for the battle: God shall make thee fall before the enemy: for God hath power to help, and to cast down. And Amaziah said to the man of God, But what shall we do for the hundred talents which I have given to the army of Israel? And the man of God answered, The LORD is able to give thee much more than this. Then Amaziah separated them, to wit, the army that was come to him out of Ephraim, to go home again: wherefore their anger was greatly kindled against Judah, and they returned home in great anger.
> –2 Chronicles 25:7–10

I had opened to a biblical example of someone who had also made a promise in error. What was the prophet's answer to the problem? He told the king that if he chose to keep his promise, he would fail. It was better to admit a mistake than to continue in his error. Yes, the king would lose his investment and perhaps make some enemies, but "The LORD is able to give thee much more than this," the prophet stated.

I read the Scripture aloud and said, "Charlie, I really don't think God wants us to go with this woman."

It was a frustrating time for Charles. He wanted to answer the vision that beckoned so brightly, and to keep his promise, but it was eluding him. He was tense with driving as he struggled to make up for lost time, and he didn't appreciate hearing this very negative passage of Scripture. It wasn't a fun trip.

We were almost there, but our detour cost us fifteen minutes. We stopped to call. The board was in a meeting and couldn't be disturbed. We continued driving, reached the city and called again. We finally reached the missionary. Curtly she informed us that we were too late, she was leaving, and it was over.

Later we learned that we were saved from a commitment that would have been very unsuitable for our family. God, in His mercy, had protected us. Amy Carmichael writes the following in her book, Gold Cord:

> Thou hast enough to pay thy fare?
> Well, be it so;
> But thou shouldest know,
> Does thy God send thee there,
> Is that it all? To pay thy fare?
> There's many a coin flung lightly down
> Brings back a load of care.
> It may cost what thou knowest not
> To bring thee home from there.[1]

We paid.

Through a series of incidents we made contact with a group of "Jesus" people living in the basement of an abandoned school building. They invited us to join them, and we did. The accommodations were meager and the food rationed. We women shared duties and took turns creating meals from the food the men scavenged or had donated to them. Never will I forget one particular bag of carrots that we sorted through to find a few good ones. I didn't know rotten carrots could smell so awful.

We met some wonderful, zealous men and women of God in rainy Washington. We also met ourselves in that dank basement as we tried not to tread on each other's feelings in our communal setting. Then I developed a bronchial cough that wracked my body and threatened the life of our unborn child. Something had to be done, *but what?*

One Sunday morning, we took our little family and went to visit an Assemblies of God church. Solemnly we sat amongst the well-dressed worshipers and awaited our fate. What would God say?

The minister read his text:

> *Then I went down to the potter's house, and, behold, he wrought a work on the wheels. And the vessel that he made of clay was marred in the hand of the potter: so he made it again another vessel, as seemed good to the potter to make it. Then the word of the LORD came to me, saying, O house of Israel, cannot I do with you as this potter? saith the LORD. Behold, as the clay is in the potter's hand, so are ye in mine hand, O house of Israel.*
> *–Jeremiah 18:3-6*

Charles and I looked at each other. The vessel was broken "in the hands of the Potter." We were still in His hands. He would make us again. We drank in the message like thirsty travelers on desert sands. Then, humbling ourselves, we called home and borrowed money.

When we arrived back home, in debt and discouraged, we discovered that our house hadn't sold, and the man who took the teaching contract had changed his mind. We had a house, Charles had a job, and we were still in the Potter's hands.

I recalled the story of a man in 1 Kings named Elijah, who took a trip to Mt. Carmel. When he arrived there, he challenged the prophets of Baal, and the assembly at the mountain watched in awe as the sacrifice and the water that had been poured around it were consumed by fire from heaven.

"The Lord, he is the God," they declared.

Elijah's triumph was profound, but his reason for victory was simple: "I have done all these things at thy word," he said (1 Kings 18:36).

I realized that the faith that succeeds is built upon obedience to a word from God.

TRUST HIM
by Fern Willner

When the years are passing by,
And your dreams appear to die;
You don't need to question why,
Trust Him!

Never trade His will for yours,
Though you see the open doors;
You'll regret mistaken chores,
Trust Him!

In your patience you possess,
Souls of men and happiness;
Seek not less despite the stress,
Trust Him!

He will speak, and not too late,
Hearing Him is worth the wait;
Father has a perfect date,
Trust Him!

We didn't have any furniture and had to sit on the floor for a while, but we were thankful that when we acknowledged our mistake, God gave us mercy.

When we feel pressed for time, it is often hard to remember that God is never late.

Faith is Effective
When There is Unity

"That if two of you shall agree on earth
as touching any thing that they shall ask,
it shall be done for them of my Father
which is in heaven."
Matthew 18:19

Agreement on earth releases
provision from heaven.

4

To Africa with Five Dollars

*By faith Abraham, when he was called to go out into a
place which he should after receive for an inheritance,
obeyed; and he went out, not knowing whither he went.*
—Hebrews 11:8

The year was coming to an end, and the school principal needed
to know Charles' intentions for the coming year. Did he plan to
renew his contract? Charles was uncertain. If he received another
invitation to work in Africa, would he be tied to a contract and
unable to follow his heart? He struggled with his sense of responsibility as a provider and his need to answer the call to missionary
work in Africa.

He finally decided to teach for one more year and then to with-
draw from teaching. He decided to make every effort to find God's
perfect will. Every day he rose as usual, dressed, ate breakfast, and
left for the church. He spent the day there, fasting and praying. His
discipline continued for weeks. Suddenly, unsolicited invitations
for meetings began to arrive. We traveled to New Mexico, California, Michigan, Illinois, Arkansas, Rhode Island, and other states.
Then, while we attended a class reunion in Rhode Island at Zion
Bible Institute, Nat Saginario, the school's choir director, invited

Charles to travel with the choir to Africa and asked if he would be a speaker.

Charles looked at me. We were both excited. It was right. We knew it. I nodded in agreement, and he accepted the invitation. Charles would have to raise his own travel and expense money, and I would be left alone with the care of four children and no certain income. We would be catapulted into a ministry of faith.

Not long after Charles left for Africa with the team, letters began to arrive with glowing reports. He was thrilled to be ministering there. The joy and musical ability of the choir were a blessing to the churches and schools where they sang. What an incredible opportunity.

It was also a ministry-training experience. The Christian fortitude of most of the members was challenged by changes in food, accommodations that kept them in close proximity, weeks of tiring, scheduled travel, and the continuing responsibility to minister no matter how they felt.

Then I received a letter from Kenya that read, "Get the children's shots and start packing. The director of a small Bible school here has invited us to take their place when they go home on furlough in a month."

God had opened the long-awaited door to a ministry in Africa. I shared the announcement at our church. A young couple took the children and me to Fort Leonard Wood to get yellow fever shots. Other friends helped me pack. A newsletter was mailed. Without realizing it, we had established a support group of friends during the previous years of traveling ministry. When Charles returned home, he made a quick ministry trip, and then accepted a job offer from a fellow church member, building a house for a couple of weeks. We didn't know it then, but he would later use the building techniques he learned on the job to help put roofs on village churches.

Friends rallied in support. Others didn't. After ministering in one church, a lady confronted me outside in the parking lot.

"What kind of a mother are you," she challenged, "to take your children over to Africa and deprive them of a decent home and a proper education?"

To the casual observer, it probably did seem like sheer ignorance for us to put our family in such a position of uncertainty. But after months of prayer, we were ready to take the step. The response of obedience filled us with expectancy but whenever we were tempted to take an "intelligent" look into the total uncertainty of it all, it was frightful.

Eventually the rest of our ticket money came from unexpected sources, and our departure day arrived. Mom and Dad must have been more than a little apprehensive as they watched me board the waiting van. It was only ten days before Baby Mina was due. Where would this baby be born? We didn't know, but we had a sense of divine guidance and protection. Our move was further confirmed when, even at that late date, my doctor willingly wrote a letter giving consent for me to fly.

Two young couples escorted us to the St. Louis airport. As we drove, Charles hid a frightening secret. Just before we left, an unexpected bill claimed most of our money. It was too late to cancel the flight or change the itinerary. Was this a Gideon move? When the host of the Midianites came against Israel, God whittled Gideon's army down to 300 men so that Israel could never say, "Mine own hand hath saved me" (Judges 7:2). The success of this mission would be of God and not of us.

Charles will never forget the quiet sense of desperation he felt as he shielded me from our dilemma. He watched two-year-old Ruth, three-year-old William, five-year-old Jeffrey, and six-year-old Deborah walk across the tarmac to the waiting plane, each trusting child carrying a shoulder bag of favorite toys, and he prayed. We would arrive in Africa with only five dollars.

As the plane descended for landing at the Nairobi airport, we pressed our noses against the oval windows, eagerly surveying our new world. The sun shone brightly on African workers in a nearby field. They stopped their work and stood to wave a welcome to their unnamed guests. Then the doors of the airplane opened, and we smelled the scent of the tropics for the first time. It was a warm, moist, earthy scent unlike any we knew. We disembarked. Richard and Ila Kirby greeted us warmly, then took us to their home on the little campus of Harvest Fields Bible School.

A few days later, Charles located a three-bedroom duplex within easy walking distance of the school. Excitedly, we moved our few belongings into the house. The Kirbys loaned us some basic furniture, a few necessary kitchen items, and a little money to live on until our own support began coming in. Each shopping trip provided us with items that helped furnish our home. Empty tin cans were converted to drinking glasses, and the cardboard boxes became our bedroom dressers. Some of Mina's cloth diapers doubled as curtains on the windows of our new home. Need was certainly the mother of design!

We found a skilled Seventh Day Adventist doctor who accepted me as a patient, and it was none too soon. A few days later, baby Mina indicated her intentions to meet the outside world. She was in such a hurry; she made her grand entrance into the labor room instead of the delivery room. Our new doctor missed most of the event, but the nurses on duty rose to the occasion. In the meantime, Peace Corps workers Ed and Kathy Putnam, who shared the room with us, were entertained by the scurried commotion, then the newborn wailing behind the curtain around my bed. They later became wonderful friends.

When Charles applied for health insurance, we were immediately accepted. The normal waiting period was waived, and he returned to the hospital in awe. Our total bill at the Nairobi hospital would be $7.00.

The hospital stay was my first real introduction to Kenyan culture. Staying in a ward with approximately 20 African women was a novel experience. As the only white woman, I created considerable interest.

"What is your name?" they asked.

"Fern Willner," I answered.

"Where are you from?" they questioned.

"Missouri," I replied.

"How many children do you have?"

"Five," I stated.

They were shocked. The concept of a white woman with five children was contrary to the western guidelines of family planning that were being widely taught in African schools and clinics. But when Charles and I adopted Psalm 127, we decided to carefully trust our bodies to God. Although babies began to arrive quicker than we planned, we still considered them to be gifts from God.

When visiting hours were announced, groups of visitors hurried in and gathered around the new mothers. Soon I heard the word *Missouri* echoed from one end of the room to the other. My, I mused, *the news of the white woman from Missouri with five children is spreading fast.*

That night, the women taught me Swahili greetings. "*Habari* means 'how are you,' and *mzuri* (pronounced like Missouri), means 'fine,'" they explained. It was then that I realized my reputation had not reached as far as I had supposed!

Language differences and voluntary tutoring were not the only things that made this an unusual hospital stay. Our simple room was charmed by tropical sunbeams and the songs of native birds. Balmy breezes blew through the open windows and wafted the perfume of brilliantly-colored flowers to our bedsides. Doctors made their rounds casually dressed in shorts and rubber sandals, and the bathroom was called a "water closet."

But for me, teatime was one of the most delightful highlights in this hospital experience. Tea was served mid-morning and mid-afternoon. Each tray held a stainless steel tea service, including a small pot of hot Kenyan tea, a little pot of hot milk, another of hot water, and a dish of dainty delicacies. It was a custom I quickly adopted into our family's lifestyle. The hospital experience was a wonderful and unforgettable introduction to many years of ministry in Africa. Evidently, our hospital stay agreed with Mina, too. She settled in quickly and slept through the night her first night at home.

What made this trip to Africa so different from the Washington disaster? There may have been many factors, but perhaps the most important one was that Charles and I were in agreement as a couple when we made this decision. God loves unity. In Psalm 133:3, He likens it to the anointing oil that flowed over Aaron's beard and down to the skirts of his garments, or to the life-giving dew that descended upon the mountains of Zion. In Ephesians 4:3, God exhorts us again to "endeavor to keep the unity of the Spirit in the bond of peace."

Why, I wonder, *is unity so important?*

The Bible says that answered prayer comes from the place of unity: "That if two of you shall agree on earth as touching any thing that they shall ask, it shall be done for them of my Father which is in heaven" (Matthew 18:19). There is strength in unity: "A threefold cord is not easily broken" (Ecclesiastes 4:12). God manifests His presence in the place of unity: "For where two or three are gathered together in my name, there am I in the midst of them" (Matthew 18:20). Life and blessing are imparted in the place of unity: "For there the LORD commanded the blessing, even life for evermore" (Psalm 133:3).

If all of these things are the result of unity, then what is the result of disunity? According to these Scriptures, God's blessing is limited, answers to prayer are hindered, strength is weakened, God's presence is missing when we meet together, and death is manifested instead of life. But I also learned that true unity goes beyond just agreeing to do and think the same thing. True unity is finding our place together in the will of God and agreeing together to do it. When God's will becomes our will, it releases a flow of faith, and the impossible becomes possible.

Faith Originates From God
Not From Good Intentions

"Examine yourselves,
whether ye be in the faith . . . "
2 Corinthians 13:5

When zealous statements of faith
have no divine origin
they bear no witness of truth,
and bring no comfort.

5

Flight in the Night

And Nathan said to the king, Go, do all that is in thine heart;
for the LORD is with thee. And it came to pass that night,
that the word of the LORD came unto Nathan, saying,
Go and tell my servant David, Thus saith the LORD,
Shalt thou build me an house for me to dwell in?
—2 Samuel 7:3–5

News and visitors from home were welcome diversions from chasing spiders, fighting deadly mosquitoes, and struggling to communicate in an unknown tongue. When two gentlemen came to Kenya on a missionary trip and asked to stay with us, we were delighted. Charles and I gladly gave them our bedroom and moved in with the children.

The men were Bible school teachers and ministers with a great sense of humor. In the evening, they retired to their room to study and pray, but the solemnity didn't last for long. We heard yelling, jumping from bed to bed, then the sound of shoes banging on the wall. The ministers shouted encouragement to one another while in hot pursuit with their shoes, and the unministerial-like activity was mixed with peals of laughter.

We knew what they were doing. Big black spiders dotted the walls of our home, and Charles and I and the children had also climbed the beds many a time, shoes in hand, chasing the ugly intruders. We finally learned it was a hopeless battle. There were more spiders than there was time to do arachnid warfare, and since we had never been bitten, we learned to cohabit. Our guests, however, continued to entertain us daily with their zeal to conquer.

Since our arrival in Africa, Charles had already traveled to a number of villages where he ministered and made friends. He decided to introduce our visiting brethren to the churches. He warned our evangelistic friends about the dangers of drinking unboiled water and eating uncooked foods. Then he took them to share the Word of the Lord in the mud churches.

It was a new experience for them to sit on seats constructed simply of a tree bough, in a church with a grass roof and a mud floor. The pastor and members of the congregation were thrilled to have guests. The program lengthened as the men were treated to special renditions of the children's choir, the youth choir, and the mama's choir. Others were inspired to testify or to sing special songs. As the service lengthened, the gentlemen leaned wearily against the whitewashed wall.

In a moment of mischievous inspiration, Charles leaned over and explained in a hushed whisper, "These people are very creative. Their nice white walls are painted with chicken dung."

Patient expressions suddenly changed to wide-eyed alarm as our friends sat bolt upright with their hip bones resting on the unaccommodating tree bough. No amount of whispered reassurance changed their minds. They were decidedly resolved to finish the service in silent suffering.

Then, one day a letter came from Mom. Dad, who had been diagnosed with cancer, was in the advanced stages and not expected to live long.

"I think you should go and see him," Charles said.

I packed quickly. Baby Mina was only a few months old and nursing, so I would take her with me. Sadly, I told the rest of the children and our guests good-bye, and we left for the airport. At the ticket counter, Charles explained our need to the agents, and they booked me immediately.

As we walked across the tarmac to the waiting plane, Charles used those last few minutes of time to give me hurried instructions about the trip. I looked at him as he talked. He was assuming a heavy load. It would not be easy for him to continue with the work of the ministry and the care of four small children, alone. It was dark as we paused at the foot of the loading stairs that lead up to the plane.

We kissed good-bye again, and I started up the steps, carrying baby Mina. Halfway up, I felt that uncomfortable sense of walking away from the will of God. As much as I loved my dad and wanted to be near him, I knew it was wrong to go. My place was in Africa with my husband and children, who were already bravely engulfed in culture shock. It wasn't right to leave them motherless now. God hadn't made a mistake in bringing us here at this time. He knew Dad's needs. Dad was safe in God's loving hands.

Turning around, I walked back down the steps.

"Charlie, I don't feel right about going," I said. "I need to stay here."

"Are you sure, Fern?"

The decision was mine, but Charles wanted to be sure that I knew he solidly backed me if I wanted to go.

"I'm sure," I replied. "Let's go home."

Quietly, we walked back to the car and drove home.

We arrived at the house and silently walked in. It felt like a funeral parlor. Then, the room exploded in a flurry of hugging, kissing, crying, grateful children. Our guests watched and cried. As the older of the two gentlemen struggled with his emotions, he said, "God is going to honor your sacrifice, Sister Willner. He is going to heal your father."

His sincerity was evident, but his words didn't hold that ring of truth that accompanies a rhema word from God. In my heart, I knew that the good-intentioned prophecy was not true. The kind-hearted man was speaking out of his emotions. Dad was dying. I would never see him again in this life. God helped me make a difficult decision, and I did not need unfounded prophetic words born of sympathy to justify my action or to give me a false hope in the midst of my sorrow. My action was an act of obedience to God's prompting, no matter what its consequences might be.

Shortly afterward, Dad did die, but I never forgot the good intentioned words of our visitor. They were an indelible demonstration to me that truth is the only real comforter. I realized that statements of faith built on good intentioned emotion are like sounding brass and a tinkling cymbal. They will not build faith in the hearer or provide solid guidance or hope in the time of need. When we speak the truth in love, however, that truth is like an anchor that holds us securely when the storms of life, like a maelstrom, threaten to draw us into their deathly whirlpool. Only truth spoken in love gives real comfort and security. Only truth is the divine lifeline of reality.

Faith Does Not Worry
About Daily Provision

"Wherefore, if God so clothe
the grass of the field,
which today is, and tomorrow is
cast into the oven,
shall he not much more clothe you,
O ye of little faith?"
Matthew 6:30

Beloved, should the brook run dry
And should no visible supply
Gladden thine eyes, then wait to see
God work a miracle for thee.
Thou canst not want, for God has said
He will supply His own with bread.
His word is sure. Creative power
Will work for thee from hour to hour,

6

The $1,512.64 Letter

But my God shall supply all your need according
to his riches in glory by Christ Jesus.
—Philippians 4:19

Charles scheduled personal weekend safaris into outlying villages as often as possible. These visits brought encouragement and teaching both to the pastors and to the congregations. We didn't own a vehicle, so he traveled by public transportation. When the bus or country taxi in which he was riding reached the village of its destination, the host pastors and elders often met him under the village trees. From there, they walked through stands of banana trees, over hillsides of growing tea, or under canopies of native trees to the pastor's home. Sometimes the walk took only a few minutes, but many times it took several hours.

"It's not far," the pastors would say to Charles encouragingly when his steps started to lag. "We just have to go over the next hill."

Eventually he realized that "just over the next hill" may mean another six hours of walking. It wasn't unusual for him to come home from those weekend meetings with blistered and bloody feet.

Charles had an outstanding ability to find his way around and made many return trips alone to remote villages that he had visited deep in the forest.

"Why do you do this when you don't have a car?" some of the people asked. "We are used to walking in the heat and dust, but it is very difficult for a missionary."

One Bible school student explained, "If God wants you to travel, He will give you a car."

"Oh, no," Charles responded. "If I travel, God will see that I need a car."

God honored his faith. One day we received a check for $500 from a woman in North Carolina.

"I was praying," she said, "and felt led to send you this money toward the purchase of a car."

Charles was jubilant when we made a down payment on a car of our own.

We had been staying in Nairobi where Charles was filling in for another missionary who was home on furlough and also had the responsibility of looking after the Harvest Fields Bible School located there. When this missionary returned, we accepted an invitation to work in Meru, one of the towns Charles had visited. Meru was approximately a four-hour drive northeast of Nairobi. One day we drove up together to see the town and to try to find a house to rent. Our search was futile.

Several days after we returned home, a car drove into our yard. It was another missionary couple.

"We just came back from Meru," they said. "We are moving up there and heard that you are, too. We went up to look for a house to rent and just happened to discover two houses built in the middle of a cornfield. They are so hidden from view by the corn that you can't even see them from the road. One of them is brand new. Both of the houses are well-constructed of cement block. They have three bedrooms, a bathroom with a bathtub, a kitchen, a dining room, and a living room with a fireplace. On top of that, they are very affordable. We chose the older one because it suits our needs better, but we thought the new one would be great for you guys."

All of us were excited. Then it dawned on us. What would we furnish a house with? After returning the items loaned to us by the Kirbys, we would have precious little to put in our new house.

We checked the newspaper and found an ad by an expatriate family. They were selling all of their household goods and leaving the country. It was the ideal answer. The only problem was, we didn't have enough money to buy anything.

"We can at least go and see what they have," we decided.

It was a lovely home, and they had everything we needed, the refrigerator, the stove, the cutlery and kitchen utensils, the furniture, everything. We made note of the items we would like to buy and the prices. Finally, we totaled the cost of our selected items. It came to $1,512.54. The prices were excellent and the opportunity seemed providential, but we didn't have $1,512.54. Now what? It was heart-rending to find such a good deal and have to walk away from it.

We told the lady of the house good-bye, suggesting that we might be back. In the car, we prayed and brainstormed. Surely there was some possible solution to our problem. We wracked our brains, but to no avail. Nothing. The money just wasn't there, anywhere. We were stymied.

Finally, tired of thinking, Charles said, "I need to pick up a part for the car. Let's drive downtown."

In a way, it was a psychological diversion to give us time to adjust to our loss. We didn't feel like going home just yet. On the way to the car parts shop, we stopped by the post office. Charles found one letter and tossed it through the window onto my lap as he passed by going to the car parts shop.

"You open it," he said dispiritedly. "I'll be right back."

It was from our home church in Springfield, Missouri.

"We just came back from a great camp meeting in Arkansas," it read. "During one service, we felt led to take up a special offering for the Willners. When we announced it, there was such a spirit of giving, we decided that you must need this money right away. We sent it immediately. God bless you. We are praying for you."

A check for $1,512.64 fell onto my lap—ten cents over the exact amount of the cost of the items that we had just selected.

The timing was perfect. It was incredible, almost unbelievable!

Quietly, I sat alone in the car, savoring the moment, holding the miracle money in my hands. Then Charles came back.

"Look at this, Charlie," I said, handing him the letter.

He opened the letter, saw the check and exploded in excited delight!

I don't remember if we peeled rubber as we took off, but we probably did. That was a shopping trip to be remembered.

According to Matthew 6:32, "your heavenly Father knoweth that ye have need of all these things." But often, from our point of view, our earthy needs seem so difficult for God to meet, we invariably factor in circumstances that we are assured will make it difficult or nearly impossible for God to keep His promise of provision. To be loosed from that bondage of faith by sight, I found, takes a great deal of effort. It doesn't just happen. But in this particular test, God showed us His mercy in the form of a providential letter. He gave us a gift of encouragement to help us learn to decide to have faith, to help us learn to determine to believe the promises rather than the circumstances.

We moved to Meru to the brand new three-bedroom house with a fireplace. It was the nicest home we had ever lived in. A local boy came and asked to be our gardener. It wasn't long before we discovered that Michael was a naturally gifted horticulturist. He created a neatly sculpted lawn with gardens of brilliant flowers surrounding our house in the cornfield. As they flourished under his care, he flourished in his achievement. What a gift he was. Later, when we left Kenya, the Methodist boarding school hired him as its gardener.

"Watch this," he said to the children one day, as he presented us with a potted green plant. It was a fern-like plant, but with broader leaves. Gently, he ran his finger over the leafy fronds. To our amazement, the fronds began to close like frightened little beings trying to hide. The once healthy plant now appeared to be wilted and dying.

"Wait quietly," Michael instructed us.

We waited. Slowly, the delicate fronds opened and formed a healthy plant again. We all loved to demonstrate the conduct of our novel plant to guests, and they were no less fascinated with its unusual response to touch than we were. We later learned that it was a type of mimosa, commonly called the "sensitive plant."

* * *

One day, four-year-old, blond-haired William came home pulling his little red wagon behind him. It was filled with flying termites he had carefully gathered. He had already learned that the insects were a favorite feast during certain seasons.

"Mama, please fry them," he begged.

I didn't want to disappoint my little cherub of a son, but just one look at the wriggling termite mass put me in a serious state of squeamishness. I honestly, seriously thought about attempting the task, but with another look at the insects, I knew it was definitely out of the question. Then I had an idea.

Just over the fence behind our house, in a mud hut, lived a busy African family with their old patriarchal grandfather.

"Take them over to the old grandpa," I suggested lovingly. "He would love to fry them for you."

What a blessing to have neighbors, I thought with relief.

Happily, William went to visit and share his bugs.

* * *

Our neighbors also nurtured a hive of bees, housed in a barrel hanging from a tree branch right near my clothesline. The African bees weren't a passive lot, and when I hung my laundry outside, I learned to do it quickly and quietly, to the tune of their angry humming. Had I been as informed about the temper of African bees as I am now, I may have done it even faster.

On the edge of town was a large Catholic compound with a well-equipped nursery and elementary school. Charles bought a big black motorcycle, and morning and afternoon, it served as our school bus. Those rides were special events. Charles carefully placed William and Ruth in front of him, astraddle the gas tank, and Deborah and Jeff behind him. With a kiss and a wave, they carefully roared off down the roads of dried red clay, powdery in the dry season and glass slick in the rainy season.

Towering fern trees dripping with lavender flowers and flame trees brilliant with red-orange blooms edged in gold gave them shade. Huge bushes of bright yellow daisies decorated the roadsides. Fascinated children and adults waved as the strange bus passed by with its passengers dressed in crisp blue and white uniforms.

"Fern, you need to learn how to drive the motorcycle," Charles said one day. "You might need to take the children to school sometime when I am gone."

The black "beast" looked formidable, but I was willing to try. One day, when the children were at school and Charles was out of sight, I made my first attempt. Carefully, I walked the machine down the drive and away from the house where I was well secluded by cornstalks. I hopped aboard, turned the key in the ignition, and gave it some gas. It leaped forward like a horse at the starting gate.

"Control it, control it," I said breathlessly to myself. "Don't let it tell you what to do. You tell it what to do."

But it didn't work. The motorized monster careened wildly between cornstalks, deposited me in the nearest ditch, and lay down beside me.

Trembling, I stood up to assert my authority. It took almost all of my might, but I hauled the resisting vehicle to an upright position, marched it back to the starting point, and tried again.

"Humans are smarter than machines. Right? I can do this. Right?"

I mounted the apparatus again, but in spite of my best efforts, the beast was determined to carry me where I did not want to go. There was an abysmal sense of impending doom before I was flung into the ditch once again.

When I was sufficiently black and blue, I concluded that driving a motorcycle was not my calling. I was content to cook, teach in the Bible school, type newsletters, and take care of children, but no amount of encouraging from Charles ever enticed me to tackle the monster again.

But the inability to transport myself or the children on the motorcycle did not dampen the joy I was beginning to feel as I realized all that God had provided for us. One day it dawned on me. I had been accused of depriving my children of a stable home and a good education if I went to Africa with my husband. Now God had abundantly provided those very things! We now had a lovely home and the children were receiving an excellent education.

We read that the children of Israel danced on the shores of the Red Sea after their great deliverance because they saw Pharaoh's army drown. But when they were instructed to cross over and conquer the land of Canaan, a land of milk and honey and enormous grapes, they declined. How could little men that looked like grasshoppers in comparison to the giants that lived there, possibly overcome such obstacles? It seemed humanly impossible. Those giants were nothing to be sneered at. Deuteronomy 3:11 tells us that the bed of a giant named Og was more than thirteen feet long and six feet wide.

Yes, it is hard to believe in what we do not see, declare what we do not understand, and receive by faith that which is unknown, because we have a promise from an unseen Father. But perhaps that is what makes the declared faith of a human being so outstanding and brings such joy to the Father.

Because faith is so important, God allows it to affect us in our most basic form of need, the need for food and clothes. And something wonderful happens when we decide we will not complain, we will not quit, we will not die. Something changes inside us when we decide to sing aloud, to praise with faith, to trust and not be afraid, to refuse to be grasshoppers because He is our God. For when we praise with faith, it lifts our hearts into the realms of divine truth and calls the angels to our assistance.

THE LIVING PRAISE HIM!
By Fern Willner

Years ago when young with childish wonder,
I discovered morning, wet with dew;
Sparkling, trembling on the leaves and grass blades
Nature's diamonds, beautiful and new.

Birds excited, singing, full of praises,
Filled my room with song and beckoned come;
How could one lie dull with sleep and silent,
While creation joined the rising sun?

Baby things all frolicking and joyful,
Scampered in the fresh unfolding morn;
All around, the creatures and creation,
Woke with life to greet a new day born.

As the morning broke with dewy splendor,
My heart beat, nor could I sleep for long;
Quickly I arose and joined the chorus,
Singing praise in happy, morning song.

Years passed by and slowly quite unknowing,
Business pressed in hard upon my world;
Duties, needs, life's daily plans and burdens,
Grievous cares across my life were hurled.

Planning, worried, wondering 'bout tomorrow,
Fitful sleeping, waking weary still;
Rising weakly, facing busy turmoil,
Robins sang unheeded on my sill.

Does our walk as Christians sometimes follow,
Such a parallel of burdened change?
As our new found love for God gets dimmer,
Peace and joy fall slowly out of range?

Soul, be still and listen for a moment!
Songs of gladness, praises fill the air;
Not of trained and cultured, proud musicians,
But of lilting, warbling everywhere.

Care they not for audience nor scorner,
Glad they are for each new rising sun;
With it comes provision by their maker,
For He knows the needs of everyone.

Loud they cry in praise and adoration,
Unconcerned if friend or foe approve;
Only knowing they were born to praise Him,
Cares and needs cannot their songs remove.

Come, wake up my soul, and join the chorus,
Sing aloud His praises on your bed;
Let the glory of His presence bless you,
For the living praise Him, not the dead.

Faith Will Not Substitute Sacrifice for Obedience

"And Samuel said,
Hath the LORD as great delight
in burnt offerings and sacrifices,
as in obeying the voice of the LORD?
Behold, to obey is better than sacrifice,
and to hearken than the fat of rams."
1 Samuel 15:22

*Our greatest sacrifice to God
is not enough
to justify disobedience.*

7

"But Lord, I Fast Twice in the Week"

But this thing commanded I them, saying, Obey my voice, and I will be your God, and ye shall be my people: and walk ye in all the ways that I have commanded you, that it may be well unto you.
—Jeremiah 7:23

Charles had an invitation to minister in Nigeria. We lay in bed in our Meru home and talked about the upcoming trip, then settled down to sleep. I had just fallen asleep when a voice spoke to me and said, "I want you to go, too." I didn't know if it was an audible voice or a dream, but I woke Charles up and shared the words with him. Because of the expense involved in taking me too, Charles decided to make Nigeria a stopover and go on home to Canada. After two years in the tropics, it was time for a break.

We had an unforgettable time of ministry in Nigeria, spent a few months in the United States, and eventually settled in Niagara Falls, Canada. We stayed busy teaching and preaching and rearing our growing family and every summer Charles spent six weeks ministering in Africa. He held pastors' seminars and took items like amplifiers, guitars, eyeglasses, clothing, and medicines to the people. His yearly summer missionary trips left us trusting God to be our provider and protector, and God never failed us.

Several weeks after Charles left one summer, I received calls from a couple of churches up north that wanted to combine and schedule a week of meetings.

"Would you come and speak for us?" they asked.

I expected it to be challenging to care for the family and speak every night, but where God guided, He always provided. The children and I would also enjoy the country scenery.

"Lord, make us a blessing," I prayed.

Studying the map, I determined the distance we expected to travel and the amount of money needed for gas. I then calculated in the luxury of one pleasure stop at a McDonalds en route that had affordable ice cream; we all liked ice cream. We were excited.

The children traveled well, although the ice cream did elevate sugar levels and give me hyper company for a while. After several hours of driving, we arrived at our destination. Our hostess took us to a small apartment in a country home that had been prepared for us. The accommodations were adequate, but not elaborate, and allowed the children and me to remain together comfortably. That evening, the gracious congregations gave us a warm, country welcome.

Studying and preparing to minister each night while caring for six active children kept me busy.

"God, please reward these people for their expense in bringing us here, but most of all, accomplish Your will," I prayed.

Prior to this engagement, I had begun fasting two days a week, Tuesdays and Thursdays. With the increased demands of our growing ministry and family, I felt a need to discipline my body, mind and spirit in order to meet the greater challenges. It was hard, but the spiritual discipline was rewarding. I experienced a greater keenness in my spirit, a renewed presence of the Lord, and an increased anointing in the gifts of teaching and prophecy.

One morning, as I placed the children's breakfast on the table, the Lord spoke clearly to my heart.

"I want you to eat today," He said.

O Lord, not today, not on my fast day, I thought. I tried to ignore the still small voice, thinking it must be my flesh rising up. *Surely God wouldn't tell me to stop doing something so spiritually rewarding,* I thought. But the little voice persisted.

"You must eat today," He instructed gently.

By now I was genuinely confused. I sincerely did not want to abort this rewarding discipline, nor allow my flesh to deceive me and cause me to lose God's blessing. Yet, I felt that I knew the voice of the Lord and He was definitely telling me to eat. Desperate to know God's perfect will, I picked up my Bible and did what we were told not to do in Bible school. I closed my eyes, prayed a quick prayer asking God to confirm His word, randomly opened the Bible, and put my finger on the page. Would God speak? I knew He could if He considered it really necessary. I opened my eyes and read the verse my finger pointed to. This is what it said:

> *The Pharisee stood and prayed thus with himself, God, I thank thee, that I am not as other men are, extortioners, unjust, adulterers, or even as this publican. I fast twice in the week, I give tithes of all that I possess.*
> *–Luke 18:11,12*

Dumbfounded, I reread the passage in its amazing clarity. Obviously, God was showing me the futility of attempting to determine my own recipe of righteousness to achieve God's blessing. Obedience today may be disobedience tomorrow. At no point in my Christian experience could I become wise enough to live without dying daily. I knew that Jesus did encourage fasting and gave instructions concerning it, but obviously today was not one of those days.

"Lord," I reminded Him, "I really need your anointing to minister. I must do everything I can to prepare myself to be used effectively for you here." But, inwardly I struggled with the knowledge that if I chose to pursue my own methods of spiritual enrichment, without the approval of the Holy Spirit, I was in danger of producing only Pharisaical self-righteousness. Was it coincidental that I had opened up to the only Scripture in the whole Bible that talks about fasting twice in the week?

Before Jesus ascended, He promised His disciples that He would send the Comforter, who would "teach you all things." The Comforter was obviously trying to teach me something that I did not understand. One thing was for sure—it was more important to eat in obedience than to fast in disobedience. I ate my breakfast.

When the meetings concluded and we returned home, I continued eating. Instead of gaining strength, however, I became increasingly weak and nauseous. Finally, a visit to the doctor confirmed my growing suspicions. I was pregnant. Now I understood. While I was busy focusing on a ministry, God was gently watching over the health and safety of a young mother and a growing fetus. In my ignorance, I would have deprived our tiny baby of needed nourishment. But God mercifully answered my prayer for guidance and kept me and our baby safe.

The Bible tells us in 1 Peter that we are guarded by the power of God operating through faith.

> *Blessed be the God and Father of our Lord Jesus Christ, which according to his abundant mercy hath begotten us again unto a lively hope by the resurrection of Jesus Christ from the dead, to an inheritance incorruptible, and undefiled, and that fadeth not away, reserved in heaven for you, who are kept by the power of God through faith unto salvation ready to be revealed in the last time. Receiving the end of your faith, even the salvation of your souls.*
> *—1 Peter 1:3–5,9*

This experience was an enlightening demonstration to me of God's careful guardianship over His children. As a child of faith, we have a divine power working on our behalf which protects us until our full salvation is revealed when the Lord returns. We often forget how powerfully guarded we are and how jealously God watches over us. Occasionally, He allows us to view an act of heavenly intervention and shows us a glimpse of His sovereignty and grace.

Faith Wavers Where There is Double-Mindedness

"Let us hold fast the profession
of our faith without wavering;
for he is faithful that promised;"
Hebrews 10:23

*If we would be unwavering,
our eyes must be focused
on the goal not the past,
and on the promises,
not the circumstances.*

8

"I Ate One of Your Apples"

*Ask, and it shall be given you; seek, and ye shall find; knock,
and it shall be opened unto you: For every one that asketh receiveth;
and he that seeketh findeth; and to him that knocketh
it shall be opened. Or what man is there of you,
whom if his son ask bread, will he give him a stone?*
—Matthew 7:7–9

"Breakfast time," Rosie called. Rose Kremblas was a talented and beautiful girl who came into our lives when we lived in Niagara Falls. She was a single young lady who needed a family. So we welcomed her into our home. We loved her. Even though she was a plucky gal and adapted quickly to the challenges of faith, this was no ordinary Sunday morning breakfast.

Charles was on another missionary trip to Africa. We had searched the cupboards, but they were bare except for a little white flour. The refrigerator was equally barren except for a can of frozen grape juice. Interesting.

"If I add water to the flour and fry it, we would have a kind of a crunchy pancake," Rosie suggested.

"It might not be too bad, even without butter or syrup, when eaten together with the sweet grape juice. If we have the right attitude when we present it to the children, they might not mind," we decided.

"But we are going to have steak for supper tonight," Rosie declared.

She made the crunchy pancakes and grape juice and set the table. The children weren't overly enthusiastic about this latest concoction, but they joined in a prayer of blessing. Charles and I had been taught that the God who calls you is the God who provides for you. When you live by faith, you don't live by begging. This might not appear to be the best breakfast in the world, but if this was all God provided, then we would be thankful.

Later, after we had eaten and I was alone in the kitchen, I walked and prayed and sang the song, "Oh, I've never seen the righteous forsaken, or His seed go begging for bread."

The doubts and discouragement came, but I fought them off and sang on, watering the song of faith with my tears. I must not give up. I had to believe.

At church that morning, someone gave us a love offering. With careful budgeting, I bought steak to honor Rosie's faith, and enough food to last a few more days.

Then, one day the doorbell rang. I opened the door. A stranger stood on my doorstep.

"Are you Sister Willner?" he asked.

"Yes I am," I replied.

"Well then, I have something for you," he said.

He turned and walked to a taxi parked in the driveway. Apparently, he was the driver. He opened a door, and I saw bags and bags of what appeared to be groceries. He brought in a bag. It was groceries. He went back for more bags. Two bags. Three bags. Four bags.

How many bags is he going to bring in? I wondered. *Are all of these groceries for us? I've never had this many groceries in my life.*

He emptied the back of the taxi and then opened the trunk.

Oh God, this is amazing, I thought.

I was as excited as the children were as we peeked into the bags to see what was in them. There were chocolate chips and nuts for baking cookies. They were a luxury I never allowed myself to buy.

There was fruit. We rarely bought fruit. It was too expensive for a family of our size. There was even candy. It was like Christmas.

"Where did all this come from?" I asked the driver.

"The donor is anonymous," the driver explained.

He deposited the last bag of groceries and started to leave but stopped in the doorway.

"Are you really Sister Fern?" he asked again.

"Yes," I said.

"Well, then," he said slowly, "I have a confession to make."

Oh no, I thought, *he must think the term 'sister' means that I am a Catholic nun and am qualified to hear confessions. The poor man must be really confused to see a nun with so many children. No wonder he asked if I was really a sister.*

"I apologize," he said sheepishly, "but I was hungry, and I ate one of your apples."

"Oh, you are most welcome to it, but thank you for telling me," I answered joyously.

Eventually, our benefactor made herself known. She was a Catholic woman who also had seven children. Her Protestant sister-in-law had told her about us. One day, she called and invited me to her home for lunch. Her husband was an architect, and their large home was a local showplace in design and decor. Then they invited the children to come and swim in their enormous indoor swimming pool and play in their amazing multilevel tree house. The children were thrilled.

"Oh God, thank you for rewarding the children for their share in this faith life too."

Our new friend continued to bless us. She made arrangements to have her egg man deliver several flats of eggs to our house regularly. She gave me fruit for canning. And then, one day she said, "I believe a woman can run a house if she has a wooden spoon and a sewing machine." I had the wooden spoon, but she bought me a beautiful new Janome sewing machine.

Through the years, this couple continued to bless us with their friendship and with material goods as the Lord directed them. If we had complained about crispy pancakes and grape juice, would we have hindered God's intended blessing? We realized later that it was a small price to pay for this reward of faith. Had I allowed my faith to waver that morning, I would have demonstrated what James had to say: "For he that wavereth is like a wave of the sea driven with the wind and tossed. For let not that man think that he shall receive any thing of the Lord" (James 1:6b,7).

We never know who or what God will use to meet our needs, but God often uses another person's obedience to strengthen our faith. Like David, we finally realize, " . . . I have not seen the righteous forsaken, nor his seed begging bread" (Psalm 37:25). When we know how much God loves us, it gives us faith to stand steadfast when things seem impossible. God is our faithful provider.

Faith May be
Jump-Started by Fear

"And others save with fear,
pulling them out of the fire;
hating even the garment
spotted by the flesh."
Jude 1:23

*God can use
whatever means He wants to
to get our attention
and to direct our steps,
if we really want Him to.*

9

"Your Car's on Fire!"

When a man's ways please the LORD,
he maketh even his enemies to be at peace with him.
—Proverbs 16:7

"Take your pictures down and prepare to move," God said to me in a dream.

Was this really God? We had only been home from Africa a few months. We were buying a new home, the children were enrolled in school, and I was busy feathering my new nest, helping Charles in ministry, and teaching women's meetings. Was God telling us to go back to Africa so soon? It was so nice to feel safe and normal.

I didn't want to argue with God. But, maybe it wasn't God. Maybe it was just my imagination.

"If it really is God, He will speak again," I reasoned quietly. "He will confirm this word."

I continued to listen in the dream, but I made no response of obedience.

Then, the scene changed, and I saw myself standing in the darkness beside the ashes and rubble of our home.

"Why God?" I cried. "Why did it burn down?"

Very gently, He answered me.

"Fern, you wouldn't take your pictures down, so I did."

It was a very unusual dream. It wasn't threatening or scary, but very specific, very clear, very factual. I shared the dream with Charles then tucked it away in my memory bank for further contemplation.

Several years passed. Charles made trips to Africa in the summer time. During the rest of the year, we stayed busy teaching, preaching, writing and rearing our growing family. A Women's Aglow chapter asked me to teach a weekly Bible study in a nearby town. The group grew, and God blessed our time together. Other invitations came in. But something strange was happening on the home front.

Day after day I went outside to find that children had plastered mud on our front door. *Why? What had we done? What was prompting some of the children that lived near us to act so maliciously,* I wondered as I patiently washed mud off the door.

Then, one day Charles went into the backyard to mow the lawn. As he mowed, the little boy next door entered our yard. He had dipped both of his hands in white paint and purposefully ran up to Charles wiping the white paint on his clothes. Charles was shocked. He picked the boy up, carried him to the fence, and carefully but firmly deposited him on the other side in his own yard. The little boy ran inside screaming and crying and told his parents that Charles had hit him.

The parents were furious, so furious they called the police. The police met with them, then came to our house and sat down to question us.

"You have a problem," the officer informed us after hearing the details of the incident. He wished us well and left.

Then, one night we were awakened by frantic knocking on our front door. It was about 4:00 A.M.

"Someone has set fire to the clubhouse in your backyard," a neighbor told us excitedly. "We've called the fire department. They will be here any minute."

Just then we heard the roar of engines and the scream of sirens as fire trucks careened around the corner racing toward our house.

The boys had worked hard to build their own clubhouse with scrap lumber. It was quite an achievement. Now we stood clustered in the dark house in silence, watching through the patio doors as brilliant yellow-red flames leaped high into the night sky. The glow silhouetted the running firemen in their hard hats as they dragged their hoses behind them. Huge streams of water finally stilled the crackling flames, but the clubhouse was totally destroyed. The firemen left, and we silently returned to our beds.

Shortly after the incident Charles was away ministering. While he was gone, I prayed about the unusual situation.

"God, please show us what is wrong? This is unreal. Why are these things happening to us?"

The next day as I was reading my Bible, one verse suddenly spoke to my heart so strongly it was as if God read it to me aloud. It was Psalm 79, verse four.

"We are become a reproach to our neighbors, a scorn and derision to them that are round about us."

When Israel's ways displeased the Lord, she became a reproach to her neighbors. Our sin may not have been as blatant as theirs, but if I had closed my heart when God attempted to speak to me about returning to Africa, then I too was living in sin. According to this example in Scripture, if I do not listen to His voice, I am walking in rebellion and am setting myself up for reproach.

In my heart, I knew our place was in Africa, but my desire for some of the finer things of life and the security of the western world had led me down a subtle path of rebellion. Lack of faith led to confusion. God's voice was now contrary to my quiet but unspiritual state of self-will.

Charles came home.

"The Lord spoke to me while you were gone," I said. "He gave me a verse in Psalms, and I think it identifies why we have been going through these problems." I read him the verse.

"That's interesting," Charles answered. "While I was away, the Lord spoke this verse to me: 'When a man's ways please the LORD, he maketh even his enemies to be at peace with him,' (Proverbs 16:7). I believe God is telling us that the reason our neighbors are treating us like this is because our ways are not pleasing to Him. I think we need to sit down and have a talk."

As a gift for the many months of teaching, the Women's Aglow chapter paid my way to a regional conference in Honey Harbor, Ontario. Several of us loaded our luggage into a van belonging to one of the ladies, and we traveled to the conference in happy camaraderie. We sang, laughed and fellowshipped as we expectantly approached our destination.

At the conference, the women were divided into groups and assigned a leader for morning prayers. The first morning I met with my group, we introduced ourselves one by one. As we did so, we noticed something very unusual. Almost every woman in the group had some sort of association with Africa. Incidents that each had never shared before surfaced in those introductions, uniting us in a common bond and focusing our attention on that far away country. If I had not believed that God directs the paths of those who love Him, it would have been uncanny. I could not ignore the fact that God was trying to get my attention again.

That night in our room, I felt a strong burden for the family at home. I lay awake thinking and praying. I wanted to call them, but there was no phone in the cottage where we stayed. What was happening? I prayed. Finally I slept.

The speaker at the conference was dynamic. Her messages challenged our unbelief and our need for security. The anointed words reached down into the depths of my heart and pulled up hidden roots of rejection, bitterness, and faithlessness. Then, one night she called us to stand before God to renew our dedication and our commitment to the call of the Lord. I stood with scores of other women that memorable night and sobbed from the depths of my heart. Many of us were baptized in our own tears as we repented before God and were bathed in the peace of His healing love. That meeting was my turning point with God.

When we reached home after the conference was over, Charles met me at the door. One hand was covered in gauze.

"What happened to your hand?" I asked in alarm.

"You won't believe this," he said. "We were in bed when a neighbor called on the phone. 'Your car is on fire,' she shouted. Someone had poured kerosene on the front of our car and set fire to it," Charles said unbelievingly. "I managed to get the fire put out, but I burned my hand in the process and had to go to the emergency room at the hospital to have it treated. Fern, we've had a fire in the backyard and a fire in the front yard . . . " We looked at each other. We knew. It was time to go back to Africa.

Some people told me that God doesn't lead us through fear. Jude doesn't agree with that. He says, in so many words, if you have to use fear to get some people saved, then do it. Some people are drawn by the love of God. Others aren't. They need the strong motivation of fear.

Who knows how many of us came to God, not because we loved Him initially, but because we were afraid of hell. As we grew, our attitudes changed, but fear may have been the hook that caught us.

Jonah is another famous Bible character whose life was turned around by fear. He spent some very miserable days at the bottom of the ocean in the terrifying squeeze of the whale's belly. There, with seaweed wrapped around his head, he repented of his rebellion. When he was ready to obey, God sent him on one of the most rewarding evangelistic missions a man has ever had. Matthew 12:41 compares Jesus to one who was greater than Jonah, whose dynamic preaching had turned a whole nation back to God and saved them from destruction.

We really don't understand God's needs or His ways, so He uses whatever means He can to get our attention and to direct our steps if we really want Him to. We wanted Him to.

We put our house up for sale. It sold. God provided money for all of our fares—Charles, me, and now six, soon to be seven, children.

Our ticket included a luxurious overnight stay in Amsterdam at the expense of the airline. The children swam and played in the hotel pool. We ate dinner in a beautifully decorated dining room where the tables were spread with velvety blue cloths and set with silver. A waiter grilled flaming steaks beside our table while the children watched in awe. We slept in comfort, then awoke the next morning to continue our trip into the unknown.

I'll never forget that transatlantic flight. As we sat upstairs in the huge airliner, I knew we no longer had a home to call our own. We didn't know where we would live in Zaire, now the Democratic Republic of Congo, or what the future held. But, as clouds floated past our windows and we flew into the great unknown, there was no peace in the world like knowing that we were in His perfect will.

Owning my own home had not given me peace. Instead, my anticipated pleasure had become my unexpected bondage. But now, because of God's mercy, I was free at last. God does not want us to become bitter when we experience trouble. The difficulties we experience may be divine roadblocks to help us change direction. When we turn to Him with all of our heart, we will find the real pathway to blessing.

Faith Makes it Possible to be Secure Anywhere

"Yea, though I walk through the
valley of the shadow of death,
I will fear no evil:
for thou art with me."
Psalm 23:4

Anyplace is safe with Jesus,
No place is safe without Him.

10

"Anywhere with Jesus I Can Safely Go"

Thou wilt keep him in perfect peace, whose mind is stayed on thee:
because he trusteth in thee. Trust ye in the LORD forever:
for in the LORD JEHOVAH is everlasting strength.
—Isaiah 26:3,4

We peered eagerly through the airplane windows as our carrier droned noisily on toward our new home. Far beneath us, picturesque villages dotted the banks of Lake Tanganyika. Tiny dugout canoes were grouped on the water's edge, and as the lake shimmered and sparkled in the morning sun, we gazed in quiet wonder.

We would soon be joining hearts and lives with our African brethren in Zaire. Our destination was Kalemie, Zaire, on the western banks of Lake Tanganyika. How would we be received? Would this baby that I carried, yet to be born, find safety in its entrance into a strange and wonderful world?

That morning I had awakened with a sudden fear. It was as if the devil himself had come into the room, sat on the bed beside me, and taunted me.

"What are you doing?" he'd questioned me menacingly. "Don't you know that you are going into a high malarial area? Your children will probably get sick and die. Where will you deliver this baby?

There probably isn't a hospital where you are going. In fact, there probably isn't even a doctor. Your baby will die, and you might die as well. And if you die, who will take care of the children?"

These were all legitimate concerns that I had already faced, and settled, when we'd made the decision to come. Now the devil was trying to resurrect them and use them to taunt me with fear of the unknown.

"If your husband wants to go, let him go. You don't have a right to risk the lives of your six children and your unborn child. You are a foolish, foolish woman. What kind of a mother are you anyway? Take these children, get on the next plane, and go home as fast as you can. Hurry, before it's too late."

A spirit of fear gripped me then. It threatened to annul a God-given call to missions and cast me down to meager faithlessness. I trembled.

What should I do? I took the next most logical step. Quietly I got up and made my way into the bathroom to wash and dress. I turned on the water tap. As I stood waiting for the sink to fill, it suddenly dawned on me that my heart was singing a song. I was amazed. My mind certainly wasn't singing. Deliberately I turned off the water and stood quietly, hoping to hear the words that my heart quietly sang with such assurance. The mental clamor subsided, and the words and music of an old hymn gently surfaced.

"Anywhere! Anywhere! Fear I cannot know; Anywhere with Jesus I can safely go."

Just as the dawning of light dispels darkness, the truth of those words brought peace. Miraculously, faith powerfully displaced the doubt. The transformation was amazing. Circumstances had not changed. We were still going into an area infested with malaria, plagued by cholera, and riddled with disease and danger, but we were going with Jesus.

Now, as we flew toward Bujumbura, Burundi, where we had to make a connecting flight to Zaire, my husband, Charles, leaned over and whispered anxiously in my ear.

"Fern, the flight from Bujumbura, Burundi, to Kalemie, Zaire, only goes once a week. The plane's seating capacity is only twenty-four people, and it's always full. It will be a miracle if all of us can get seats on that plane. If we don't get seats today, we will have to spend a week or two in Burundi waiting for seats on another flight. We can't afford that. We need to ask God to give us seats on that plane today."

He paused, and then continued, "When we arrive in Kalemie, we will need to find a ride from the airport into town. There are very few vehicles in the town of Kalemie and no airport service. The distance from the airport into town is too far for you and the children to walk. Fern, I don't know what we are going to do. It will be a miracle if we can just get a ride, but to get a ride in a vehicle large enough to carry all eight of us and our luggage will really be a miracle."

He closed his eyes and continued praying quietly. He was very worried.

A good wife will share the burden and worry and pray, too, I thought.

Halfheartedly, I attempted to join him in praying for this need, but my recent victory was too new. I didn't want to enter into the stress. Hadn't I been promised just this morning that Jesus was going with us? Hadn't He said that there is safety when we are with Him? Hadn't I been reminded that I didn't need to fear?

I breathed another prayer and returned to my view out the window. We were close enough to the ground to have ringside seats in this tropical panorama of native life. *Awesome!*

We landed in Bujumbura and joined other travelers in the airport lounge. The airport had been a place of beauty at one time, but attractively tiled floors lacked attention and the spacious bar in the departure lounge was deserted and barren. The children twirled the tall bar stools playfully as they curiously investigated their new surroundings. Concern was etched on Charles' face as we watched our inquisitive offspring and waited with the others for news of a flight to Kalemie.

Suddenly, a scream pierced the monotone of conversation. The whole lounge came to life. I looked around, and my heart stopped. There, lying on the floor, was our four-year-old, Bethanie, her head already soaked in blood. Charles rushed to her side and gently gathered her up in his arms. While playing with the bar stools she had fallen and hit her forehead on the hard floor.

"Is there a doctor in the airport?" we asked. "Or is there a bathroom where we can wash off the blood?"

A young man hurriedly guided us to a small adjoining room. There was no running water in the airport, but the young African proudly produced some penicillin powder. As he carefully sprinkled the white powder over the bloody wound, we heard a flight to Kalemie being announced.

"Get the kids quickly and follow me," Charles said. He carried Bethanie, white and blood-soaked, out onto the tarmac to the waiting plane. We followed.

"What happened?" asked the pilot.

Charles explained briefly, and the pilot hurriedly gave orders for all of us to be given seats.

We boarded.

As the plane taxied down the runway and climbed into the clouds over the lake, we knew that God had organized a miracle. *Incredible.*

Charles breathed a sigh of relief. Phase one of our problem was solved. The family was all on the plane. Now we faced the newly urgent phase two, the imminent need of a family physician, and phase three, transportation after arrival.

We hadn't been flying long when someone tapped Charles on the shoulder. It was a French-speaking woman seated directly behind us. She was obviously upset as she watched little Bethanie lying across our laps, pale and matted with blood.

"How is she?" she asked earnestly. "My husband is meeting me at the airport with our Land Rover," she said. "He works for Filtisaf Cotton in Kalemie, and he will take you to our company doctor at the factory dispensary. Afterward he will take you wherever you want to go."

Charles thanked her in French, and we marveled.

Upon arrival in Kalemie, we were introduced to the husband of our new benefactor. They escorted us to the largest Land Rover we had ever seen. We, and our luggage, all fit!

The company dispensary was located near the airport. We stopped and went inside. Our friends introduced us to Dr. Blanpain, a young Belgian doctor who generously agreed to treat Bethanie.

"We won't need to take any stitches," he said after cleaning the wound. "I can close the cut with a butterfly bandage."

Then, turning to me, he said, "I'm more concerned for you. Where do you plan to have the baby? If you would like, I will be glad to help you."

Bethanie's accident was not serious, but because of it, we were all given coveted seats on the airplane, an excellent family physician and friend, and transportation from the airport to town. The chain of events leading to our provision reminded me of the story of Joseph.

Joseph was chosen of God, loved by his father, and bitterly en-vied by his brothers who sold him to be a slave. He was falsely ac-cused by Potifer's wife and imprisoned for ten long years. But when Pharaoh had a dream, God had Joseph in a position to interpret it. In one day's time, he was transferred from the prison to become the ruler of Egypt, second only to Pharaoh. Under his guidance, the powerful country of Egypt survived a seven-year famine and provided food for Israel and his children. God allowed an inconsol-able father to mourn for his son for many years and a young man to suffer injustice and imprisonment. Why? Because His priority was to protect the fledgling nation of Israel.

Later, Joseph said to his brothers, "But as for you, ye thought evil against me; but God meant it unto good, to bring to pass, as it is this day, to save much people alive" (Genesis 50:20).

Even the demonic realm was fooled by the events of the crucifixion. They thought that the pain, betrayal, desertion, public disgrace, and death of Jesus would lead to destruction. They never dreamed that it would lead to the salvation of the world. It is described in 1 Corinthians 2:8 as that "which none of the princes of this world knew: for had they known it, they would not have crucified the Lord of glory."

When we walk with God, the adverse circumstances of our lives are never an indication of failure. Sin, breaking the commandments of God, is always evil, but pain, suffering, financial reversal, or loss, may only be a means used by God of turning one's direction onto a more productive path. Each step will unfold with His divine provision in His divine timing. The provision of God is not dependent on our resources, and the ways of God are not subject to our approval. Our security lies in trusting. And no matter where we are, our faith can stand sure when it is based on the promises of God and not on our own understanding.

ANYWHERE WITH JESUS
Jessie B. Pounds, 1861–1921

Anywhere with Jesus I can safely go;
Anywhere He leads me in this world below;
Anywhere without Him dearest joys would fade;
Anywhere with Jesus I am not afraid.
Anywhere with Jesus I need fear no ill,
Though temptations gather round my pathway still;
He Himself was tempted that He might help me;
Anywhere with Jesus I may victor be.

Anywhere with Jesus I am not alone;
Other friends may fail me, He is still my own;
Though His hand may lead me over dreary ways;
Anywhere with Jesus is a house of praise.

Anywhere with Jesus over land and sea,
Telling souls in darkness of salvation free;
Ready as He summons me to go or stay,
Anywhere with Jesus when He points the way.

Anywhere with Jesus I can go to sleep,
When the darkening shadows round about me creep;
Knowing I shall waken, never more to roam,
Anywhere with Jesus will be home, sweet home.

Chorus:
Anywhere! Anywhere! Fear I cannot know;
Anywhere with Jesus I can safely go.[4]

Faith Born in the Light
May be Tested in the Night

"And the Lord said,
Simon, Simon, behold,
Satan hath desired to have you,
that he may sift you as wheat:
But I have prayed for thee,
that thy faith fail not:
and when thou art converted,
strengthen thy brethren."
Luke 22:31,32

While Satan sifts,
Jesus prays.

11

Culture Shock in the Night

*And I will give thee the treasures of darkness,
and hidden riches of secret places, that thou mayest
know that I, the LORD, which call thee
by thy name, am the God of Israel.*
–Isaiah 45:3

The tropical sun shone brightly as we bumped along the rutted, dirt road leading from the dispensary into town. Bethanie was feeling much better, and I was tremendously relieved to have a new family doctor. We looked about our new surroundings wonderingly as we rode. A few palm trees swaying gracefully offered little shade to the occasional pedestrian, but the people seemed friendly. Some of them waved and smiled as we passed.

Where would home be?

We were told that during the time that Kalemie was under Belgian rule, beautiful homes were constructed, complete with swimming pools and flowering terraced gardens. Well-supplied shops offered imported foods. A theater provided entertainment. The train station boasted uniformed attendants and faultless punctuality. A well-equipped hospital provided excellent medical care. Two and three-decked lake boats lay in the harbor.

Now, the town of Kalemie consisted of thousands of mud huts in various sectors, surrounding the core of the town. The one-time pride of Belgian colonialists lay a skeleton of its former beauty. African residents did not have the money or the expertise to continue the prosperous lifestyle.

Our Land Rover pulled onto a sandy church compound and parked in front of a weather-beaten frame house. Its windows seemed like empty, lidless black eyes staring vacantly out of its poverty.

Why are we stopping here? I thought. *Surely no one lives here.*

To my amazement, a hand waved from the frame window, and a cheery face appeared. Presently, the little woman came bounding outside, hugged us all soundly, and greeted us as if we were long lost friends.

"You can stay with us until you find a place, though it isn't much," she grinned as she led the way inside. Beulah Gardner and her husband, Fred, had arrived only three weeks earlier.

Curious children, chattering excitedly, gathered in a swarm to view the newcomers. They followed us to the entrance as we were guided inside the house, then clustered about the door and vacant windows watching our every move.

As our eyes adjusted to the darkness, we surveyed the mission home. The rough cement floors were cracked and bare and the walls needed paint. There was no electricity or running water. The furniture consisted of several worn, wooden chairs, a simple wooden table, and a bed. Our hostess happily seated us, then busied herself heating water for tea over her little African charcoal burner that sat on the floor. We looked hesitantly about us. *So this was Zaire.*

The Gardners were excited for us when Charles came in with a joyful announcement a few days later.

"The Lord has provided us with a home of our own," he exclaimed.

Everyone was anxious to see it, so off we trekked down the sandy road, across the bridge spanning the Lukuga River, and up the hill to Kankomba. At the top of the hill lay a mission station that had been built by Brethren in Christ missionaries twenty years before. The compound consisted of a red brick church with wooden shutters and a cement floor, three houses constructed of burned mud brick with tin roofs, and several outhouses. The landscaping was typically meager. Scraggly crabgrass struggled to live in the sandy soil. There were several palm nut trees, some guava trees, and some mango trees that provided shade and food for the compound residents. Two huge trees, similar to elms, stood in front of the house that would soon be our home.

Charles explained that when the local pastor and elders of this church heard of our arrival, they wanted us to live in one of the houses on their compound. Their representative led us inside. The walls and floors were cracked and covered with black soot. Rusted screens on the windows had gaping holes which extended an open invitation to hungry, malarial mosquitoes.

Something hung down over our heads that appeared to be rotted canvas. Evidently, it was once a ceiling. Little hands sought mine, and a timid voice half whispered, "Mama, are we going to live here?"

"Yes we are, Honey," I answered as cheerfully as possible, "and we are going to make it look pretty."

We moved in and busied ourselves trying to make our home "pretty" and safe. Searching through the village stores, we were elated to find foam mattresses and nylon mosquito nets. Bedroom spaces were designated on the floor, and soon, neat mattress beds canopied with billowing mosquito nets adorned the appointed sleeping areas. Someone lent us a single bed that was assigned to me and our unborn baby of seven months.

A single pipe with a spigot on the end of it brought water into the kitchen. But we soon discovered that water only came twice a week, generally around 3:00 A.M. We found a large, metal oil drum, cleaned it and placed it under the tap to be filled whenever water came. We boiled some of the water for drinking and used the rest for laundry, cooking, and cleaning. Water was a precious commodity.

The small room adjoining the kitchen became our pantry and bathroom. We kept a metal basin filled with water on the lowest shelf in which to wash our hands. On the edge of the shelf, Charles pounded nails to hang towels and wash cloths. Our bathtub was a bucket. We learned to shampoo last or our wash water would be filled with suds.

At the end of one busy day, I retired to the bathroom for a bucket bath. The water was cool and refreshing, even if it was scant. Finally, I plunged my head into the bucket, soaked my hair, and applied shampoo. I attempted to rinse but got soap in my eyes. Blindly groping for a washcloth I knew was hanging on a nail, I felt something fuzzy. It wasn't the washcloth. I hesitated, opened one eye a little, and peeked. There, with his hands carefully folded above his head clutching my nail, hung a little bat. How had he gotten there so quickly and quietly?

We had heard unusual sounds in the ceiling. Now I knew what it was. We had moved in with a community of bats. One set of tenants was going to have to vacate the premises, but how does one give an eviction notice to bat attic residents?

One evening, as we stood outside talking, we noticed small flying creatures emerging from under the eaves of the house in droves. It was a bat exodus. Evidently, the tiny residents felt our noise level was too high for their liking and found quieter quarters. We quickly took action to block their return.

After busy hours of work and planning for our growing family, sleep was a welcome time of renewal. One night after Charles tenderly kissed me good night and securely tucked in the mosquito net, I fell asleep only to be startled awake when the quiet of our makeshift haven was pierced by foreign sounds. From the valley below, beating drums and drunken voices rose as some kind of orgy began. Evidently, local beer, called *pombe*, was contributing to the volume level of native revelry. The sounds of chanting rose ominously. They were accompanied by driving drum beats that drove winds of fear into my heart.

Hour after hour the chanting voices continued, and the pulsing drum beats throbbed relentlessly. Fear of the unknown etched its own dread into the scene. It had been twenty years since missionaries fled from Kalemie or were killed during the Simba Rebellion. Local church members welcomed us as new missionaries with open arms, but we weren't sure if the unchurched residents endorsed that welcome.

Were some of the people still carrying animosity toward whites? Did our presence revive repressed resentments from colonial rule? Were they angry with the arrival of foreigners? Would roots of bitterness rise unrestrained and emotions become inflamed while under the influence of locally-made booze? Would this party remain in the valley or were they planning a visit that would express their disapproval? When recalling past atrocities, this wasn't outside the realm of possibility.

In the solitude of darkness, I had a much more enlightened view of the situation we had come to be a part of. The prophetic words that had been proclaimed over us during the glory of church conventions didn't mention confrontations with the forces of darkness and ignorance. The promises only sounded wonderful.

I tried to sleep, but the atmosphere was sodden with sultry sin. My heart froze. I prayed, then dozed. More drums. Another hour passed. *When and how would this end?* Delving into my store of memorized Scripture and hymns, I began a quiet recitation.

Not by might, not by power, but by my Spirit saith the Lord.
—Zechariah 4:6

Perfect love casts out fear.
—1 John 4:18

"Anywhere with Jesus I can safely go."

I will trust and not be afraid.
—Psalm 56:11

He that dwelleth in the secret place of the most High shall abide under the shadow of the Almighty.
—Psalm 91:1

Thou shalt not be afraid for the terror by night.
—Psalm 91:5a

The Word worked, and I slept. When I awoke again, at 4:00 A.M., the party was finally over. In the stillness, I had time to think.

Our situation resembled the word that God gave to Abraham, Moses, and Joshua. He showed them the land, gave them a promise, and then told them to go and walk it out. He said to Abraham, "For all the land which thou seest, to thee will I give it, and to thy seed forever. Arise, walk through the land in the length of it and in the breadth of it; for I will give it unto thee" (Genesis 13:15,17).

To Moses he said, "Every place whereon the soles of your feet shall tread shall be yours" (Deuteronomy 11:24a). Then, He passed the same promise on to Joshua, "Moses my servant is dead; now therefore arise, go over this Jordan, thou and all this people, unto the land which I do give to them, even to the children of Israel. Every place that the sole of your foot shall tread upon, that have I given unto you, as I said unto Moses" (Joshua 1:2,3).

When God gives us promises, they are never really ours until we walk them out. The problem is, the promises given on the sunlit mountaintop of glorious church conventions may not gleam as brightly in the valley of obedience when enshrouded by clouds of opposition. However, the end result of victory is not dependent upon the circumstances surrounding it. It is dependent on the truth of the Word of faith. Though circumstances seemingly change for the worse, the Word remains the same. Truth cannot lie.

King Cyrus did not understand the ways of God, but God sent His servant Isaiah to explain some principles of divine authority to him.

I will go before thee, and make the crooked places straight: I will break in pieces the gates of brass, and cut in sunder the bars of iron: And I will give thee the treasures of darkness, and hidden riches of secret places, that thou mayest know that I, the LORD, which call thee by thy name, am the God of Israel.
–Isaiah 45:2,3

Does God allow darkness? The Word says He does! In fact, He explains that treasures are found in the darkness, that hidden riches are found in secret places. A natural example of a treasure found in the darkness is the diamond. A diamond is formed under high temperature and pressure. It is the hardest naturally occurring substance and one of the most valuable. The most valuable diamonds are completely colorless. Imitation diamonds may resemble genuine diamonds so closely that only a jeweler using scientific testing can tell them apart. However, imitation diamonds are softer than genuine diamonds and may show scratches and other signs of wear.[5]

God knows exactly how much pressure and heat we need to make us scratch-resistant. If our scratches are on display, or if we are clouded by sin, unbelief, self-centeredness and fear—we can expect more heat before we become genuine. Isaiah 45:7a says, "I form the light, and create darkness." When God is finished turning up the heat in the darkness of our trials, scratches won't mar the reflection. Cuts and blows will only serve to create a more beautiful jewel, a many-faceted jewel that reflects the wisdom and precision of the Master Craftsman.

Moses knew what darkness was. In Exodus 20:21, "the people stood afar off, and Moses drew near unto the thick darkness where God was." The people were afraid of the tangible darkness that they saw. The magnitude of this divine phenomenon terrified them, but God was there and Moses knew that He was.

He entered into the darkness with confidence; he met with God and returned with the greatest governing laws that man has ever known, the Ten Commandments.

God used darkness as a means of protection when Pharaoh pursued the Israelites (Joshua 24:7). "And when they cried unto the LORD, he put darkness between you and the Egyptians, and brought the sea upon them, and covered them." The darkness was a tool of deliverance in the hand of God. It became a hiding place while the sea rolled back and a miraculous path was laid to liberation.

Faithful Daniel, who prayed three times a day, was betrayed by his peers and thrown into the lion's den by a misguided king. This Daniel, who had interpreted the king's dream, had boldly declared, "He revealeth the deep and secret things: he knoweth what is in the darkness, and the light dwelleth with him" (Daniel 2:22). Did those words come back to mock him as he sat in the dirty darkness? This man of integrity and sterling character believed his God to be of even greater integrity, and He was. God sent His angel into that darkness to shut the lions' mouths.

David experienced the darkness as he was pursued by jealous king Saul. He had been anointed for rulership by the prophet Samuel, but the caves he hid in were a far cry from palace living. Where was the prophetic word that promised honor when he feigned madness in order to escape from a heathen king and spittle drooled from his mouth? Where was the promise of greatness when only discontented men, in distress and in debt, sought his leadership in the cave of Adullum? (1 Samuel 22:1) Yet, it was David who wrote in Psalm 139:12, "Yea, the darkness hideth not from thee; but the night shineth as the day: the darkness and the light are both alike to thee." And in 2 Samuel 22:29, he announced his faith when he said, "For thou art my lamp, O LORD: and the LORD will lighten my darkness."

No one knew more than David the darkness of the human heart, the deceit of the enemy, and the frailty of man. But when the love of God exceeded all expectations of mercy, and grace restored the repentant king even after an adulterous affair, David wrote, "Unto the upright there ariseth light in the darkness: he is gracious, and full of compassion, and righteous" (Psalm 112:4).

As we follow God by faith through the unknown paths of divine guidance, may patience protect us from aborting His plan when darkness hides the victory from view. Every great man or woman of God has learned that God is the God of the darkness as well as the light. Therefore, be strong and of good courage. Arise! Go with God!

Faith Without Charity
is Worth Nothing

"And though I have the gift of prophecy,
and understand all mysteries,
and all knowledge;
and though I have all faith,
so that I could remove mountains,
and have not charity, I am nothing."
1 Corinthians 13:2

Any attempt to follow Jesus' example
of ministry will be ineffective unless
we also follow His example of love.

12

God Speaks in a Mud Church

*And I will sow them among the people: and they
shall remember me in far countries; and they shall live
with their children, and turn again.*
–Zechariah 10:9

After days of diligent effort making a livable home for our family, we were anxious to meet new friends and to give more time to the ministry that God called us to.

Charles had purchased an old Volkswagen bug which made it possible for us to accept an invitation to speak in a village church. Gleefully, we piled inside our little vehicle: Dad, Mom (being great with child), Deborah, age fourteen, Jeff, age twelve, William, age eleven, Ruth, age ten, Mina, age eight, and Bethanie, age four. We needed our interpreter and the accordion, so our African "bug" was introduced to cramming.

Spirits soared as we embarked on our maiden voyage, as missionaries, through the surrounding villages. The valiant little "bug" putted along bravely as we followed our interpreter's directions down winding tracks through the elephant grass.

Keen ears of the village children picked up sounds of our arrival as we approached each village. Word spread from mouth to mouth like wildfire. By the time we arrived, crowds of people stood expectantly by the sides of the road. We stopped to greet them and curious hands reached shyly in the windows to touch our skin and feel the children's hair.

Our interpreter introduced us to new friends, then shared news of his relatives living in Kalemie. Since there was no telephone service, and mail service was via the courtesy of travelers, sharing news in this way, through the human grapevine, was deeply appreciated.

As scantily-clad, giggly boys and girls chattered excitedly and the adults attempted to converse with us, one old mama came hurrying to the car and jubilantly presented us with a large papaya. My heart melted, knowing that this gift was given out of her poverty. Amidst our own sacrifice, we still had lessons to learn in giving.

As we resumed our journey, we were suddenly confronted by a locally-built bridge. Four logs spanned a meandering river that we were expected to cross.

"Everyone out," Charles said.

We evacuated the bug. We would have to walk the logs. Gingerly, we made our way across to the other side, then Charles went back for the car. I watched as he approached the logs.

"You can't do that," I hollered. "It isn't safe."

"Direct me," he yelled.

"Oh God!" My heart pounded. His life is in my hands. I didn't want that responsibility, but I had no choice. Fixing my eyes on his front tires, I motioned directions.

A challenge to Charles is an invitation to success. Never say never. His adrenaline would start to flow as his mind kicked into overdrive. Often it was like watching a miracle in the making as he, by the grace of God, made a way where they said there was no way.

Cautiously, coupled with the enthusiasm of our delighted boys and the assistance of his terrified wife, Charles maneuvered the car to the other side. Jubilantly, we returned to our assigned seats and resumed our safari.

As we chugged along under swaying palms, the quiet bliss of this strange, native utopia seemed to ease itself into our beings. We reveled in moments of pure joy as we melted into the tropical scenery.

Arriving at our destination, eager friends flocked to greet us. Our limited Swahili was disregarded in the flurry of enthusiasm as we heartily shook hands and exchanged hugs.

Graciously, our host led us to a hut that had been prepared for our arrival. Homemade chairs and a simple wooden table adorned with a handmade tablecloth awaited us. To our delight, we were served African chai, a simmered mix of tea, sugar, and powdered milk, before being taken to the large church hut.

Inside the church, the Willners were seated in carefully selected chairs all along the front of the church on a two-foot high, dried-mud platform. Oh, what a spectacle: Daddy, pregnant Mama, and six children on display. It was delightful for the congregation, I'm sure, but I wasn't confident that our training in church etiquette could stand this test.

The local mamas and children were seated on the right side of the church and all the men on the left. As we waited for the program to begin, my attention was drawn to the pastor's wife. She sat in the front row holding their baby girl. Tenderly, she nursed her child, but little, thin arms that normally would have been plump and cuddly by now, drooped pathetically in a kind of apathy that was frightening.

Did their baby have malaria? Was she dying? I was trained as a teacher, not a nurse, and I could only guess.

Little barefooted children with runny noses, ignoring the pesky flies drawn to their dirty faces, eyed us curiously. What a contrast to my own children sitting washed and scrubbed in neatly ironed clothes.

We had carefully worked to protect our children from disease, but suddenly we were surrounded by it. The gospel that we came to preach and the love that we came to share threatened to be overpowered by dirt, disease, and fear. Maternal instincts of protecting the young stir valiantly when an enemy lurks, but all of our efforts for survival suddenly seemed fruitless in the face of such overpowering deprivation. Cleanliness may not protect us from malaria carrying mosquitoes or the stray germ from a friendly handshake.

Slithering subtly into the consciousness of my maternal dilemma, old fears began to surface. *Will my baby survive its entrance into this beautiful, deadly world? What about the danger to my children, surrounded by dirt and disease? Will they survive? Will I? Will my husband?*

The beauty of the landscape faded against the poverty of the village as fear, with apparent logical reasoning, attempted to gain control of my heart and mind. Quietly, I reached for my Bible and opened it. In the dim light of the little mud church, my eyes sought for the life of the Word. God spoke. He spoke as clearly as if He had walked into the room.

> *And I will sow them among the people: and they shall remember me in far countries: and they shall live with their children and turn again.*
> *–Zechariah 10:9*

It was a rhema word from God. God didn't send us here to die. He sent us to this far country to live. We may be surrounded by malaria, cholera, hepatitis, dysentery, dirt, parasites, and thieves, but we would live. Nudging my husband, I showed him the verse. It became our verse, our lifeline to security. Over and over, when circumstances promised disaster, our verse remained the same: "They shall live."

The service started. Homemade musical instruments accompanied native voices as they blended in typical Zairois harmony. Excited by the rare opportunity of performing in front of foreign visitors, we were treated to renditions by the youth choir, the children's choir, and the old mama's choir.

Animated faces glowed as they sang the songs they loved. We attempted to show appreciation even though we didn't understand a word they said. This was before our Swahili language study. It was clearly apparent that although traveling with an interpreter was a blessing, we did not want to be limited to assisted conversations. We wanted to personally know our friends and talk with them freely.

As the service progressed, I watched the people from our little mud platform. Just outside the side door on our right, I spotted the nursery. A group of ladies sat on the ground laughing and talking in an undertone while they shared feminine interests and nursed their young.

Meanwhile, from the platform, it was announced that it was time to collect the offering. Two of the ladies from the nursery group were asked to pass the baskets. Carefully, they passed their nuzzling offspring to friends, picked up a couple of baskets, and hurried obediently inside.

Halfway down the aisle, one of the ladies became aware that she had forgotten to put "baby's dinner bottle" away. Nonchalantly, she tucked a dangling breast back inside of her dress as she continued on down the aisle in her ministry of receiving tithes and offerings. Obviously, in this little corner of the world, our western symbol of sexuality is more casually regarded, with a healthy appreciation for the utilitarian purpose it serves.

Our children were asked to sing, and I played the accordion in accompaniment. Everyone was delighted, even though they didn't understand the words that we sang.

Finally, it was time for the message. Charles and his interpreter ministered the Word of the Lord to our own hearts as well as to a grateful, receptive audience. It was nice to be able to understand the words of inspiration and challenge.

It was a long service for six fidgety children, and when it ended they were ready to look for new adventure. They didn't have long to wait. Above the din of the exiting congregation, we heard a commotion. Two chickens were being chased by several Africans. Around and around the huts they ran with the natives in close pursuit. The scramble ended with one captured chicken. Its legs were tied, and to our surprise, we were presented with the chicken as a token of their appreciation.

Our new friends watched with interest as we tried to figure out where to put our gift aboard the bug. In the process, I glanced down and noticed that the pastor's wife didn't have any shoes. I had brought along my favorite, most comfortable shoes to change into as soon as the service ended.

"Give them to her," a little voice inside me said.

How could I argue when it was obvious that this little lady was so much more destitute than I? But I did. Suddenly, I thought of so many reasons not to give the shoes away. These thick-soled rubber shoes were my protection as I walked on the hard concrete in our house. Being pregnant made the cement harder and my feet hurt worse. I loved these shoes. They were so comfortable. Besides, they probably wouldn't fit her.

But God wasn't speaking to me about rights, He was speaking about obedience. Deep in my heart, I knew that if I did not give her those shoes, I would never forget this moment of selfishness.

Her face lit up in gratitude as I carefully laid my treasures in her hands. And even though as I did the enemy loudly whispered to me that I would greatly regret this act, my heart was filled with the joy of surrender to divine love. We could sacrifice, and preach, and deprive ourselves and our children of the luxuries of life for nothing if our actions did not come from a heart of true love. Faith for giving does not lie in the condition of our circumstances but in the condition of our hearts.

Faith is the Source of Quiet Confidence

"In quietness and in confidence
shall be your strength."
Isaiah 30:15

*Strength is not born of power
but of the quietness and confidence
of indwelling faith.*

13

Having a Baby Without a Hospital

And the life which I now live in the flesh I live by the faith of the Son of God, who loved me, and gave himself for me.
–Galatians 2:20

Days passed swiftly as we continued to work creating a secure home base for our children and ourselves. Frogs and strange creatures roamed the floors unbidden at night, so we needed beds. The African carpenters in the little wood shop in the village offered to build what we wanted, but they needed drawings and exact measurements. We started drafting plans but were suddenly amazed at what we didn't know. How high is a bed supposed to be? Exactly how wide and how long is it? We didn't learn things like this in Bible school. But, slowly our new home took shape.

We found whitewash and painted and repainted the walls. Carefully, I bent and twisted scrap wire which had been given to us by our missionary friends to form a frame for a swag lamp. A supporter sent a lovely picture to embroider with yarn. When it was finished, I took it down to the little carpenter shop, and we made a wooden frame for it. We cut up foam mattresses and made covered cushions for the living room chairs.

Then I discovered yarn in one of the shops. After a little experimenting, we turned it into attractive scatter rugs and a brightly colored afghan. A lady came to the door selling mud vases. I bought one and painted it with shellac we brought from Nairobi. It was the dry season and we didn't have any flowers, but we did find an interesting array of dried weeds and made a unique floral arrangement. Charles surprised us with a smooth, round toilet seat for our outhouse. He had it specially made at the little wood shop as a luxury for the family he loved.

Not long afterward, Charles came into our room one evening and found me standing beside our new bed holding onto the footboard. He watched me quietly for a few moments.

"It's time to go," he said gently.

The children were asleep, but we woke up our oldest daughter, Deborah, and told her that we were going to the dispensary.

"Our baby is coming," we explained.

Without telephone service in our unique foreign town, we couldn't call the doctor. Charles carefully helped me into our little Volkswagen bug, and we began our trek into the unknown. *How do you have a baby without a hospital?*

The unkempt roads were rocky and full of potholes. He tried to hurry, but it was difficult on this kind of road. He glanced at me out of the corner of his eye and saw me gripping the seat in discomfort.

Then, in the blackness of night, bumping over rugged potholes, surrounded by uncertainty, and in pain, my faith started to waver. In fact, I started to panic. Sensing my mounting fear, Charles began to sing softly, "Anywhere, anywhere, fear I cannot know; anywhere with Jesus I can safely go." Miraculously, the electric tension melted. As subtly as it came, it disappeared and was replaced by quiet confidence.

Fortunately, our trip to the doctor's house was only a couple of kilometers long. When we arrived, Charles knocked on the door. It was approximately 11:00 P.M., March 31, 1981. The doctor appeared and exclaimed, "Go directly to the dispensary. We'll meet you there."

Minutes later, we all arrived at the little white cement building on the shores of Lake Tanganyika. It was surrounded by a few palm trees, tropical flowering shrubs and crabgrass struggling for survival in the white sand. The young doctor and his new bride, a nurse, led us inside to his office and helped me onto the examination table. Then, while Charles cradled my head in his arms and whispered words of encouragement, they assisted Christine Amarylis Willner as she made her way into our lives.

About 3:00 A.M., after making sure that both mother and baby were fine, Dr. Blanpain and his bride bid us a happy good-bye. As we bumped our way homeward in the darkness, under a canopy of starlit skies, I held our tiny baby in awe. The devil had taunted me with death, but he was a liar. We lived, both of us. We were wonderfully, gratefully aware of divine assistance.

We expected to slip into the house and quietly to bed, but when we arrived at the house, the lights were on, and the girls were sitting, waiting in eager anticipation of the new arrival. Carefully, we passed baby Christine from one to the other as they admired their new little sister, but the two boys staged an absentee protest because we didn't bring home a boy. Their protest didn't last long before they were equally captured by her charms.

Finally, amidst the joy and excitement, Christine and I were carefully tucked into bed beneath our protective mosquito net. We made it!

The life of Christ living within us continually calls us to die to our own security because He wants to lead us divinely, through the unknown paths of life. Every time we do submit our needs to Him, we experience the quietness and confidence of the living Christ who dwells within us. That surrender gives us the strength to go where we could not go and do what we could not do. Like

Paul, we discover that our strength does not come from the capabilities of our flesh, for when he felt the most incapable, the Christ within rose up and manifested His power in the midst of weakness. "Therefore I take pleasure in infirmities, in reproaches, in necessities, in persecutions, in distresses for Christ's sake, for when I am weak, then am I strong" (2 Corinthians 12:10).

Faith May be Challenged
When God Wants
to Encourage Growth

"And he arose,
and rebuked the wind,
and said unto the sea,
Peace, be still.
And the wind ceased,
and there was a great calm.
And he said unto them,
Why are ye so fearful?
how is it that ye have no faith?"
Mark 4: 39,40

*It is very rarely convenient
to walk by faith.*

14

Life in a Refugee Camp

Whether it be good, or whether it be evil,
we will obey the voice of the LORD our God.
–Jeremiah 42:6a

A tall African man knocked on our door. He had kindly features and a gentlemanly conduct that indicated a good cultural upbringing. He was dressed in European clothing, and we recognized him as an African businessman that we occasionally saw in town.

As we talked, he explained that his family and many members of his tribe had fled from Rwanda. They were refugees living an eight-hour drive away in the village of Vyura. They existed by farming and raising cattle. When they heard of the arrival of missionaries in Kalemie, they were eager to have us come to their village for a weekend of meetings.

"Bring the whole family. You will be safe," he assured us, "because I will take you there myself in my pickup truck."

My mind began to rapidly assess the possible dangers to my family. As a mother, was I prepared to subject our children to an eight-hour ride in the back of a pickup truck, to live in a village for a weekend without boiled water, eat who knows what, and sleep who knows where?

Baby Christine was only about a month old. Little Bethanie was five, and Mina was eight. They had already experienced several attacks of malaria and were as scrawny as their African peers. Jeff, age 12, and William, age 11, were adventurous preteens ready for new thrills. They had no qualms about such a safari. But what about delicate 10-year-old Ruth, who had already had her share of illness in Africa? Fourteen-year-old Deb was not yet certain what her place was in this African ministry, but she was game for a new experience.

Charles and I both had valid concerns, but, understanding my maternal qualms, he let me make the final decision. I had already learned that obedience to God does not necessarily guarantee comfort or convenience, and since God had called us as a family to minister, I decided we would go, by faith, together.

We packed as wisely as possible, considering our ignorance of living conditions in the refugee life we were entering. I made hats for the children to protect them from the sun and prepared fresh food to eat en route.

At 6:30 A.M., on the scheduled date of departure, the pickup truck arrived. The family was stowed on board along with our luggage. With such precious cargo, Charles asked to drive. Our host assented, and we were off.

We hadn't gone far on the badly potholed, blacktop roads, when Charles was asked to stop. Beside the road stood several men with large gunny sacks full of provisions. These were loaded onto the back of the truck to take back to the camp.

"Oh well," I reasoned, "perhaps the children will be more comfortable sitting on these gunny sacks than on the floor of the truck."

A little further on, Charles was asked to stop again to pick up more passengers.

Are you kidding? I thought. Charles and I and the baby were comfortably seated in the cab, and the children were excited about riding on the back of the truck; but I became more and more concerned for their comfort as our new friend continued to pick up passengers. *What about weight limits? What about overcrowding? How could we travel safely over rutted, dirt roads with this kind of a load?* We now had seventeen people on board, plus luggage and supplies! We were fast becoming "engulfed" in the culture.

I discovered that compassion for one's fellow man was more important than the technicalities of maximum weight loads or personal comfort. There were no local transportation systems here, no buses, no taxis, no trains; so, somehow, they always made room for one more.

After traveling for several hours, the passengers asked for a rest stop. We found a shady cove beneath some palm trees by a stream and stopped. In this native setting, there were no McDonalds, Burger Kings or Pizza Huts to offer the convenience of fast foods or clean restrooms to weary travelers. The passengers simply scurried off to find a bush or tree to conceal themselves as they took advantage of the potty stop.

Our children learned quickly. As I watched, they grinned mischievously and darted behind their own private bush. After everyone returned, we passed out drinks, and then double-checked to make certain that no one had fallen overboard or gotten lost in the luggage. Off we went again.

At noon we came to a small, almost deserted, village. Six or seven mud huts were built in a semicircle beneath a canopy of tall trees. In the center of the semicircle stood a carved wooden pole, painted white with chicken dung. A tin dish holding food sat untouched in front of it. We were told that the post was their village god. It was expected to protect the residents from evil spirits.

Our fellow travelers extended greetings to a couple of elderly men who were seated near the mud huts. The more able-bodied villagers had evidently gone to tend gardens, fetch water, and hunt meat. When we disembarked, these village elders graciously brought chairs from their mud huts for us to sit on. While we ate, they sat and visited with the African passengers, who interpreted some of the conversation for us. But, our offer of *muzungu*, "white man's food," was politely refused.

Looking around, I observed the frightened black eyes of small children peering at us from behind huts and trees. They were scantily-clad or naked and carefully watched our every move. Cautiously, I approached the frightened children and offered them some cookies. They timidly received them but did not eat them. After thanking me courteously, they retreated a short distance and sat down, watching to see what we would do next.

As I served my family, I heard the drone of a large airplane far overhead. For a moment, I was caught up in the fascination of the two contrasting worlds. I envisioned the men and women above us using laptop computers, watching in-flight movies, enjoying catered meals. Most of them had never seen what I was experiencing as I sat with men and women in a village of mud huts, living in conditions similar to those two thousand years ago. The stark contrast of cultures, both ignorant of the other, was unforgettable.

When we finished, we packed up, called the roll, and started out again. Late that afternoon, we topped the last hill and entered the village of Vyura. Hundreds of people were waiting. Their faces were radiant, and they shouted for joy as they hurried to greet us. Some of them carried Bibles. Our coming had been planned for over a month, and they had looked forward to our arrival with great expectancy.

Now, they crowded carefully around the truck and watched as we unloaded. In the excitement and crushing curiosity, curious fingers touched our skin and patted our hair. But, one woman excitedly rushed forward and happily scooped five-year-old Bethanie up in her arms, stroking her long, silky blonde hair. The children later admitted they felt like exhibits in a human petting zoo.

While helping to unload the truck, I passed Bethanie's doll to a little, old lady to hold for us. When I turned around to retrieve the doll, the little lady was holding it in her arms as carefully as if she were holding a newborn baby. I seized the moment to demonstrate dolly's abilities to open and close her eyes and cry. Poor granny and friends were almost overcome with awe. Never before had they seen such an amazing replica of a human baby. Obviously, she was much more attractive and intelligent than a post. It was easy to envision dolly usurping the position of a village god.

We looked around the compound. Mud huts were different here. Unlike the square huts we were used to, these were round with the typical straw roof. Grouped in clusters, they formed a village of several hundred people. Tropical foliage provided a little shelter from the equatorial sun's rays, while banana and papaya trees produced needed fruit for these struggling members of the Tutsi tribe.

A central, three-room hut had been selected as our guest house. The mud floor had been thoroughly swept with a grass hand broom, then dampened with water and allowed to dry. It was as clean as native housekeeping could get. Someone carried our luggage into the three-room suite.

Curiously, we inspected our new quarters. The handcrafted beds were built of slatted poles lashed together. There was a dining room table made of wood on which they had placed a tablecloth and a pop bottle filled with little fresh flowers. Someone had made wooden chairs.

The hut boasted two doors, a front door and a back door, with a shuttered window in the third room. It was to this room that I was ushered and instructed to lie down and rest for a bit. It felt good to stretch out, even if the bed didn't compare in comfort to any of the mattressed resting places of our past.

As I attempted to relax, an agitated hen strolled in and scolded me soundly. A little amused, I got up, shooed her out of the room and closed the door. Wearily, I lay down again. Finally, I found a comfortable space between the slats and began to doze. A sudden, sharp peck on my back made me bolt upright.

There stood a mother hen, her eyes blazing in defiance. Obviously a believer in my mother's old adage, "Where there is a will, there is a way," she had flown in through the window, determined to regain her perch, my bed.

My will was strangely challenged by this indigent hen. Though sympathetic to her displacement, I decided that my jealous feathered impostor would have to bow to the decision of her owners. I closed the door and locked the window of my weekend boudoir.

Soon there was a knock on the front door. Our hostess greeted us, handed us a large basin and informed us that warm water was coming. Sure enough, steaming pails of warm water arrived and were poured into the huge basin. We didn't need to be encouraged to scrub away the many hours' worth of dust and red dirt we had accumulated on our safari.

Outside, preparations were under way for our evening meal. Chicken was a favorite meal for guests, though it was tough and hardy from chasing after its own food supply. The chicken was served with a dish called *ugali*. To make *ugali*, white maize meal is cooked in boiling water, steamed till it has "ripened," then shaped into a large ball. Each person at the table takes a bit from the central dish, rolls it into a ball, and presses it with the thumb to form a small indentation. This is dipped into the chicken broth and then eaten.

As meal time approached, one of the women came to our hut. She was obviously excited to have a part of the honor of caring for us as she carefully set our table with someone's choice dishes and utensils. Then waiters came with the food. As we observed, we realized that this meal had been carefully planned. Sugar for our tea had been brought from town, chickens were sacrificed, and hoarded eggs cooked. Even drinking water had been boiled for the children. We were touched by their sacrifice and care of us.

We had rice, chicken in oil, *ugali*, and an egg omelet in oil. We began eating eagerly. Everyone was hungry after the long trip. But something was wrong. It was the strange oil the food was cooked in. It was thick and red. It made the inside of our mouths pucker. We tried washing it down with tea, but finally resorted to eating mostly rice. We later found out that it was palm nut oil.

A specially built outhouse had also been prepared for us. Charles made many trips to the new facility that night. He wasn't sure if his problem was the result of our new diet or a reaction to the spiritual darkness we encountered at the village where we had eaten our lunch.

Early the next morning, the Lord awakened me. I slipped out of bed and into the other room for a quiet time with Him. As I read my Bible and prayed, the Holy Spirit began to stir my heart with a message for the people. I was making notes as I nursed baby Christine when a beautiful African mother knocked at my door. She wanted to visit.

The lady was one of the most gracious women I have ever met. Poverty did not destroy her grace. She was tall and elegant and carried herself with a dignified charm. She was also pregnant and yearned to hold baby Christine.

Understanding her mother's heart, I gently laid my baby in her arms. During our sketchy conversation, I learned that she had given birth to several babies, but most of them had died during her difficult deliveries. Childbearing was a life-threatening ordeal for her and her babies.

Her beautiful face glowed as she cuddled baby Christine and cooed native love sounds. Finally, she confessed that she was afraid of her up-coming labor and asked me to pray for her. We prayed together.

It amazed me how the Holy Spirit connected our spirits in that moment to bring about a sacred sisterhood. This God-giv-en kinship spanned differences in skin color, cultural diversity, and financial status. It was a bond born in the midst of adversity because of Jesus' own adversity, His death. It was a miracle of love.

Church time came, and we were driven to the church. When we arrived, more than 1,000 people had gathered from five area churches. The church was filled, and the yard was dotted with brightly-colored umbrellas as men, women and children huddled beneath their shade to escape the rays of the tropical sun.

Our hosts led us through a side door and seated us at the front of the large mud-brick church. Never in my life have I seen a church so crowded. The doors had been locked, but as I looked out over the congregation, I noticed movement at one of the windows. A mother passed her baby through the window to a friend; then, to my amusement, I saw the woman herself crawl through the window. Somehow, the people inside made room for one more person.

After the song service and announcements were completed, Charles was introduced. Bodies moved aside as he carefully picked his way to the front. People sat in the aisles and on every available bit of floor space, and even at the podium, he had to stand with care because people sat on the floor all around his feet.

Charles began preaching. He still felt ill, and his face was pale from his night of discomfort, but he had no intention of leaving his call of duty. Suddenly, however, he turned to me. His face was ashen as stomach cramps gripped his body.

"Fern," he whispered, "You'll have to take over."

He had ended where my notes of the morning began. Quickly taking his place at the podium, I began to speak as the Holy Spirit anointed the word He had given me from Hosea, "And I will betroth thee unto me for ever" (Hosea 3:19a).

The love of the Lord reached out through me to the struggling refugees. He loved. He healed. He challenged. He exhorted. Then, with an even greater unction, the Lord directed me to speak to the pastors. A large group of church leaders sat behind me, and I turned to address them.

"Be ye strong therefore, and let not your hands be weak: for your work shall be rewarded" (2 Chronicles 15:7).

Elderly pastors, tired deacons and weary leaders wept as the Holy Spirit moved among us all in a divine manifestation of encouragement.

Later, they confessed that they had grown weary. The heart-breaks of life were draining the strength from them. Their young people were discouraged. They needed a touch from God, and God came.

That afternoon as I talked with our interpreter, he told me, "The men respect you because of your large family. You are an example to us."

The weekend passed quickly, and before we knew it, it was time to load the truck for our return trip. We said good-byes amidst hugs and tears, knowing that our new friends would never be forgotten.

On the trip home, we added more passengers, a young pregnant woman, her husband, and their friend. She was seriously ill, and they feared for her life. When we arrived in Kalemie, we took them to the government hospital located just down the hill from our house. Though sadly deficient in equipment, staff and medicines, there was a lab where they tested for tropical diseases. Doctors' prescriptions were sometimes available in the market.

Not long after our return home, we discovered lice in the children's hair. Wal-Mart was continents away, and there was no medication for this kind of treatment in our small town. We washed each child thoroughly and picked nits by the hour. Even our pet monkey, Kiki, joined in the search.

Waist-long hair had to be cut into shorter styles. *Why, oh why hadn't I taken a course in cosmetology? We might be poor, but we didn't have to look like it,* I thought as I picked up the scissors and prayed for wisdom. The silky, blonde tresses slowly fell away, but gradually fear of failure gave way to inspiration and new styles emerged. When we were done, the girls actually looked good. On a later visit to Bujumbura, Burundi, another young missionary mom admired the girls' haircuts and asked me for instructions.

Weeks passed, and one day I learned that my new friend in Vyura had died in childbirth. *Why, God?* My own life felt emptier because of her death, but I thought of the sorrow in her village. We prayed for a safe delivery and a healthy baby, but God took her home instead. I don't know why. Perhaps He decided it was time to give this gracious woman a new life, to exchange her mud hut and refugee status for a mansion. How grateful I was for that eight hour ride that gave me a chance to meet her in our early morning rendezvous, to pray with her, to share my family, my love, and my faith with her and her refugee camp.

Then word came that the young lady we took to the hospital had given birth to a healthy baby boy. Both mother and baby were fine. I remembered the day we received the invitation to Vyura and the struggle it was for me to let go of the little bit of security we did have in exchange for a weekend of ministry. There are times that the Lord's voice seems evil, Jeremiah says. Even Jesus had no illusions about His ministry for the world.

"And he went a little farther, and fell on his face, and prayed, saying, O my Father, if it be possible, let this cup pass from me: nevertheless not as I will, but as thou wilt" (Matthew 26:39). In retrospect, I saw that when we choose to hold the call of God in higher regard than the apparent reality of dangerous circumstances, God rearranges the ingredients for pain and somehow brings blessing instead. I cannot base my obedience on anticipated blessings, because they may not come when I expect them. I must base my obedience on eternal values.

Faith Unifies Strangers and Foreigners into Fellow Citizens

"Through wisdom is an house builded;
and by understanding it is established."
Proverbs 24:3

A man through wisdom may build a house,
beautiful, bright and new;
But he will only establish it,
through understanding, too.

15

The Tea Predicament

*Now therefore ye are no more strangers and foreigners, but fellow
citizens with the saints, and of the household of God; And are built
upon the foundation of the apostles and prophets, Jesus Christ himself
being the chief corner stone; In whom all the building fitly framed
together groweth unto an holy temple in the Lord: In whom ye also are
builded together for an habitation of God through the Spirit.
—Ephesians 2:19–22*

"Ni *napenda ku ununua sabuni ku safisha maneno,*" I said carefully
to the East Indian shopkeeper.

Jeff and I were in search of toothpaste. I was far from fluent in
the Swahili language, but with a little ingenuity, I made myself understood. Jeff's daily contact with his African friends on the compound, however, had increased his vocabulary far beyond mine.

The local shopkeeper discreetly made no comment, but with a
twinkle in his eye, he produced a tube of toothpaste.

Once outside, Jeff grinned.

"Mom, I wonder what they think of missionaries who ask for
soap to wash their words," he asked.

I had confused the word *meno,* meaning "tooth," for *maneno,*
meaning "words."

Our efforts to speak the local language were rewarded with so
much enthusiasm, we sometimes thought we knew more than we
did. Our new friends bragged on us to their friends.

"Oh, you can talk to them yourself. They know Swahili as good as we do," they said proudly.

Word had spread that new missionaries lived at Kankomba, and we began to have visitors. One day, we heard singing far down the road. As the music came closer, a procession came into view. The people appeared to be ranked according to position, with the leaders at the head of the line.

Up the hill and onto the compound they came, still singing, until they stood in front of our house. Charles and I went outside, and their spokesman greeted us. The group was orderly but clearly excited. Several elders had been appointed to make speeches of welcome, and then we were presented with such gifts of sugar cane, sugar, eggs wrapped in banana leaves, rice, papaya, chickens, mangos and even a goat.

In faltering Swahili, Charles greeted them and made an acceptance speech. Then, while we attempted conversations with our guests, we became aware that hearts speak louder than words. Though we were sadly deficient in language skills, our hearts were knit together in a warm glow of friendship.

For days, we received groups of gracious Africans bringing gifts and greetings. I learned to begin my day by heating large kettles of water which we used for making tea for everyone. This was served with a locally made, arrowroot type cookie which we discovered that our new friends enjoyed.

One day, a large representation from one of the village churches came to visit. After the speeches were made, we invited everyone inside for tea and cookies. Most villagers are accustomed to sitting on the floor and actually find it more comfortable. So our little living room was filled with chattering guests seated on the polished cement floor, observing everything.

As we drank tea together, I noticed one little lady who seemed to be having difficulty. Her eyes darted about the room as she struggled to solve some sort of dilemma. Wondering, I watched. There was just a little tea left in the bottom of her cup, and she was at a loss to know what to do with it. Suddenly, she flung the remaining tea onto the floor in the corner of the room.

Why did she do that? I wondered.

Gathering from the experience I had gleaned, I knew that water is a precious commodity in most villages. Women leave early in the morning with plastic water containers on their back and walk long distances to a local water source. After waiting in line to fill their containers, they carry the meager supply back home for their family's use during the day.

But the water sources are not always clean. Combined with the fact that local tea is made with tea leaves which settle in the bottom of the cup, it was probably a habit never to drink the settlings in one's cup. Normally, emptying her cup would not be a problem in a mud hut with mud floors. But what do you do in the white man's house? She settled the dilemma, the old habit remained intact, and my clean, waxed floor was initiated.

As our guests visited and ate, enjoying this time of refreshing after their journey on foot in the tropical heat, several of the nursing mothers began to feed their babies. I finished serving, then brought newborn Christine out of the bedroom.

Excitedly, the mamas begged to hold her. In quiet awe, they took turns cradling the tiny white baby in their arms. Then, sitting down among the nursing moms, I took baby Christine and began to nurse her. Their eyes opened wide in shock, and an undertone of conversation began. What was the matter?

There generally seems to be one in a group who is brave enough to confront issues head on, and soon their spokesperson plied me with questions. Struggling to understand, I discovered that they did not believe that white women breast-fed their babies. They then concluded that the act of nursing was primitive and placed them on a lower social level.

As they watched and talked, shock slowly gave way to approval of themselves and approval of me. They understood this type of motherhood. We were alike after all. We did have a common bond. I was a friend.

Learning why our new friends lived as they did was often a challenge. Ignorance eventually produces contempt and division. So, to effectively preach love, we must not live in ignorance. We must pursue understanding and search for answers.

Using the wisdom of our training, we knew we could teach the Zairois a few things such as how to build better buildings, construct proper outhouses, incorporate more protein into their diets, operate dispensaries, and study the Word, but it takes an understanding heart to link the old with the new and establish lasting change.

The Bible says, "Through wisdom is an house builded; and by understanding it is established" (Proverbs 24:3). If we hoped to build anything of enduring value, we must learn to see and hear and feel with the faith of an understanding heart. We can never substitute wisdom and materials for the intimacy of time and understanding.

Faith is a Fight

"Fight the good fight of faith,
Lay hold on eternal life."
1 Timothy 6:12a

Fight! Get a grip! Don't let go!
The enemy would love to steal your faith,
but you can have it, if you want it.

16

Uniting to Fight Mama's Malaria

Be sober, be vigilant; because your adversary the devil, as a roaring lion, walketh about, seeking whom he may devour: Whom resist stedfast in the faith, knowing that the same afflictions are accomplished in your brethren that are in the world. But the God of all grace, who hath called us unto his eternal glory by Christ Jesus, after that ye have suffered a while, make you perfect, stablish, strengthen, settle you.
–1 Peter 5:8–10

We discussed various prophylactics with the doctor and our missionary and Belgian friends, but in spite of following their advice about taking proper precautions, I became ill with malaria. The fevers were followed by shaking chills. The smell of food was nauseating. Uncontrollable diarrhea left me feeling like a baby, but with too much maturity to be ignorantly blissful of my dilemma. It was humiliating to be a mother and missionary shaking with chills and wrapped in towels to protect me from my own incontinence.

At first the disease felt very uncomfortable but not dangerous. I fully expected to recover in a few days. As the days passed, however, I became weaker.

In the evenings, after their work was done, groups of people from the compound came to visit me. They had lost children and family members to this deadly disease, and they well knew the feeling of desperate weakness and incapacitation. Quietly, they knelt around my bed and prayed. As the urgency of their prayers increased, their voices grew louder. Tears streamed down their cheeks and dripped from their chins unheeded as they petitioned God on my behalf. It was a loving and humbling experience to be the recipient of their prayers, but I wondered why they cried so hard. I still expected to recover.

Then came the day I was unable to lift my head from the pillow. It was an effort just to open my eyes. Suddenly, unquestioning expectations of recovery began to be overshadowed by a menacing possibility of death.

"Are you kidding, Lord? You wouldn't allow that, would you? You wouldn't let me die, would you? I have to live. I have seven children, and they need me." But I floated into a state of semi-awareness, too tired to plead my case.

Mr. Bishalanga, his wife, and family lived next door. They were mature Christians who loved the Lord and were busy rearing a family to follow in their faith. Mr. Bishalanga not only worked at the cotton factory, but he and his wife were industrious at home as well, planting vegetables on any available garden space. He was also musical, and the whole compound was blessed during the evenings when two of his friends joined him on his front porch to sing hymns. One of them played an accordion in skilled accompaniment to their masculine harmony, while children on the compound gathered around to sing or gleefully dance during the upbeat tunes.

These men, trained abroad, had returned to share their skills with the local community. They were gifted men of integrity whose faith in God ran deep, exhibiting lives of faithfulness and devotion in the midst of much adversity.

One night, the crisis came. *What would happen?* The group from the compound came as usual. They knelt around my bed and prayed more earnestly than ever. But I was very ill. Another guest arrived; it was Mr. Bishalanga. Quietly, he asked to come in and pray for me. He laid his hand on my head, prayed a simple prayer and left. I didn't hear most of what he said or understand his Swahili, but suddenly, like the dawn of revelation, I knew that tomorrow I would be much better.

"Charlie," I murmured, "I'll be much better tomorrow."

He was startled. "That's what Mr. Bishalanga prayed," he said, "that you would be much better tomorrow."

The next day, I was well on the road to recovery. The enemy had come. He had sought to kill and to destroy. But, in love, our friends united with us to keep a nightly vigil of faith. God heard our cry, and together we withstood the enemy.

The discomfort of the disease was soon forgotten, but the bond of friendship that was strengthened by dripping tears of love, the acceptance that was established through our mutual sorrow, and the deep settled peace that came when God replied, will never be forgotten.

Faith will not always shield us from pain, but it will sustain us through the suffering as we are strengthened, established and settled on a higher plane in God. Jesus did not pray that we would be taken out of the world, but that we would be kept in it as we share in the sufferings of our fellowmen. John 17:15 says, "I pray not that thou shouldest take them out of the world, but that thou shouldest keep them from the evil."

Friends and elders, who stand steadfast in the faith with us, are a gift from God. The lion rarely risks the pounding hooves of a herd when he is seeking his prey, but woe be to the straggler who runs, weak and alone. Don't let the enemy seek you out and cut you off when you are hurting. Stay with the pack. Hebrews 10:25 admonishes us, "Not forsaking the assembling of ourselves together, as the manner of some is; but exhorting one another: and so much the more, as ye see the day approaching."

The enemy roars. Faith is a fight, and no good soldier tries to fight independently of the others.

Faith Can be Steadfast Under Pressure

"I have fought a good fight,
I have finished my course,
I have kept the faith:"
2 Timothy 4:7

Faith will try, but fear will cry.
Don't give up when it's tough.
Finish well.

17

Alone With a Madman

"Preserve me, O God: for in thee do I put my trust."
—Psalm 16:1

It wasn't long before more invitations began to come for Charles to speak and teach in various village churches. An itinerary was arranged, and Charles left for a short tour of ministry.

The children and I were challenged by our new lifestyle, but we were surrounded by friends on our compound who were eager to help. We still groped for words to surmount the language barrier and puzzled over different customs. Charles had more expertise than we did in these areas, and he was our buffer. Now, while he was gone, we faced the changes alone.

With limited finances, Charles and I had attempted to make our little home safe and secure. The window in our living/dining room now boasted new green and white gingham curtains. The table was covered with a matching tablecloth and napkins, all made from my maternity dress that had been carefully ripped apart.

Our old wooden door had no latch or lock, but Charles found a good-sized nail, pounded it into the door frame, and bent it. Now the door could be closed and locked from the inside by turning the bent nail to secure it. Hopefully thieves were not aware that the missionary's family and goods were protected by so fragile a security system.

Our budding watch dog was a little puppy that someone gave us, but we had high hopes for it. We were also very grateful that we lived close enough to the main part of town that we had the privilege of having electricity. That made it possible to keep a security light burning all night on the front verandah.

After Charles' departure, all went well for several days. Then, late one night, I awoke with a start. Eerie sounds from somewhere nearby made my spine tingle. Stealthily, I crept out of bed to investigate. Peering out of the front window, I saw a sight that made me gasp. There walking back and forth on our verandah was a man, stark naked. His hair was matted with mud, his eyes were glazed, and he held our "budding watchdog" in his arms. He sang something like a drunken man, but the sounds were unintelligible and strange.

Quietly stepping away from the window, I stood in the darkness and tried to still my quaking heart. How could I protect my sleeping family? There was no telephone to call 911 in this underdeveloped land, and we had never kept a weapon of any sort.

Our tiny baby was sound asleep, and thankfully, the rest of our children had not been awakened. If I was quiet enough, I might be able to slip out of the back door undetected and run for help. Dare I leave them? That bent nail wasn't much protection between my children and a madman.

"Oh, God, help me do something." I must not allow fear to paralyze my faith.

In the dark, I gingerly opened the back door, praying that it wouldn't squeak. The strange man apparently had no accomplices, for I didn't see anyone else. Cautiously, I stole outside and ran to the nearest house.

Because thieves were so prevalent in this area, the Africans had wooden shutters on their windows which they closed and locked at night. Silently, I worried, "If I knock loud enough to waken someone, I might attract the man's attention. Suppose my new friends can't understand my struggling Swahili?"

I knocked gingerly and then desperately louder. A voice finally asked what I wanted. I struggled with my broken Swahili, but Mr. Kiete understood. He quickly gathered several other men, sending one to the village to get the help of a policeman.

Carefully, they approached the man and discovered that he was mentally deranged. With the help of the police, he was led away and quiet was restored. But my own heart still pounded, and questions filled my mind. What would St. Paul, the great biblical missionary, have done? He probably would have laid hands on the man and healed him. Should I have tried to do that? Was the devil accusing me, or was God convicting me? Did God want me to speak a word of deliverance to humanity such as this, so poor and broken in mind and spirit?

Slowly it dawned on me that Jesus did only what the Father wanted Him to do. He said in Luke 11:20, "But if I with the finger of God cast out devils, no doubt the kingdom of God is come upon you."

What God pointed out to Him to do, He did. As Jesus met with His Father morning by morning, He received His instructions and was certain of the results. God doesn't need brave faith, He needs obedient faith.

And in the morning, rising up a great while before day, he went out, and departed into a solitary place, and there prayed.
–Mark 1:35

For he taught them as one that had authority, and not as the scribes.
–Mark 1:22

For with authority commandeth he even the unclean spirits, and they do obey him.
–Mark 1:27

As I continue to spend time in His presence, He may instruct me to cast out devils, I thought. But I knew that He wanted me to have the faith to stay alone in strange surroundings and guard the heritage He had entrusted to me. I had sought His wisdom and I had acted accordingly.

"Lo, children are an heritage of the Lord: and the fruit of the womb is his reward," Psalm 127:3 says. There are seasons in our lives. Whether we are given the responsibility of guarding the home or casting out devils, our Father will give us faith sufficient for the need. That faith will also protect us from the fear that paralyzes and the enemy that condemns.

Faith is the Launching Pad for Divine Solutions

"Through faith we understand that
the worlds were framed by the word of God,
so that things which are seen were not
made of things which do appear."
Hebrews 11:3

We're made in the image of God,
Who tossed out the stars into space;
We too have the gift to create
When joined to God's wisdom by faith.

18

Cholera and Buggy Flour

For the LORD giveth wisdom: out of his mouth
cometh knowledge and understanding.
—Job 36:5

Kalemie, Zaire, Africa did not have the snows of winter, the thaws of spring, or the colored leaves of fall. We did have a season of light rains, a hot season, a season of heavy rains, and a dry season.

In Kalemie, July and August were dry. Without rain, the earth turned to powdery dust, grass withered and died, and trees lost their leaves. That is when water supplies ran low, and people began to go to the lake to get drinking water.

The water taken close to the shore was not clean, and it needed to be boiled. Although people were warned about the danger of drinking lake water, most people did not have enough wood or charcoal to boil their drinking water. It was a hardship to find enough wood or purchase enough charcoal to cook meals, let alone boil water. An outbreak of cholera resulted in epidemic proportions.

Officials quarantined our town in an attempt to isolate the epidemic and keep it from spreading. The railway line which serviced Kalemie was closed down. Boats, which normally brought supplies from Burundi and Tanzania, were refused entry. The weekly Air Burundi flight was discontinued.

Our house was situated close to the road which led to a local cemetery. As funeral processions passed by day after day, our hearts grew heavy. We would hear them coming up the dusty hill, the non-Christians wailing, the Christians singing. The lead person generally carried a cross in front of him as he walked. Sometimes a truck was hired to carry the funeral party, and as many of the mourners as possible climbed onto the back of the truck. Those standing nearest the front of the truck bed held up a large cross indicating that the group was a funeral procession.

Some corpses were fortunate enough to be placed in rough wooden coffins, but most were simply wrapped in a sheet and carried to the grave site on a litter. Mourning friends and relatives followed along behind. As the mourners passed, we followed the lead of the other compound residents. We stopped whatever we were doing and bowed our heads in respect.

With the passing of each mournful company, uninvited fears assaulted my mind.

"What if that were one of my children, or my husband, or me? I almost felt guilty to be alive. What right do we have to live, and them to die? Will we die too?"

Then death struck our compound. It claimed the life of a young male relative of one of our neighbors. The dead man was washed, wrapped in cloth, and laid on chairs at the front of the one room home. Family and friends gathered at the house. Since furniture was scarce, most of the guests sat on the cement floor.

I was sorry for our friends and went to show my sympathy. Quietly, I entered the room, found a place on the floor with the mourners, and cried. Occasionally, someone began singing a hymn, and everyone joined in and sang together. Sometimes they took turns praying, shared selections from Scripture, or gave words of comfort. This was a special time with the deceased and his family because the young man would be buried in the after-noon. Tropical heat and danger of disease made it imperative to bury a dead person on the same day as his death.

This assembly was called a *kilio*. It was a native wake, when friends and relatives came to the home of the bereaved family and stayed with them from three to seven days. Day and night the home was to be filled with visitors so that the bereaved would not to be left to mourn alone. During the wake, some people sat outside in small clusters visiting. Other visitors cooked, washed clothes, or did dishes. Others cried.

While I sat and wept and prayed, I became aware that, for some people, these stark moments of mourning had become a ritual. Several mourners sitting near me were making the sounds, but they were watching me out of the corners of their eyes. My genuine sorrow intrigued them. Perhaps their rugged lifestyle had made them more accepting of death and dying, while my western culture had sheltered me from such glaring realities. The death and disease that surrounded us was appalling to me.

As the quarantine continued, food behind closed borders be-came scarce. Businessmen were angry that all supply routes had been cut off. Prices escalated. It was no longer possible to send or receive mail, since mail traveled by airplane via Burundi. Phone service was nonexistent. We were totally isolated.

Finally, the most basic commodities were unavailable. There was no sugar, no potatoes, no flour. The situation was desperate. We began praying for flour.

Then, one day two women knocked on our back door. One of them carried a large bag of flour on her back which they offered to sell us. We were thrilled. The price was high, but it was worth it. Gladly, we paid for this answer to prayer.

The next morning I decided to celebrate with the family by making pancakes, but when I opened the bag of flour, it stank so bad I was almost overcome by the smell. Closer examination revealed that our treasure was full of bugs and worms. Not to be deterred from my surprise, I determined to hide the buggy taste. Carefully, I sifted out the bugs and worms, then added cinnamon to the batter.

Yuk! My cinnamon didn't camouflage the foul taste and stench the worms had left behind.

We tried gagging the pancakes down, but the surprise was a failure.

The next day, I tried again.

"This flour needs something stronger than cinnamon to hide the essence of bug," I reasoned.

This time I added garlic. *Garlic pancakes? Well, you never know till you try it. It just might be good.* "Need is the mother of design," I'd been told.

Yuk! Even garlic was defeated in camouflaging the wretched aroma.

In desperation, I prayed, "God you gave us this flour in answer to prayer. Please show me what to do with it so we can use it."

I was sure that God doesn't play cruel jokes. I was also learning that His treasures are often hidden so that only the wise can find them.

"Lord, I need your wisdom. Please reveal your answer for this problem to me," I prayed.

A few days later, as I watched the sun sparkle and dance on the lake below us, I had a sudden thought.

The sun purifies. Maybe the sun can purify my flour.

We sifted all of the flour twice to remove as much of the "protein" as possible. Then we spread a large white sheet out on the grass in the sun. Carefully, we covered the sheet with the buggy, wormy scented flour and let it sit all day. That evening we gathered up the flour, resifted it, and put it in a clean bag. Now for the test. *Would our experiment work?*

We made pancakes again—yummy, delicious pancakes with our God given flour. *It worked!* I was awed. Faith in God's promise of protection and provision had made me resolutely sure that pancakes could be made from buggy flour. It also kept us believing that we could survive, and help, in a cholera-infested community.

Several years later, I was asked to speak for a women's meeting in Ontario, Canada. The Holy Spirit prompted me to speak on "buggy flour." My text was from Romans 5:20b: "But where sin abounded, grace did much more abound."

Most of us have special things that we yearn for in life. It may be a husband, a child, a job, or a friend. Sometimes these gifts are granted to us. With high expectations, we prepare to enjoy our dream come true, but something happens. Bugs appear. The new husband may have a disturbing habit. The baby may cry continuously with colic. The long sought for job may be dominated by a tyrannical boss or difficult associates. The new friend begins to exhibit irritating personality traits. The choice possession suddenly becomes "buggy flour."

Western culture encourages us to discard the unwanted and replace it with something better, but God discounted that philosophy long ago. His experience with Noah and the flood made Him determine that He would never again discard in order to change. He sent Jesus into the midst of the fallen race to redeem it instead. "Where sin abounded, grace did much more abound" (Romans 5:20b). He provided grace, mercy, forgiveness, new hope, even everlasting life to every person who would allow the life of the Son to purify them.

Jesus then asked us to do the same. He didn't expect us to know how to accomplish this healing, cleansing task of redeeming that which is polluted by sin. He knows all too well the frustration of dealing with the human spirit and the complexities of life in a fallen world. But through the Son, the Holy Spirit was sent to impart enabling gifts and power sufficient for the task. Through His enablement, help is available in "buggy" situations. But it involves faithfulness, intercession, and divinely imparted creativity. Often, the best gifts emerge out of the greatest difficulty.

Don't throw out the buggy flour. Be patient. Keep on seeking God for a divine remedy until the answer comes. Don't give up on the buggy flour. Be an intercessor as you spread the situation before the Son and wait for Him to intervene.

Don't focus on the impossibilities of the buggy flour. Receive the spirit of inspiration that the Holy Spirit wants to impart to you. Then, step out in faith using that wisdom, and work together with God to transform your buggy flour into the treasure that it was meant to be.

> *Ask, and it shall be given you; seek, and ye shall find; knock, and it shall be opened unto you: For every one that asketh re-ceiveth; and he that seeketh findeth; and to him that knock-eth it shall be opened.*
> *–Matthew 7:7,8*

Whatever our buggy situation may be, it is a divine invitation for supernatural creativity. We will become frustrated if we focus on our short-sighted expectations and disappointments, but when we can turn to Him with all of our heart, He will reveal His divine solution.

Faith Entitles Us to Abraham's Covenant Blessings

"So then they which be of faith
are blessed with faithful Abraham."
Galatians 3:9

*We can choose
to break covenant with God,
but God will never
break covenant with us.*

19

Two Women in White

And it shall come to pass, that before they call,
I will answer; and while they are yet speaking, I will hear.
—Isaiah 65:24

Before we left Canada, I had tried diligently to gain information on how to live in the tropics. When our application to a missions jungle training course was denied because of denominational barriers, I phoned the Tropical Diseases Centre in Toronto for information. They responded by sending us some brochures with valuable information. It wasn't a lot, but it would help. Finally, as a last resort, I completed a St. John's Ambulance First Aid course.

Now, three-month-old Christine was sick. I fought the chills, the fever, and the diarrhea, but it looked like a losing battle. Finally, her fever went down, but the diarrhea continued and she was growing dangerously weak. Doctors at home had told me that disease-resistant antibodies were passed on to the baby through the mother's milk. Since I was a nursing mother, I assumed that the malaria pills I carefully swallowed each week were protecting both me and baby Christine from the disease. Too late, we discovered they weren't.

My limited information didn't equip me to deal with the crisis we faced now. We desperately needed help. There must be a way. God had promised us life. Hopelessness and frustration were an obvious reaction to our apparently hopeless situation, but I had learned from the past that self-made pity parties were a destructive activity to be avoided.

Don't think about the negatives. Don't focus on what things look like. Pray. God has said He will never leave us nor forsake us. God has answers that we know nothing about. Fight this enemy. Don't give up. Keep trying. Look for an answer, I exhorted myself.

As I stood outside on our front verandah holding onto faith's lifeline in the midst of the circumstantial evidence of growing failure, I suddenly spotted two European women walking uncertainly up our driveway. They were both dressed in white. Apparently puzzled, they looked around hesitantly. *Who were they?*

Slowly, I approached the strangers and greeted them in English. They didn't understand me. They paused, then greeted me in French, but I didn't know French. I tried a greeting in Swahili. Their faces lit up. None of us were fluent in Swahili, but with effort we made ourselves understood.

Apologetically, they explained that they were nurses from Montreal, Quebec and had come to Kalemie to work with the Catholic church. They were sent on a mission, but while searching for a certain village, they somehow got lost and ended up in our front yard instead.

I was amazed. All the while I was struggling to believe, God was planning a medical house call. Who would have ever thought of losing a couple of Catholic nurses in our front yard? The divine blessing was so obvious, I envisioned God grinning in heaven.

"Can you help me?" I asked.

They listened as I explained Christine's condition to them. She would die of dehydration if I didn't stop the terrible diarrhea, a common problem in third world countries.

Assuredly, they were no longer lost. Now at home in their field of expertise, they carefully explained how to make a rehydration drink by boiling water with a little rice in it, adding a tablespoon of orange juice and a little salt and sugar. Then, with my profound thanks ringing in their ears, we parted ways under the waving palm nut tree—they in search of a village and me to my kitchen where I prepared a lifesaving drink.

Though we may be surrounded by the miseries of a world immersed in sin, God knows the personal address of every child of faith. While we persevere, He makes plans for the delivery of the promises of the Abrahamic covenant. Annie Johnson Flint expresses it well in her poem:

> "The devil may wall you 'round
> But he cannot roof you in;
> He may fetter your feet and tie your hands
> And strive to hamper your soul with bands
> As his way has ever been;
> But he cannot hide the face of God
> And the Lord shall be your light,
> And your eyes and your thoughts can rise to the sky,
> Where His clouds and His winds and His birds go by,
> And His stars shine out at night.
>
> The devil may wall you 'round;
> He may rob you of all things dear,
> He may bring his hardest and roughest stone
> And thinks to cage you and keep you alone,
> But he may not press too near;
> For the Lord has planted a hedge inside,
> And has made it strong and tall,
> A hedge of living and growing green;
> And ever it mounts and keeps between
> The trusting soul and the devil's wall.
>
> The devil may wall you 'round,
> But the Lord's hand covers you,

And His hedge is a thick and thorny hedge,
And the devil can find no entering wedge
Nor get his finger through;
He may circle about you all day long,
But he cannot work as he would,
For the will of the Lord restrains his hand,
And he cannot pass the Lord's command
And his evil turns to good.

The devil may wall you 'round,
With his grey stones, row on row,
But the green of the hedge is fresh and fair,
And within its circle is space to spare,
And room for your soul to grow;
The wall that shuts you in
May be hard and high and stout,
But the Lord is sun and the Lord is dew,
And His hedge is coolness and shade for you,
And no wall can shut Him out.[6]

Faith Works by Love

"For in Jesus Christ
neither circumcision availeth any thing,
nor uncircumcision;
but faith which worketh by love."
Galatians 5:6

*The power behind faith
is love.*

20

The Sore that Killed Grandma

*And thou shalt love the Lord thy God with all thy heart,
and with all thy soul, and with all thy mind, and with
all thy strength: this is the first commandment. And the second
is like, namely this, Thou shalt love thy neighbor as thyself.
There is none other commandment greater than these.*
—Mark 12:30,31

The elderly African grandmother was sitting on our cement cistern when I came out of our back door. It was a sunny day, but this grandmother's face didn't reflect it. She was in pain.

"Mama," she said, "I have a sore on my leg. Will you fix it?"

After examining it, I gently explained that we were not equipped to treat her.

"We are not trained as healthcare givers but as Bible teachers," I said. "Your *kidonda*, "sore," is much too serious for me to attempt to treat. Please go down the hill to the hospital," I instructed her. "They can help you there."

Reluctantly, Grandma left. Several days later, she returned and asked again, "Mama, will you fix my sore?"

Another examination and quick mental evaluation of my medical expertise brought me to the same conclusion. I didn't have enough training. The St. John's Ambulance course I had taken did not include instructions for treating infected tropical wounds like this poor mama had.

"I'm sorry, Mama. Your sore is much too serious for me to try to treat. Please," I urged her, "go to the hospital."

Days passed, and I inquired about Grandma's health. I heard that her condition had deteriorated and she had gone to live with relatives in another area of town.

Why didn't Grandma go to the hospital? I wondered.

I wasn't aware, in my new missionary naivete of the impoverished conditions at the local hospital or of their acute lack of supplies. I later learned that no bedding or food was provided in the hospital. Even the gauze and bandages used after surgery had to be supplied by the patient. Obviously, Grandma had not had the resources for a hospital stay.

Occasionally I met someone who knew Grandma, and I was able to obtain information about her condition. Finally I heard that the infection had spread up her leg. In the tropical heat, the flesh rotted. It became infested with maggots, and Grandma died.

The horror of her death haunted me. I had stacked my qualifications against the circumstances and reckoned myself inadequate. It was true that my professional training was limited, but it was also true that we would never have sufficient professional training to meet the overwhelming needs that surrounded us here. Obviously, my lack-of-training, lack-of-faith mentality needed to be readjusted. If my faith to help was limited to my ability, then where I lacked ability, I lacked faith. If I was going to be of any help in this needy culture, I needed another basis for faith, "faith which works by love."

The Bible confronted me with the fact that, "The things which are impossible with men are possible with God" (Luke 18:27). *Dare I trust God to make a way where there seemed to be no way? Was it feasible to believe in the possibility of stepping beyond the conditioning of my western culture that classifies medical needs and restricts treatment to the proper caregiver? Could I have more faith in divine guidance than the necessity of scientific data and expertise? Could I enter into a dimension of love that would unleash faith and produce creative medical solutions?*

When Jesus was moved with compassion, miracles followed. "And Jesus went forth, and saw a great multitude, and was moved with compassion toward them, and he healed their sick" (Matthew 14:14). Grandma's death brought me face to face with my need of Jesus' kind of problem-solving faith, a faith that was moved by compassionate love.

Was it presumptuous to believe that with God's help I too could step beyond the limitations of my own knowledge into a dimension of divine enablement? Would it work? I had to try. Never again did I want to turn someone away without at least trying to help.

It wasn't long before my decision was tested. One day, I heard a knock on our front door. A mother stood there holding the hand of her little girl.

"My little girl's arm is burned," she said. "Will you help us?"

Gently, I examined the child. The right arm from the wrist to her shoulder was red and raw. The severity of the burn sickened me. How could we treat such a severe case? In spite of my commitment, I was still tempted to send her for help elsewhere. Instead, we prayed together, then quietly I asked God to guide me.

Carefully, I cleansed the wound with boiled salt water, applied Silvadene cream for burns that I found in our little stock of medicines, and wrapped it in gauze. After instructing the mother to give the girl plenty of liquids and the medication for pain if needed, mother and daughter were sent home.

Several days later, the pair returned for a check-up. Carefully, I removed the gauze and was astounded. The burn was healing beautifully. I treated her arm again, rebandaged it, and prayed over her. The little patient and mother left, and I never saw them again. But when I asked about them, I was told that the burn had completely healed.

The decision to help opened the door to a greater scope of heavenly assistance. A book that we did not know existed, passed from country to country and hand to hand until it was given to us. It was entitled, *Where There is No Doctor*,[7] a layman's medical guide for people working in situations where professional treatment is unavailable.

The man who worked for us as a cook began drinking and had to be fired. The lady we hired to take his place mentioned that she had trained in France as a nurse. She gladly added suturing cuts, lancing boils, and drug dispensing to her job description.

Letters arrived from two young women who wanted to come and work with us. Rose Kremblas had lived with us in Canada. She was a former marine and nurse and was gifted with an ability to diagnose and treat disease. When Rose arrived, our daughter Deb became her avid student and assistant. Darlene Abrey, who had been sent to us by a minister in Canada, assumed duties as Bethanie's home-school teacher, giving me more time to help. Our front verandah became an outpatient clinic.

Word of the medical service spread. Charles ordered more medical supplies and counted pills by the score. Rose and Deb helped fill prescriptions. Soon our services included giving out medication for malaria and parasites, treating burns, stitching up cuts, lancing boils, and passing out rehydration drink packets for diarrhea patients. Charles became known as the doctor, and I was the nurse. Any attempt to disclaim the titles was to no avail.

God used my encounter with Grandma to teach me a memorable lesson. Love can inspire faith to reach beyond the inadequacy of human resource into the realm of divine assistance, discovering miracles. We never know when God will superimpose His ability over ours and manifest Himself in a supernatural, creative act—an act of transcending love.

The love that produces a persistent faith, a faith that is willing to try the unknown, was also demonstrated in the life of George Washington Carver. Mr. Carver was born into slavery on a farm in Missouri. The plight of his people prompted him to believe that God would help him to unlock the secret of the peanut. He made more than 300 products from peanuts and received national attention when he presented his findings before a committee of Congress.[8]

The faith which works by love isn't stopped by seeming impossibility. Thus, it is faith that makes men and women great. When the rich young ruler in the book of Matthew came to Jesus, Jesus informed him that if he would be perfect, he needed to go, sell what he had, give it to the poor, and then follow Him. Jesus said that with "men it is impossible for a rich man to enter into the kingdom of God, but with God, all things are possible" (Matthew 19:26). Total reliance upon God is necessary for entrance into the kingdom.

Security in and dependence on our own provisions and abilities tend to seclude us from realms of divine enablement. The faith which works by love contradicts humanism, disallows exclusiveness, and reduces one to total humility. But miracles follow the one who dares to walk there. The Jesus of compassion was the miracle Jesus. Faith works by love!

Faith is Not Based on Sight

"For we walk by faith,
not by sight."
2 Corinthians 5:7

*Our faith should not be
judged by the apparent
failure or success of our work*

21

God Cares About Umbilical Cords

For my thoughts are not your thoughts,
neither are your ways my ways, saith the LORD.
—Isaiah 55:8

The children and I were sitting around the dining room table eating lunch when we heard a knock on the door. One of the ladies living on the compound entered with a tiny baby that she proudly introduced as her new granddaughter.

After the introductions were over, she sobbed.

"Mama," she pleaded, "please help us."

The baby's mother had delivered the child in her mud hut. The navel cord was probably cut with a dirty razor blade, and now, although the newborn was fine featured and beautiful, her navel and little belly were terribly swollen. This little grandbaby probably had tetanus.

Carefully, I bathed the area and prayed, knowing that only a miracle could save her. The case before me was, again, definitely beyond my medical training. How frustratingly helpless I felt as I bathed and disinfected the area.

"Please God," I prayed, "do a miracle and let this little baby live."

Several days later the grandmother came with the sad news that although they had taken the baby to the local hospital for treatment, the baby had died.

"You're a failure," the devil whispered in my ear. "You couldn't help and God didn't answer your prayer. You don't have enough faith. What are you doing here anyway trying to offer these people something that you yourself don't possess?"

Sorrowfully, I murmured words of sympathy. My heart ached for the young mother I had never met. I felt that I had failed her. What right did I have to claim to be a missionary when I didn't have the power to produce the needed results?

Oh, God, I groaned inwardly, *please help us all. Forgive us and help us somehow to truthfully represent you in this needy world. Lord, please help this young mother. You know how much I wanted to help, but I failed. Oh, God, please let me do something for her.*

Sadly, I searched through my belongings and selected a green dress, a favorite. Giving it to the grandmother, I asked her to please give it to her daughter as a token of my love to her and sorrow for her loss.

Many months had passed when I heard that a young couple had moved onto the compound. Late one night, Deborah came and woke me up.

"Mom," she said, "Mama Matolo just knocked on my window and wants us to come and help the new lady. She is in labor. They want us to come and help and also cut the umbilical cord. They are afraid to do it because her last baby died."

Quickly, I found our copy of the book, Where There is No Doctor. With the help of this well-used book, Deb and I briefed ourselves on umbilical cord cutting procedure, then prepared our utensils. We put string, scissors, and bandaging material on a cookie sheet and put it in the oven to sterilize it. Then, carefully covering it with a clean dish towel, Deb and I made our way through the darkness to the little one-room home.

We entered the nearly barren room and found the young mother lying on a bamboo mat on the floor. Several local women were gathered around her and a newborn baby. Carefully, they handed the tiny infant to us, then watched intently to see what we would do.

We washed and disinfected the area, then Debbie whispered, "Mom, you measure and tie, and I'll cut." That suited me fine. I measured and tied, and as Debbie cut, we heard the ladies murmur questioningly. According to their custom, we had cut the cord too short, but they trusted us.

After bandaging our tiny patient, we bowed our heads and prayed that God would bless our efforts, cover our ignorance, and let this baby be healthy and strong. Finally, amid a chorus of thanks, Deb and I made our exit. We felt like we had climbed Mt. Everest as we wound our way back home in the dark. We had done our best. Now we trusted that God would let our tiny patient survive.

Several days later, we had visitors. The same grandmother that had brought me the tiny little girl, so sick with tetanus, was back. Proudly, she introduced me to her daughter and new granddaughter. In amazement, I found myself gazing at the young mother we had just helped and my little namesake. They had named the baby after me.

Though God has millions of people to guide and worlds to order, He saw the grief of two young mothers and heard our prayers. In answer to our prayers, He arranged a move and the birth of a second baby girl for one. Then He allowed me to be given an invitation to help cut the umbilical cord. It was the only umbilical cord that we ever cut. Now, the young mother had come to thank me for a green dress and a healthy baby girl, who they named after me.

After returning home to Canada, I heard Randy Clark speak in a prophetic convention in Toledo, Ohio. He recalled a time when he had assisted a brother as he prayed for the sick. Though they had prayed for many people that evening, to their knowledge, no one was healed. Later, in their hotel room, Randy asked, "How can you handle it? You prayed for all of those people and not one was healed?"

The man replied, "When someone is healed, I don't take the glory; therefore, if they are not healed, I don't take the responsibility. God didn't tell me to heal people, He just told me to pray for them. All I do is obey!"

It is interesting that the famous Hebrews 11 faith chapter includes in its list of great men and women, those who were destitute, afflicted, and tormented. God didn't consider it a disgrace to be destitute, afflicted, and tormented, as long as faith in God's promise remained unshakable. Hebrews 11:39 tells us, "These all, having obtained a good report through faith, received not the promise."

What happens when we don't see the results of our faith? Doubting Thomas couldn't believe that Jesus arose from the dead. And when Jesus appeared to him and proved the power of the resurrection, He made this statement, "Blessed are they that have not seen, and yet have believed" (John 20:29).

Faith is never in vain. Although we may not see the results we had hoped for when we prayed, God still has an answer. Somewhere, somehow, sometime, my faith is sure to be rewarded. When present circumstances do not indicate any assurance of evidence to come, just wait. The answer, still unseen, is being prepared.

Faith is Not Limited
by Time or Space

"He sent his word,
and healed them,
and delivered them
from their destructions."
Psalm 107:20

A word sent by God,
to those far away,
Can overcome time, space, and fear;
It flies with a power,
unrivaled on earth,
To answer a saint's fallen tear.

22

"The Babies Are Dying Like Flies"

The centurion answered and said, Lord,
I am not worthy that thou shouldest come under my roof:
but speak the word only, and my servant shall be healed.
—Matthew 8:8

It was a balmy day. The sun splashed brilliant beams of light over the lake, creating a panorama of sparkling diamonds against the watery blue. The world continued as usual, but not at our house. One-year-old Christine had been sick for several days. Prayer and vigilant nursing hadn't stopped the ruthless illness. Diarrhea, vomiting, and fever wracked her tiny body. Today we had to try something else. Gently carrying the frail little form, we drove as carefully as possible over the rutted, dirt road to the Filtisaf dispensary.

Concern focused our attention on our little daughter as we drove beside the sparkling lake. The scenery went unnoticed. We parked beside the small, white-plastered dispensary sitting on its plot of sand, walked past the palm sentinels, and went inside.

The rustic chairs that lined the hallway were filled with anxious patients waiting to see the doctor. We waited our turn. Finally, Dr. Blanpain's nurse called us into the simple examination room.

Carefully, the young doctor inspected Christine. Then he turned to us and said, "A virus has hit Kalemie, and it's killing the babies like flies. We don't know what it is, and we don't know how to treat it. There is nothing we can do. Take her back home and care for her as best you can."

We stood to leave, but as we were standing there holding Christine, she experienced another attack of diarrhea. The watery stool ran out of her diaper and onto the floor. Dr. Blanpain saw it.

"Just a minute," he said. "Come with me." He led us into a small room with a single bed, a small wooden table under the lone window, and a wooden bench. Gently, we laid baby Christine on the bed. Dr. Blanpain left and returned with an intravenous apparatus and a bag of fluid. He skillfully inserted the needle into her tiny arm, and the fluid began to flow.

"Don't let her pull it out," he instructed.

Deborah stayed with me all day and through the night. Talking in hushed voices, we grappled with our emotions as we watched the hanging bag dripping liquid into baby Christine's arm. Sadly, in her weakened state, it took little effort to hold her still when she tried to move. Most of the time, she lay practically lifeless. Deborah and I softly prayed together and encouraged one another. The next evening, I sent her home to help care for the family and to get some rest.

Another baby lay in an adjoining room, a little African baby boy. His mother, like me, kept vigil over her tiny offspring. But, unlike me, family members and friends accompanied her. My family members and friends were hundreds of miles away. As I sat alone, watching my struggling baby, my heart hammered as waves of fear rose to staggering heights.

Why, God? Why us? Why them? Have I sinned? I'm so scared, God. Do You really see us in this little far away dispensary? I'm even too afraid to cry, God. Are You there?

I was secluded in the tiny room with Christine and couldn't see what was happening in the rooms nearby. But, suddenly, I heard a piercing shriek, and the African mother ran past the door of our room, clutching her baby boy and wailing the all too familiar death cry. Her family and friends followed her wailing in accompaniment, and the little dispensary echoed with their anguish.

Oh God, are we next? Jesus, have mercy. Show us how to stand in the face of death? Jesus, is there a purpose for us being here in the hospital? Do you want me to see something that I haven't seen?

Suddenly, a verse of Scripture rose in my mind: "And I sought for a man among them, that should make up the hedge, and stand in the gap before me for the land, that I should not destroy it: but I found none" (Ezekiel 22:30).

Silently, I knelt, and as soon as I began to pray for the babies of Kalemie, a powerful focus overtook me. *These were His babies. He cared for the tiny innocents like the one who just died so tragically. He died for them, too.* The love He felt flowed through my heart and out through my words as I cried for their deliverance.

Fear fled in the face of the anointing as I fought against the ruthless devourer. God's presence and His peace came. When the burden lifted, I rose from my knees and walked quietly to the lone window. Gazing out over the sunlit lake, I prayed softly, "Lord, I'm so tired. I've prayed for your babies, and now Lord, will you please have somebody pray for mine?"

I had heard stories of how He spoke to people and prompted them to pray for needs thousands of miles away. Miracles happened when they obeyed. *Would God put it on someone's heart to do that for me? Would He actually answer my prayer?* I wondered. It was getting dark, and I felt very alone and far away.

Christine stirred and I returned to my vigil. The doctor came in to check on her, but she rarely moved so there was little danger of her attempting to pull the intravenous needle from her arm. He changed bottles of fluid, and the long night continued. Sleep was difficult, but the young doctor was also sacrificing sleep as he joined forces with us in our fight for life. I was deeply grateful.

He returned with another liter of fluid and a baby bottle.

"Give her this by mouth," he instructed. "She needs to drink all of it by morning."

Christine was a nursing baby and would never have anything to do with a bottle of any sort. This would be an impossible task, I was sure. If I could get her to drink even one eight-ounce bottle full of fluid, it would be a miracle.

I prepared the bottle. Then, gently holding Christine in my arms, I put the bottle to her lips. She drank greedily, without hesitation. It was as if she had heard the order and knew it must be obeyed. She drank the whole liter of fluid. It was then I knew God had heard our prayers.

The next day when Charles came to check on us, Dr. Blanpain released Christine. We laid her on a pillow and carefully carried her home. She seemed relieved when we lay her in her own little crib. We covered it with a mosquito net and placed it outside on the front verandah in the fresh air. She slept all day. It was a long road to recovery, but she made it.

Almost a year later, I had an unusually clear dream that I went home to visit my mother. Charles felt the dream was significant and urged me to make the trip with baby Christine. It was difficult to leave the children behind, but they encouraged me to go. Carefully, I wrote out personal notes with special Scripture verses for each child and bought little gifts. The day we left, I hid a gift and a note under each pillow.

We drove through our little town, down to the port, and joined the mob seeking passage on the crowded boat to Uvira, 180 miles to the north along the shore of Lake Tanganyika, the first leg of our trip. I was in no hurry to join the din of pushing travelers, and the children were beginning to regret their decision to encourage me to go. Gently, I hugged and kissed each child good-bye. As I did, I whispered, "You have a surprise waiting for you under your pillow when you get home."

It made the parting so much easier as I watched their faces light up with anticipation.

Because we lacked mail and telephone service in Kalemie, we arrived in Bujumbura, Burundi unannounced, but the Johnsons greeted us warmly. With the help of God, Missionary Carl Johnson worked miracles to secure updated visas, a passport for Christine, and arrange our flight.

Our arrival home in Springfield, Missouri, was purposefully unannounced. Carrying baby Christine and trembling with anticipation, I approached the house, quietly opened the door, and walked inside to discover a carefully guarded secret. Mom was seriously ill. My family had tried to protect me. She was lying in bed with my faithful sister Gail sitting beside her.

Mom heard us enter, turned, and saw us. Wonder and joy lit up her face as she cried out, "Is it really you, Fern?"

Our coming was like a shot of new life. It was sheer joy just being together again, sharing our love, praying together, and catching up on the news. We both reveled in our unexpected time of shared healing and renewal.

God allowed the time at home to be like a missionary "pit stop" for Christine and me, too. We were treated to wonderful meals. Church supporters collected and boxed up clothing, household items and toys. Some of the ladies in the church organized a sewing bee and made several new outfits for our girls in one day. Money was provided to buy us a much needed computer and printer. One family bought an expensive Lego set for the boys.

My sister Gail was engaged to Timothy Turra. Their wedding date was already set, but they changed it so I could be a part of the wedding party. We only had a few days to find dresses and plan the entire event, but friends offered to help, and the wedding was a beautiful success.

Then God arranged another special event just to show me how precisely He had answered my solitary plea for prayer for Christine that day in Kalemie.

One morning, my sister Emily invited Gail and me to her home for breakfast. As we chatted over bacon and eggs and other deliciously prepared breakfast foods, Gail said, "Fern, I want to ask you something. I had an unusual dream one night. In the dream, Christine was very sick." Gail paused, slightly embarrassed, then added, "It seemed that Christine had diarrhea really bad. I thought about the dream all day," she said, "and finally in the afternoon, I shared it with Mom."

"Gail," Mom said, "we had better pray."

"As soon as we started to pray," Gail explained, "we felt such an unusually strong presence of the Holy Spirit, we were sure God had definitely directed us to pray. We realized that this must be a very important need. We prayed earnestly until the burden lifted. It was such an unusual experience, I marked the day on the calendar. Was Christine really sick?"

I told them how Christine almost died and how I had stood at the window in the little dispensary and asked God to please have someone pray for my baby. We cried in awe of what God had done.

In his article published by *Reader's Digest* in their September 1996 issue, Larry Dossey, MD asked, "Does Prayer Heal?" and concluded "Scientists are discovering what believers have always known".

While working as chief of staff at a large urban hospital, Dr. Dossey began to come across studies that showed prayer bringing about significant changes in a variety of physical conditions.

"Had the medical technique being studied been a new drug or surgical procedure, it probably would have been heralded as a breakthrough," he says, "but scientists, including doctors, can have blind spots."

Dr. Dossey has since given up practicing medicine to devote himself to researching and writing about prayer and how it affects our health. In his observations, he notes that "Love increases the power of prayer. Virtually all healers who use faith and prayer agree: Love is the power that makes it possible for them to reach out to heal even at a distance."[9]

Could it have been that our critical need required the intense, godly love of those that loved us most? The long-distance ministry of healing is a mystery to us. We don't know how it works, but we saw it demonstrated when Gail and Mom responded to a supernatural alert, joined their hearts with the heart of God in loving intercessory prayer, and produced a miracle.

Then Gail went on.

"Fern," she said, "I saw something else in my dream. I saw you walking down a sandy road with stones. It seemed like you were very discouraged. You walked over to the edge of the road and sat down on a log."

I was shocked. I remembered that day. Thoughtless words had been spoken that hurt me deeply. I felt emotionally molested and abandoned of a love I needed and trusted. *How do you live a life of faith when you hurt so deeply?*

It was twilight. All alone, I ran down the hill on the rocky, sandy drive. One of the ladies on the compound happened to see me, and ran after me.

"Mama, don't walk alone," she begged. "It is very dangerous for you. I will go with you."

"It's all right, Mama Matolo. I'm not going far," I replied.

Hesitantly, she returned.

Slowly, I walked out of sight to the edge of the road where I spotted a fallen log and sat down.

I just need a few minutes alone, I thought.

Could I go on any longer? I didn't have the energy. It was like the thoughtless words had opened my soul and let the life drain out. I felt so lost, so alone.

No one but Mama Matolo ever knew about those lonely moments.

Now, months later, my sister was telling me something I could hardly comprehend. God saw me in my lonely grief. He was so concerned and loved me so much, that He gave Gail a dream and a burden to pray for me. I had asked God to have someone pray for my desperately ill baby. That was very important. But God considered my own personal, emotional need of equal importance and included it in the "call to prayer" dream.

Jesus knows how important it is that our "faith fail not" (Luke 22:32). *Could it be that as He interceded before the Father on my behalf, my pain grieved Him so much, He let Gail share His grief and join with Him in intercession? Then, just to make sure I knew how much He loved me, He arranged a visit with my sisters so I would hear about it?*

Yes, God is concerned for the intricate affairs of the world, but He is also concerned for us. We are the beloved children for whom He died such an agonizing death, in order that we might be saved and healed. Our tears are so important to Him, He records them and saves them in a bottle. Psalm 56:8 says, "put thou my tears into thy bottle: are they not in thy book?"

Jesus felt the agony of desertion, misrepresentation, and abandonment in the desolate garden of Gethsemane when He went alone to pray. No wonder He intercedes so earnestly for us in heaven now. He knows what it's like. When we feel overwhelmed by wounded relationships, He wants us to know that someone is praying. It may be Jesus Himself, it may be a near or distant friend, but somewhere, someone is praying that our "faith fail not." God cares!

1973 | *The Willner family in Kenya*

1974 | *Visiting Calabar, Nigeria*

1981 | A *"welcoming party"* in Kalemie, Congo

1982 | Kalemie, Congo

1986 | *The Willner Family*

1992 | *Arriving in Meru, Kenya*

1993 | *Visiting Meru, Kenya outside a church build in
1973 by Charles Willner*

1993 | *Visiting Meru, Kenya in front of the second church built in 1974.*

1993 | *Fern preaching out in the open air in Meru, Kenya.*

1998 | *Fern and Charles dancing at a Valentine's Party*

Charles and Fern

Fern C. Willner

Faith is Rewarded by God

"But without faith it is impossible
to please him:for he that cometh
to God must believe that he is,
and that he is a rewarder of them
that diligently seek him."
Hebrews 11:6

*God will never send you into the
wilderness without His miracles."*

23

Kindness in Kongolo

For the LORD thy God hath blessed thee in all the works of thy hand:
he knoweth thy walking through this great wilderness: these forty years
the LORD thy God hath been with thee; thou hast lacked nothing.
—Deuteronomy 2:7

In my letter to Gail and Mom I wrote:

Dearest Gail and Mom,

We just had some miracles in our wilderness. About a month
ago, we saw a white man in town. All excited, we introduced
ourselves and found that he and his family are from the
States and are living about a half-hour flight from here, in
Kongolo. They are working with a U.S. Aid government program, and he is the finance manager of the project there.

We invited him for supper and discovered that he and his
wife are from a Mennonite background. They have three
children, the oldest is Ruth and Mina's age. He was so excited to discover our girls that he wanted to take them right
home with him to meet his daughters. Charles had a meeting scheduled not too far from them, so we made plans for
all of us to go for a visit.

Finally, the day arrived. We waited in the train station with hundreds of people for three hours. Debbie played her guitar and we sang while the children played. About 6:00 P.M., we began trying to board the train. People fought as they climbed over each other trying to get in the doors or through the windows. One very attractive lady, well-dressed and wearing high heel shoes, climbed over the backs of those in front of her, stepping on their shoulders, and scrambled in through the train window. It would take pages to describe the scenario that followed, but the train finally started, leaving many behind.

We stopped at a number of villages along the way. In the semi-darkness of the full moon, we watched as villagers excitedly rushed to sell dough balls and fruits and greet passengers through the windows of the train. Even when we didn't stop in a village, we spotted moonlit scenes of people lined up in front of a group of mud huts waving as the train sped by. Most of the people who spied our family of *muzungus*, "white people", in the semi-darkness were very friendly. Only once did we meet with jeers, a glowing cigarette butt, and a man who leaped up quick as a wink and struck Jeff and William as they waved from the window of the train.

We arrived in Nyunza about 11:30 P.M. and were greeted by a crowd of African brethren. They led us over dirt roads to the U.S. government project compound. There, we were given a message sent by short wave radio, greeting us and inviting us to stay overnight in the simple guest room. We were delighted. We would have mattresses to sleep on and even running water from their water tank. Mr. Ackerman was scheduled to arrive in the morning on the project's six-seater Cessna airplane. In the meantime, the company's vehicle, a Blazer, was waiting, ready to carry us overland to Kongolo in the morning, four and a half hours away.

We ate the rest of our sandwiches with milk made from our can of milk powder and some boiled water that we carried in a plastic container. After figuring out how all nine of us, and our interpreter, could fit on the four single mattresses, we blew out the lantern, said happy goodnights to each other, and settled down for a few hours sleep.

In the morning, we dressed hurriedly, then walked to the local market to buy bread. Tea with our bread would make an excellent breakfast, so when we found a little wooden frame building with one wooden table that served tea, we felt that we had fallen into the lap of luxury. We ate breakfast then bought some oranges, bananas, and bread for the safari to Kongolo.

Though preparing outwardly, inwardly I was concerned. Christine was over a year-old, but she only weighed 22 pounds and was not very strong. How would she handle the long dusty trip? Then, an unexpected message came by short wave radio. Mr. Ackerman was due in at 8:15 A.M., and there would be space for Christine and me to fly on to our destination with him. It was an answer to my silent prayer. We said good-bye to the children as they started their safari in the Blazer with Mr. Ackerman's trusted chauffeur.

Charles and Deborah would join us later after going to minister at some scheduled meetings in Nyunza to which they were headed. Deborah often ministered to the young people when Charles was invited to churches to preach.

Soon Robbie Ackerman arrived. We waited until he finished his business, then we drove out to the little runway. We taxied down the runway.

Our time in Kongolo with Robbie and Susan and their children was wonderful. Robbie and Susan showed me how to make a stove-top oven out of an oil can. The children watched movies when the generator was on in the evenings. They played games on the battery-operated computer and listened to a Walkman stereo for the first time. Then, all too soon, it was over. We had planned to return by train, but we received word that the pilot had to do a test flight and would fly us all the way to Kalemie. Ruth and Mina would stay with the Ackermans until the end of the month and come home with Robbie when he was scheduled to come to Kalemie for business.

The flight back to Kalemie was a miracle in the desert for Jeff, too.

"How would you like to fly, Jeff?" the pilot asked.

How would a 14-year-old aspiring pilot like to fly? Jeff was thrilled. The pilot gave instructions, arranged Jeff's ear-phones and let him act as copilot. What an unforgettable experience. We just couldn't get over how beautifully the Lord arranged this vacation. Robbie took pictures of us, then offered to develop them and send copies to our mothers during their upcoming vacation in the States. So, if you get a letter and pictures from a strange person, it's just a new member of the family of God that we finally got to meet.

Gail, I love the gem you enclosed in your letter. I hope I never lose it. "God will never send you into the wilderness without His miracles." It's true, Gail. Let's encourage ourselves in the Lord, take our eyes off the wilderness, and look for the manna in our own backyards. No desert is barren enough to prevent God's abundance.

Faith Can be
Exemplified in Youth

"Let no man despise thy youth;
but be thou an example of the believers,
in word, in conversation,
in charity, in spirit, in faith, in purity."
1 Timothy 4:12

*God challenges youth to be an example
in the words that they speak,
in the actions of their daily lives,
in their acts of charity,
in the kind of spirit they exhibit,
in the faith that they demonstrate, and
in the purity of their moral character.*

24

"Are We Sacrificing Our Daughter?"

Yea, for thy sake are we killed all the day long:
we are counted as sheep for the slaughter.
—Psalm 44:22

"Jeff and William, time to get up!" hollered Kasuku, our pet African grey parrot. Charles was almost dressed and ready to go call the boys when our pet parrot decided it was his turn to make the morning wake-up call. We looked at each other in astonishment. He even had the time right, precisely, eight A.M.

As residents living outside of Canada, we were fortunate to be able to receive free correspondence materials from the Ministry of Education in Ontario. The program was designed for students to work independently or with minimal supervision so the older children could do most of their work without help and we were free to assist the younger ones. Charles is an organizer. Together with his experience as a former army sergeant, he had sufficient expertise to keep us all in line, and he also had a degree in math and physics which was a tremendous help since the children required more assistance in that area of study.

The children rarely complained, but it was obvious that Deborah was having difficulty accepting her new surroundings. Did Dad and Mom have a right to make such dramatic changes in her life, to take her from home, friends, and glory as a high school track star? What does a 14-year-old girl do on the mission field?

Before deciding to become angry and miserable, she determined to find some answers for herself. She began getting up at 6:30 every morning. I watched as she took the little guitar that I bought for her at a garage sale before we left, her Bible, and a notebook. She walked over to the cement-block church on our compound and went inside to meet with God. Morning after morning, she kept her sunrise rendezvous with God. She read her Bible, made notes from quickened Scriptures, and learned new chords on her guitar as she worshiped. As her relationship grew with God, she felt very sure that He had called her too. But what could she do?

One day, she asked for a Swahili Bible. Although she didn't know the language, she decided to compare the two Bibles and translate the Scripture choruses that she knew into Swahili. Before long, some of the youth on the compound approached her and asked if she would have a youth meeting with them. Though struggling with her limited knowledge of Swahili, she agreed to try. Daily family language study was improving our communication skills, and Deb knew the kids would be patient with her.

She began weekly meetings on the compound. Kids were saved. Some were filled with the Spirit. Deborah taught them the new choruses, and soon the whole compound was singing the Word. Scripture verses echoed from home to home as Mamas sang while they cooked, washed, gardened, and tended babies.

The local hospital, sanitarium, and leprosarium lay at the foot of the hill where we lived. Deborah and her newly-formed youth group decided to take their faith beyond the little church and down the hill. The group met and prayed. Then, armed with the "faith of a little child," they set off for the hospital. Undaunted by the danger of the diseases they faced or their lack of ministerial experience, they marched forward to "set some captives free."

With the permission of those in authority, Deb and disciples sang and preached, then divided up into teams of twos for individual counseling and prayer for the sick. Twelve-year-old Ruth helped to preach, and 10-year-old Mina helped in praying for the sick and leading them to Christ. New hope sprang into the eyes of many. Loneliness and neglect gave way to smiles as love broke through the clouds of their solitude. Songs lifted their hearts, and the Word paved the way for faith. When this little band of believers laid hands on the sick and prayed, to their delight, some were actually healed.

One lady in particular will never be forgotten. She lay helpless and crippled on her bamboo mat. But when the little band of believers prayed, she grasped a ray of truth, she believed, and she was made whole. She arose from her helpless, crippled position on her bamboo mat and walked. The joy on her radiant face more than repaid the enthusiastic little evangelists.

But Deb's budding ministry had only begun. She began taking solitary walks around the nearby area, asking God to lead her in her mission of personal evangelism. Day after day, she returned home to tell of people who had given their lives to God. We began a house meeting to disciple new believers in our community. And they came.

Carefully, I watched our zealous offspring. *Was she genuine, or was she doing what she thought was expected of a missionary? Was she overburdened by the needs around her? Had we deprived her of too much? What was really in her heart?*

Then, one night, I had a most unusual dream. I dreamed that I was in a slaughter house where a group of sheep were standing in line waiting to be slaughtered. As I watched the line move forward, I was startled to see that the next sheep in line was Deborah. Meekly she knelt. Without a word, she tilted her head back and opened her mouth in preparation for the slaughter. The machete-like knife, with a large curved blade would cut through her open mouth. She was calm and submitted. She was ready for death. Trembling, I watched my daughter, my firstborn. Her silent surrender and impending slaughter were terrifying.

Suddenly, I awoke. *God*, I agonized, *have we forced our daughter to sacrifice herself? Is she dying?*

"No, Fern," He said, "I am showing you her heart. She has presented herself to me as a living sacrifice."

In the early morning stillness, I crept out of bed. Quietly, I stole into Deborah's room and climbed up onto the bunk bed beside her.

"Deb," I said, "God just gave me a dream, and He showed me your heart."

As I related the dream to her, Deborah began to cry. "Mom," she said, "I want to serve God with all of my heart, but I wondered if God really knew how I felt. Now I know that He does. Thank you, so much, for telling me about your dream."

God saw her sacrifice and honored it. Within a few months, eight young people, including her own sister Ruth, were filled with the Holy Spirit in her meetings. The lives of some of the youth, the boys especially, were dramatically changed. She was invited to teach a group of 120 primary school children every Monday. She met some wives of local business men, including the wife of the army colonel who lived near us, and began a house meeting for married couples, which we added to our own responsibilities.

When it was time for Deborah to enter her senior year of high school, we sent her to Rift Valley Academy, a missionary boarding school in Kenya to help her make the transition from home-schooling to university. She graduated with honors and after commencement, flew to Springfield, Missouri to become a student at Evangel University.

While working as a waitress to help pay her way through school, she was "discovered" and asked to compete in the local Miss Springfield pageant. She won. Later, she became Miss Trenton, Miss Lake of the Ozarks, and a runner-up to Miss Missouri. Then she was selected to spend several months in Japan promoting the United States as part of the American Train Project.

Finally, back in Canada, Deborah met and married Erik Kiezebrink, a ministry intern. After four years of ministry in Canada, they flew to the Philippines and began a new period of missionary service. Deborah writes:

Had a great four and a half hour service yesterday at ICS for their anniversary celebration. The Lord gave me a prophetic word for the church regarding the need for people to keep pursuing and pressing in for their relationship and the promised blessings of God. We need to be like Jacob who wrestled with God and Naaman who bathed seven times in the Jordan. We need to keep acting in faith even when we don't see immediate results. God will bless us and strengthen us through that process as we press in through, pain, pressure, circumstances, fear, and many other hindrances.

After this there was joyful shouting, thunderous singing and dancing by a number of people near the front and on stage. I danced vigorously without my shoes. We look forward to all that God is going to accomplish.

During those days of difficulty in Kalemie, were we sacrificing our daughter on the altar of personal achievement as the devil tried to lead us to believe? No! Thankfully, Deborah listened when God spoke to her heart. He told her that it was no accident that she was born into a family that was called to Africa. God knew where she was, and He would use her in Africa too, if she was willing.

As the children joined us in our call to minister, they realized that you don't have to be a college graduate to be used by God. God had the stories of overcoming youth recorded for all of us to read. For example, young David slew the giant and liberated his nation from Philistine oppression. Young Timothy was commended by the apostle Paul as an example of faith. And, young Joseph demonstrated outstanding moral integrity in a pagan land where he was sold as a slave. Even youth are called to present themselves as living sacrifices to God, to be transformed by the power of God, and to remain unconformed to the evil of the world.

> I beseech you therefore, brethren, by the mercies of God, that ye present your bodies a living sacrifice, holy, acceptable unto God, which is your reasonable service. And be not conformed to this world: but be ye transformed by the renewing of your mind, that ye may prove what is that good, and acceptable, and perfect, will of God.
> —Romans 12:1,2

God has not excused any of us from the effects of sin because of our age, sex, or race. Sin still kills. The wages of sin are the same for the 14-year-old as they are for the 60-year-old— "death"(Romans 6:23). And likewise, God will not deny any of us salvation through faith in Jesus Christ or the power of the Holy Ghost to live a victorious, overcoming life. "But as many as received him, to them gave he power to become the sons of God, even to them that believe on his name" (John 1:12).

Age does not need to be a hindrance to the power and anointing of God. A young person under divine control can be a blazing example of morality, integrity, and righteous power.

Faith Cannot Survive
Without Patience

"In your patience
possess ye your souls."
Luke 21:19

Patience is a virtue,
Needed for salvation;
Grows when faith is tested,
Or during tribulation.
James 1:3 & Romans 5:3

25

Fourteen Flat Tires

And that which fell among thorns are they, which,
when they have heard, go forth, and are choked with cares and riches
and pleasures of this life, and bring no fruit to perfection. But that on
the good ground are they, which in an honest and good heart, having
heard the word, keep it, and bring forth fruit with patience.
–Luke 8:14,15

"Dad, let us bring the *piki*, Swahili for 'motorcycle,'" the boys begged.

We were going to spend the weekend in a village that we had never been in before. They asked us to help them dedicate their new church. After packing our red Lada automobile with items we would need, we started out in convoy. Dad and I led the way, and the boys happily followed along behind, on the *piki*.

The road we traveled was one that had been blazed by foot, then extended by occasional trucks bringing supplies into the region. We passed solitary villages, secluded by their primitive existence, but for most of the trip, we were nearly cocooned in our two-track passageway by elephant grass and tropical foliage.

"Charlie, the boys are stopping."

We stopped and went back. The *piki*'s innards were malfunctioning. It is amazing what mechanical skills emerge in boys and men when presented with an automotive challenge. *Does our society's as-*

signment of skills to specialists repress these instincts? Perhaps. But in our situation, devoid of professional help of any kind, hidden talents surfaced. The guys put their heads together, solved the problem, and we were on our way again. Their success was short-lived.

"Charlie, they've stopped again."

We stopped, fixed the *piki*, and started out again.

"Hmmm, Charlie. The boys aren't following."

What was causing the problem? Dirty gas? Very possibly, considering we could only buy gas from men who sold it in bottles and barrels, who got it who knows how, who knows when, and from who knows where. At any rate, the *piki* had finally died. The guys hauled its dusty corpse up onto the top of the car, tied it down securely with rope and rode the remainder of the anticipated *piki* safari with Mom and Dad. What a disappointment!

Finally, we reached the village. It was a large village with huts built in a circle around an open courtyard. The villagers heard us coming, and by the time we drove into the courtyard, more than 200 people were lined up to greet us. They shouted and ran and yodeled with joy. They were so excited, it was heartwarming. We got out of the car and were immediately surrounded by a myriad of hands outstretched to greet us. Some of the mamas held their babies and attempted to get the little ones to shake our hands, but the poor babies were terrified. They had never seen a white face or white hands before, and they wailed in terror. The mamas were undisturbed and laughed with amusement as the babies cried.

The elders led us to a square mud hut with a thatched roof that had been prepared for us. We parked the car and went inside. The hut had dirt floors which had been swept clean, and was divided into two small rooms: a bedroom/living room and a bedroom. We heard a noise and peeked into the second bedroom where we spied two baby baboons tied up. They jabbered excitedly at the strange looking visitors, but our host quickly captured them and took them outside. The rooms were sparsely furnished. Each had a bed and a couple of wooden chairs. There was a table in the living room. The beds were frames made of wooden poles covered with a layer of split bamboo lashed together.

We brought our overnight bags inside. While we were getting settled, someone came to the door and hollered, *Hodi*, meaning "I am here."

"*Karibu*," "come near," we responded.

Two ladies came inside. One carried a large porcelain basin, which she placed on the floor. The second lady poured hot water into the basin.

"This is to wash your feet," they said as they set up two more chairs.

Charles, Jeff, William, and I sat in a circle, took off our shoes, and dipped our feet in the water.

"Now this is real togetherness," said William as we sat back, blissfully wriggling our toes together in the steamy basin. We couldn't believe how good the warm water felt to our dusty feet.

There was no meeting that night, so after a meal of rice and chicken with the village elders, we prepared for bed. We gathered all of the clothing we could find to cover the bamboo slats and create a makeshift mattress for the bed that the boys slept on in the bedroom/living room. But as I bent to tuck them in and kiss them good night, I was startled to see a large black tarantula on the wall beside their bed. Grabbing a shoe, I aimed. I couldn't afford to miss the hairy target in a situation like this. Neither the boys nor I would sleep well if I did. Thankfully, my one prayerful whack was successful, and we all breathed easier after I carried the dead critter outside.

As the boys settled down, I made an inconspicuous search for the tarantula's mate. It had been my observation that tarantulas and scorpions generally traveled in pairs. But, my anxious search was futile. "What the boys don't know probably won't hurt them," I hopefully decided. Reluctantly, I abandoned the search, silently prayed for their protection, and went to fix our bed.

All we had left to cover our own bed was a *kikwembe*, a piece of native cotton cloth used as a full-length, wraparound skirt. I spread it on the bamboo bed, and we laid down.

Can people actually sleep on these beds? I wondered. The split bamboo was no invitation to comfort. *How do you snuggle into a bed of wood?* "Ouch." I laid on one side until it went numb, then I laid on the other side. Once, I woke up surprised that I had fallen asleep.

Then, strange noises caught my attention. Something was right outside our bedroom wall. I held my breath and listened. What was making those garbled noises and bumping against the wall? The compound was quiet. Had a wild animal strayed into the courtyard? I listened. Then it dawned on me. They were the baby baboons. They were tied to the outside of the house. The poor little guys probably wanted their bedroom back.

At the break of dawn, the whole compound was in a commotion—people running, yelling and laughing, an animal bawling. What was happening?

When our "room service" breakfast arrived, we questioned our hostess.

"O, they're just catching the goat that we are going to make for your dinner," they replied.

"Please don't kill a goat," we begged.

Our hostesses were adamant. The guests must be fed goat they explained, as they served us some *booey*, porridge made of cassava flour, and hot tea. We thanked them. After they left, we took a bite of the porridge. It was white and slimy and tasteless. We assumed that its closest relative was wallpaper paste. Something needed to be done to give it some flavor. I dug into my travel supplies and found the margarine. We stirred some in, but it didn't help. We tried adding sugar, but it was worse. Salt? *Uggggg. It was awful.*

Suddenly, William remembered that in all the excitement we hadn't prayed. We bowed our heads.

"Lord bless this *booey* to my body," he quipped.

We looked up, and he grinned sheepishly.

"You know," he said, "I felt a check while I was praying that."

Finally we abandoned the porridge and drank our tea. We decided you just have to grow up with some things to like them.

The morning service in the new church was held in a wonderful atmosphere of excitement and pride. The people had worked hard. Now they were blessed to share their achievement with guests from far away. Charles preached well, and afterward we spent time ministering to those who came forward for prayer.

Time was flying. It was dangerous to travel after sunset, so we needed to get home before dark. We returned to the compound and ate a quick lunch. Finally, after lingering farewells, we left. But speed was impossible on the tropical trails. We hadn't gone far when Charles decided to check the tires. He stopped the car and got out to look. One tire was flat. The boys happily scrambled out to help fix it. They didn't mind the travel break as they cut a patch from the tube which they had taken from the spare tire. They scrubbed the patch, applied glue, and stuck it on. Finally, it was fixed. Now we really needed to hurry. It wasn't good to be out alone in the forest at night.

Then we felt the symptoms again. Bump. Bump. We stopped. Checked. Sure enough, another flat tire. They took off the tire, took out the tube of glue, scrubbed, glued, patched, and reassembled.

Drive. Hurry.

Bump. Bump.

The boys got out good-naturedly. This was now our fourth flat tire, and by this time, they had the procedure well established.

Oh, no. We were out of glue. There was no need to hurry now. It was midnight. The moon shone serenely overhead, scattering moonbeams over the sheltering trees, the steamy elephant grass, and the helpless travelers sitting alone in their car, in the wild. What a unique experience to be stranded in the middle of Africa, with a flat tire and no glue, under a moonlit sky. *Now what do we do?* We had not met any other vehicles on this road, so there was no likelihood of getting help. There was nowhere to go and nothing we could do.

In spite of our predicament, neither of the boys, nor Charles seemed disturbed. Through it all, they remained cheerful and un-complaining. Maybe they had determined, like I silently had, not to lose their patience.

Then a noise broke the stillness, a deep, slow, rumbling sound. A form appeared. It was a truck. A big truck. The driver drew up alongside, and Charles explained our plight.

"No problem," said the driver. He had glue. He handed a tube to Charles, then slowly drove out of sight. The guys fixed the tire, and we started out again.

Bump. Bump.

As the boys scrubbed and glued in the moonlight, I silently mused, "You know, we could write an article for *Guideposts*, 'The night we had five flat tires and still kept our peace.'" In the midst of my musings, William appeared at my window.

"You know what, Mom?" he said grinning. "That guy in Guide-posts thought he had trouble when he had four flat tires. I could write a story for *Guideposts* and say that we found that we had peace even in the most distressing circumstances."

Was our peace the result of somebody's prayers? I wondered. *Was it a reward from God for being faithful? Or were we actually learning the patience that tribulation is designed to teach us?* Whatever the case, it was wonderful that we all shared the same sense of peace.

The tire was finally fixed again, and we continued our "tire-ing" journey home.

Eleven flat tires. Twelve flat tires. Thirteen flat tires.

We had just reached the bottom of our driveway when the four-teenth flat tire occurred. By now, the sun was coming up, its new-born rays sparkling on the droplets of cool morning rain. We got out, locked the car, and laughingly walked home in the rain—in peace.

Funny, I don't remember the tiredness of that all-night trip. I don't remember hunger or fear. I just remember the peace, the beautiful morning sunshine sparkling on the rain drops, and walking home in the tropical shower together.

The noble, enriching feeling of overcoming, shines like sunlight in our hearts in comparison to the bleakness of failure. The tribulation, the test of faith is a vehicle to the joy of triumph. Though the process of overcoming may not seem worth the effort at times, that's not true. No joy is like the joy of victory. No trial is worth the loss of faith. Tribulation, tested faith, patience, and overcoming, are the natural progression of faith for every child of God, but God sends His Holy Spirit to comfort us through it all.

Faith is Always Rewarded
by More Than it Gives

"Give, and it shall be given unto you;
good measure, pressed down, and shaken together,
and running over, shall men give into your bosom.
For with the same measure that ye mete withal
it shall be measured to you again."
Luke 6:38

God keeps accurate books.
He never shortchanges His people.

26

The Millionaire's Miracle

*Trust in the LORD, and do good; so shalt thou dwell in the land,
and verily thou shalt be fed. Delight thyself also in the LORD:
and he shall give thee the desires of thine heart.*
—Psalm 37:3,4

"Mr. Willner, I must send my son away to get a better education, but he needs to learn English. Please, will you teach him English?"

Charles understood the need of the Arab businessman, but could he add another responsibility to his already busy schedule? Finally, when requests continued to come from people begging for English classes, he decided to open a class on the Kankomba compound using the Bible as a classroom textbook.

It was early in the evening. Dinner was over, and Charles was teaching at the church. The children and I were talking in the living room when we heard a car drive up the hill and park in front of the house. The children watched curiously as I went outside to investigate. Two well-dressed gentlemen stepped from a beautiful black Mercedes and greeted me. We had never seen these men before or a car like this in our sandy little town of Kalemie.

"Hello," they said in English. "We are looking for the home of the Gardners and were directed here."

I gave them the directions that they needed, then invited them inside to meet the children and have a cup of tea. They accepted, and we escorted them into our simple home. The knitted throw rug helped to cover some of the cracks in the cement, and you would never guess that the neatly ironed gingham curtains were made from my retired maternity dress.

Everyone was delighted to have guests, and our guests seemed equally fascinated to find us. We discovered that the men were in town on business from Bunia, a town in northeastern Zaire. One was a business man, and the other was his personal pilot. The children kept them entertained as I fixed tea and cut wedges of freshly made squash pie. Deborah sang a song she had just written. It spoke volumes, revealing to the men the spiritual depths of this 14 year old. They were fascinated. Time flew as they laughed and joked with the kids, enjoyed seconds of the pie and tea, and finally rose to leave.

"I want you all to come and visit me at my hut," the businessman stated. "My wife carries water on her head, too," he informed the children, grinning.

I caught the wink that he gave his pilot and knew that this man was no hut-dweller.

"I will be in touch," he said, with an emphasis that let us know that the invitation was more than a joke. After shaking hands with each of us, they bid us a warm farewell, started the Mercedes, and with a wave of their hands, the rare touch of wealth disappeared down the hill.

They were hardly out of sight when Charles came from the church wondering who the guests were. We explained the visit, and Charles exclaimed, "Do you know who that was? That was Victor Engezio, a millionaire!"

"Oh," Jeff said, holding up his hand and looking at it unbelievingly. "I shook the hand of a millionaire. I'm never going to wash it." To further establish association, he ran and sat in the chair where Mr. Engezio had sat.

"I sat in the seat of a millionaire," he declared with boyish glee. If he had anything to do with it, the spirit of prosperity would rub off on him.

About a month passed, then one day when Charles was in town, he was approached by a stranger.

"I am Victor Engezio's secretary," he explained, "and I have an invitation for you and your family to visit his home."

He showed Charles a three-week detailed itinerary that had been arranged for us. We accepted the invitation and embarked on the most incredible vacation we have ever had.

When we arrived in Goma, Zaire, we were booked into the modern Masque Hotel. We didn't know such places existed in Zaire. Our clothes were laundered by the hotel laundry service, and we dined in the attractively-decorated dining room with distinguished foreign guests and tourists.

One evening as we ate, the dining room lights suddenly dimmed. Flames leaped, and the children gasped in awe as the waiter prepared flaming crepes beside the table of one of the guests.

"Can he do that here?" the children asked eagerly.

"Of course," Mr. Engezio's brother, the proprietor and our host replied, entertained by the children's enthusiasm.

Passion fruit juice was another exotic discovery, and he served the children all they could drink with their gourmet meals. It had been a long time since we had eaten strawberries and ice cream, and we had never been able to afford meals of lobster or chicken cordon bleu for our family of nine. He urged us to order anything we wanted on the menu, and like everything else on this trip, it was gratis.

After two days of rest and lavish meals at the hotel, it was time to leave. Mr. Engezio's personal secretary became our appointed chauffeur and safari leader. He carefully seated us in a large green Land Rover, and we drove off through the lush foliage produced by the black lava fields of Goma. He pointed out the region's smoldering volcano. The boys would have loved to hike to the top to check out the molten mass for themselves, but I was thankful we didn't stop.

Several hours later, we spotted white, thatched, round houses resembling mud huts. When we entered the area, we discovered it was a tourist game preserve and the round houses served as motel units. The park also housed a restaurant and a large, well-maintained swimming pool. Several of the mud hut units had been prepared for us, and we hurried to unload and investigate. Once inside, the huts did not resemble those we were used to. They were modern and clean with comfortable beds and bathroom facilities.

Because of the threat of wild animals, our activities outside were limited to daylight hours in designated, safe areas. The next day, the children were taken by Land Rover to a fishing site. Armed guards stood by protectively as the children fished in a river that housed more than fish. Huge hippos rested lazily in the cool water. Their tiny eyes occasionally peered casually at the intruders, but they were content to sleep in the deep.

The catch was plentiful. Suddenly, the aroma of grilled fish filled the air, and hunger pangs diverted the children's attention. A resort chef, complete with a white cook's hat and jacket, had arrived from the restaurant and was busily cooking their catch of the day. They watched as he arranged the cooked fish on silver platters. Then, to their amazement, he spread a lavish table and served them lunch by the lake. This kind of life was for the rich and famous, not missionary kids that had been bathing out of a bucket for the last year. They were impressed!

When we left the reserve and resumed our drive through the jungle, we were suddenly surrounded by baboons. Some of them jumped on top of the car and peered upside-down through the windows at us. Others sat on the front of the car and stared at us through the windshield. We were their personal zoo. The children were as fascinated with them as they were with us.

Searching through our travel supplies, the children found some pineapple slices and, rolling down the windows just a little, they carefully passed them out to the inquisitive spectators. The baboons fought and screamed at one another as they tried to get possession of the tasty treats. Then the triumphant winners, clutching their piece of pineapple in both hands, sat on the hood in front of us and ate while juice dripped down their whiskered mouths and onto their fur.

Our Mount Hoyo stop was fascinating. Its caves house thousands of migrating butterflies, and its tropical rain forests shelter the legendary pygmies. As we drove beneath the dusky canopy of foliage, lit by filtered sunlight, we passed compounds of tiny mud huts. The little people heard our vehicle coming and hurried outside to line up and wave at the strangers. They were naked or wore tattered loin cloths. It looked like a village of children, but when we looked more closely at some of their faces we saw the wrinkled skin and aging features of tiny parents and grandparents.

Slowly, we drove up the side of the mountain until we reached a resort that still showed evidence of its lavish past. It was almost deserted now, but rooms had been prepared for us. As we unpacked, small groups of pygmies gathered to watch. They wanted to touch our skin, feel our hair, and talk. What a shame that a language barrier prevented us from communicating with each other. Once inside, we again became the zoo, as they peered in the windows at us.

Dinner was served in the main building, in the hotel's formal dining room. Soft candlelight gave a warm glow to the wood paneled hall and reflected off ornately framed pictures of famous men who had visited the site. The outside wall was banked with windows, and as we ate, we could look out over the moonlit jungle.

At each unique stop on our scheduled safari, homes had been prepared for our arrival. Elaborate meals were hot and ready to serve, and servants were waiting to serve us. Finally, we arrived at Mr. Engezio's home. His family was unexpectedly called away, but before he left, he gave us a tour of his house and instructed his servants to be at our disposal. The pantry had freezers of meat, both wild and domestic. His cook, formerly the head chef of a large Ugandan hotel, was instructed to cook anything we ordered. Mr. Engezio was sorry that they could not be with us, but he gave us the keys to his Mercedes and urged us to make ourselves at home.

Charles had meetings scheduled within the week, but Victor Engezio insisted that the children and I stay longer. He arranged to have us flown to Bukavu to meet Charles, in one of the planes that belonged to his charter fleet. We wouldn't have to make the long drive back.

Every morning, we were served breakfast in the gazebo by the pool, under the shade of palms and avocado trees. As we enjoyed platters of eggs, sliced meats and cheeses, homemade breads, real butter, jams, native fruits, and Kenyan tea, their African gray parrot kept us entertained by his chatter.

The children swam for hours in the crystal clear pool, and as I sat and acted as lifeguard, I sewed little dresses by hand from material given to us by new-made friends on the trip. This trip was a godsend. Gradually, the sun turned the children's skin to golden brown. The nourishing food strengthened us, and we regained the weight we had lost after months of struggle with tropical illnesses and food shortages.

Our amazing vacation ended when we were flown to Bukavu. We met Charles there and had one last elegant meal of lobster, before we drove back home to Kalemie. Who would have ever guessed that an African, Christian businessman would get lost, find some needy missionaries, and minister to them? We gave God our best for Africa, and God allowed Africa to give back to us in the most unexpected way.

Faith in God will take the fear out of giving. When we live in fellowship with God, giving is a natural response. It is a godly characteristic. God gave. We give. He gives back. It is a circle of love and only we can break it, for He will not.

Faith Cannot Please God
When it Cowers

"Now the just shall live by faith:
but if any man draw back,
my soul shall have no pleasure in him."
Hebrews 10:38

*May we never live to
regret that we traded our faith
for comfort.*

27

The Hepatitis Conflict

I can do all things through Christ which strengtheneth me.
—Philippians 4:13

Since coming to Zaire, the unusual events and illnesses we experienced made interesting entries in my journal:

July 26: Kiki, our monkey, is making the parrot a nervous wreck, chasing him around, trying to pull out his tail feathers.

July 31: Ephraim came over and said that the monkey had got in the church and was disturbing them very much. I went and caught him and tied him up.

August 1: We haven't had any water in our cistern for several days. Debbie took Mama Matolo down to a safe place to wash clothes. She had become afraid to go back down by the river. Last Saturday a young man was caught by a crocodile. He lost his arm, and even though they carried him to a hospital, he died.

August 3: The weather is very cool and dry now, and windy. There are many *funzas*. A funza is a parasite that burrows into the skin, generally near the toenail. It then sets up housekeeping in its little sac, which grows bigger and bigger as it hatches out scores of eggs. When the sac is removed, it leaves a good-sized crater in the toe, which miraculously heals. Even baby Christine has had two in her toes. William's toe is all infected from them. Bethanie has had many.

I took Bethanie and Christine and went to town. We found a parcel at the post office from a Sunday school class in Ontario. It took one year and four months to arrive. Everything was either stolen or eaten by rats, except for the toothpaste (which they had evidently sampled and didn't like), the shampoo, and a jump-rope.

August 4: Got up early and wrote another small article. Christine has been having diarrhea again and tonight is running a temperature. Found out that ten-year old Jeff has bought a parcel of ground for his friend nicknamed "Colonel" and has hired him to make mud bricks. They plan to build houses on the parcel and sell them. He needed something to do in his spare time.

I went to town. Was stopped by a policeman who was drunk and wanted a ride. I stopped at the outskirts, but he insisted that I take him all the way to his destination because the crotch of his trousers was ripped and he had a pin in them. So I did. Couldn't find any sugar in town.

Leon, the nurse at the missionary dispensary, tested Charlie's blood and found four microbes. Says he knows the cause of the disease and will get medicine for him.

August 10: Christine had a bad night. Bethanie went to stay overnight with Hennie and Ruth. We took a funza out of Christine's toe and washed her infected mouth again.

The ladies from the Bible study came today. We are still working on their handbags. More ladies are learning their memory verses. I showed Mama Vicki how to make cinnamon rolls. Mama Arne moved from the compound today. We will miss her.

It has started to rain. That will help put the funzas to flight.

Kiki should be named Curious George. Today, when Masangu came, Kiki jumped onto his lap, peered up his shirt sleeves, tried to unbutton his shirt to see inside, then finally stuck his head in the neck of Masangu's shirt to see what he could find.

August 11: Kiki is chasing the crows out of his tree. He is trying to grab them by their legs and they are screeching and screaming at him.

Darlene took Debbie to the Filtisaf dispensary on her motorcycle. Debbie seems to have strep throat. Jeff and William both have colds and are blowing their noses and coughing a lot. Now Kasuku, our parrot, has learned how to imitate them, coughing and blowing his nose. He sounds like one sick bird.

Sunday, August 14: I stayed home with Bethanie and Debbie. Christine is eating well now. Darlene and Ruth spoke at the Sympho church this morning. Charlie and the boys went to a little village to minister. "Colonel" and Kipe helped me pick over peanuts and fix them for the safari.

Charlie and I went out to see a new church nearby. It is located on a beautiful site with a panoramic view of the lake. On the other side, hundreds of huts are perched on a surrounding hillside. Simply breathtaking.

I treated some little children for fever when we got home.

August 22: Charles and the boys have gone to Fizi. About 2:00 A.M. thieves cut the screen in the front window, after turning the bulb and putting out the light on the front porch. They stole the stereo and the Grundig shortwave radio. Bethanie heard footsteps and woke me up.

I sneaked out into the living room and found the window left wide open. I went and called Baba Matolo; then we all knelt and prayed and Debbie asked the Lord to return our things. It occurred to me later as I lay praying that the Lord has given us ministering angels. I asked the angels of the Lord to go with the radios, to watch over them and protect them and bring them back. The thieves also took Bethanie's little red flip-flops and the window curtains. Thank the Lord that no one went into the living room while they were still there. They evidently carried a very sharp knife.

August 23: Some neighbors came to offer their condolences when they heard about our theft. Deb and I went to town on the motorcycle and got more wire mesh to fix the window and some material to make a curtain. Deb and I fell in front of the post office. We didn't fall hard, but it did bend the bike a bit. A crowd quickly gathered to see the injured.

This afternoon we bandaged a little boy who had been bitten by a monkey.

Pastor Lulika came over to help Debbie plan for another youth meeting in the theater next week.

John Lwenyeke is sleeping overnight here tonight. The girls gave him the baseball bat to use as a weapon. We all prayed very much for protection in our devotions tonight.

August 24: The cat woke me up trying to get in the window. I thought it was the thief. I crept to the window, yelled at the shadow and then saw it was the cat. With my heart still beating, I crept back in bed.

Pastor Esessa came this morning. A thief stole his door and window.

Today I taught for the first time without a Swahili textbook. I taught about giving, and the Lord blessed us together.

August 25: Thieves came again last night and stole the covered bucket out of the outhouse. Hennie said thieves were at her place too but they discovered them before the thieves could take anything. The thieves seem to like to come about 2:00 A.M.

August 28: Debbie and I had a good time sharing the wisdom of the Word. I so desire to pour into her those things that will keep her in righteousness as she goes out on her own.

Darlene and Ruth went to Sympho to work with their Sunday school. I sent a loaf of bread with Mama Matolo to the prison.

A couple of young boys came to talk to Debbie. One was convicted of sin, and we ended up having a real earnest time of prayer with him on the front porch. I believe God did a real work in his heart as he wept before the Lord.

We had a nice birthday party for Darlene, a young woman volunteer from Canada who is living with us. Ruth fixed the cake. I made supper, and Debbie decorated. We played games afterward. Still no word from Charlie.

*   *   *

One day much later as I meditated on the Scripture "they shall run, and not be weary; and they shall walk, and not faint" (Isaiah 40:31b), I wondered why it didn't say, they shall walk and not be weary, and they shall run, and not faint. It seemed to me that it is much harder to run than to walk.

"Why did you say it that way?" I asked the Lord.

"Because you are more likely to faint during the times of daily difficulty," He replied. "When you are running, things are happening quickly, and excitement surrounds you. When you walk, it is often slow and tedious. You need persistence, steadfastness, courage, and patience to continue when nothing much exciting is happening and the long lonely road does not appear to be the fulfillment of your calling. It is during the walking that many give up and faint by the wayside."

We had certainly learned that being in God's will did not exempt us from experiencing tests and trials. We were also having to learn not to get so focused on our circumstances that we lost sight of our goal.

Our VW bug suffered a complete breakdown when it was hit by a runaway river in the middle of town one day. Tropical rains had turned the large ditches beside the roads into swift running rivers. Charles, with two of our children, was driving home from a Sunday morning service when a flood of water overran the banks of the ditch uphill from them. They just happened to be in the wrong place at the wrong time.

The flood of water swept down the hill and around the bug, inundating the car. Asian shopkeepers and bystanders saw what was happening and rushed to rescue the children. The rescuers graciously washed the sand off of the little flood victims and treated them to candy and goodies from their shop. The episode became a novel memory for them, but the car didn't fare as well.

The wall of flood water carried tons of sand, which found its way into the car's motor and every part of the interior. The bug was pushed home in disgrace, never to run properly again. The loss of our bug was difficult indeed. Charles had to walk beneath the tropical sun to the Bible school, the church, to town. Eventually he found a bicycle, but biking on sandy paths was hardly an option. Finally, our prayers were answered when a Filtisaf executive offered to sell us their family car, a little bright red Lada. The Tree of Life Church in Grimsby, Ontario worked particularly hard to help raise funds to buy it.

Deb and Jeff had gone to Kenya to school when Mina began to complain of nausea. She didn't feel like eating and didn't have much energy, but in spite of her discomfort, she wasn't a complainer. She continued to carry on her little girl activities but with less vigor. Then, Charles began to experience similar symptoms. He attempted to keep up his teaching schedule but found it impossible. As the illness progressed, he was practically consumed with fatigue. Only his tenacious disposition kept him moving.

Finally, we decided that Charles must get to Nairobi where more adequate medical facilities were available. Although we knew of no scheduled flights, we went to the airport/airstrip to see if there were any planes coming in or going out that might have seating available. As we stood near the runway discussing the situation, we noticed an unfamiliar plane. The pilot, a stranger, saw us and came over to introduce himself.

He informed us that he was a company pilot and had come to Kalemie on unexpected business. He needed to replace a damaged tire while in town, but all attempts to find one had proven fruitless. The delay was frustrating. During our conversation, Charles gave him some useful information which solved his problem. Gratefully, he offered to fly Charles out of Kalemie, free of charge. What a blessing!

Charles finally arrived at the hospital at Rift Valley Academy in Kenya where Deborah and Jeffrey were students. He was admitted to the hospital. Tests were run, but they couldn't find the problem.

Although it was frustrating not to be able to identify the debilitating disease, he certainly appreciated his visit with Deb and Jeff and the well-deserved rest in a comfortable, well-equipped guest house. When he returned to Kalemie however, he found that I had turned yellow, a very pronounced yellow! The mysterious disease was finally diagnosed. It was hepatitis.

It was a diabolical illness. Food, or the smell of it, made me ill. The poison in my body made me itch. I scratched so hard that my skin turned black and blue. The blue bruises that resulted from my scratching combined with the yellow hue of my skin to give me a martian-green color. I rarely went out, but when I did, people pointed and talked and avoided me. Our African friends were fascinated by my new color.

The feeling of total exhaustion was awful. As a busy missionary mother, I took periods of bed rest interspersed with childcare and homemaking, but the long nights were torment. Daytime activities kept my mind off of the need to scratch, but at night the itching was torture. It took all of the self-restraint I could muster to keep from scraping my skin raw.

Days went by, and the illness raged on. Would this disease never end?

One day, I sat down exhausted on the chair in our bedroom. Suddenly, I had a most unusual experience. My body shouted at me in a voiceless demand, "Take me home; I can't stand this anymore!"

Taken aback, I replied aloud, "Flesh, you aren't going anywhere until God tells you to."

When God calls you to do something, you don't change directions until God gives you further instructions. God had called us here, and He had not given us word to leave Kalemie yet. Even hepatitis would not make us leave until God indicated otherwise. My flesh must take its orders from God, not the devil. I decided, if living in Kalemie was our God-called station, God could heal me there as well as anywhere else. This disease was an attack, not a directive.

It was not an instantaneous healing, but God did heal me. He healed all of us. Nevertheless, this test brought mental challenges from the enemy. He attempted to make us doubt God's ability, the probability of survival, even our right to triumph. But never have I seen an incident like that day when my flesh rose up from its subtle depths to scream a demand for its rights. Such an intense demand could only be confronted by the Spirit of Truth, which Jesus sent to guide us, in the person of the Holy Ghost. That day I experienced a living demonstration of Isaiah 59:19b, "When the enemy shall come in like a flood, the Spirit of the LORD shall lift up a standard against him."

According to Webster, truth is defined as reality. What was reality to the flesh, was in fact deception when confronted with Truth. God loved us. God had never forsaken us. God was still a healer, and somehow, obedient faith would be rewarded.

DELIVERANCE OR GRACE?
By Fern Willner

Is the highest calling, God has planned for you;
Often filled with trouble, trials the whole way through?
Have you felt forsaken, all alone and blue,
Seems that there is no one, to share the load with you?

No one understanding, why you persevere;
In adverse surroundings, circumstances drear?
All alone you sought Him, earnestly in prayer;
Heard His gentle urging, "Child, I need you there."

"Yes, if you just ask me, angels I can send,
Speak divine deliverance, all your needs attend.
I am there beside you, I'm with you everywhere;
I will never give you, more than you can bear."

"But Daughter, if you're willing, this is your chosen place;
I can send deliverance, but, I'd rather give you grace."

Jesus was our pattern, once He faced the same;
The choice between deliverance, or agonizing shame.
God in love is faithful, He'll give you what you choose;
But earth's reward is meager, if the Victor's crown you lose.

Faith's Security Lies in Obedience

"But if ye will not obey the voice of the LORD,
but rebel against the commandment of the LORD,
then shall the hand of the LORD be against you,
as it was against your fathers."
1 Samuel 12:15

Never sacrifice obedience
on the altar of common sense.

28

A Sinking Boat and a Waterspout

That thou mayest love the LORD thy God,
and that thou mayest obey his voice,
and that thou mayest cleave unto him:
for he is thy life, and the length of thy days.
—Deuteronomy 30:20a

Baby Christine was only four years old. Life in Africa had not been easy for her, but prayer and diligent care had protected her from death, time and time again. Now she was recovering from *schistosomiasis*, also known as "bilharziasis," a tropical disease almost as prevalent as malaria. Schistosome larvae are found in contaminated water and enter the body of a human or an animal through the skin. They invade the bloodstream and can eventually destroy vital organs.[10] At that time, the only drugs available in our area to kill the larva were often as deadly as the disease.

A local Arab businessman met me in the store one day and offered to try and find a newer, safer drug in Lubumbashi, Zaire. He contacted a business associate there, who found the drug, and he made arrangements to have it flown up to us along with his next delivery. Thanks to their kindness, Christine was saved from almost certain death.

Christine's front teeth had turned black, possibly from the effects of fever and medication, and she had developed a large abscess on her gum. I held her and looked at her little swollen face. We didn't have any dentists in our area, and I couldn't bear to see her suffer any longer without proper medical treatment. Charles was away at an annual council meeting of the British Assemblies of God in Fizi. There was no way for us to communicate once he left home. So, as is the case with many missionary wives, I made the difficult decision alone.

The older children were in boarding school in Kenya, so I decided that eight-year-old Bethanie and I would take Christine across Lake Tanganyika to Bujumbura, Burundi, where she could receive the dental care she needed. The decision was not easy to make considering the travel conditions we faced. The weekly flight service to Kalemie from Bujumbura had been discontinued, so we would need to secure tickets on the aging lake boat going to Uvira.

In Uvira, we would get a taxi to the Zaire border, travel on the back of a bicycle taxi through the no-man's zone between the two countries of Burundi and Zaire to the Burundi border, clear customs, pay for a visa into Burundi, and get a taxi to the home of our friends, the Johnsons. We knew that if we could get to the Johnsons, they would help us find a dentist.

The lake boat was a product of the Belgian occupation. At one time, it had carried the Belgians, and wealthy Zairois, up and down the famous lake. Lack of proper maintenance and overcrowding, coupled with dirty, insufficient facilities, had reduced travel on the once elegant lake boat to a rather unpleasant experience.

I planned carefully in order to make this trip as comfortable as possible for the two girls and me. *Since they don't serve meals any longer, we will need to bring boiled water and food for the "cruise"*, I thought, as I stood in the pantry surveying my stock of food supplies. Suddenly, in the midst of my deliberations, the still small voice of the Lord spoke to my heart. "Wait until you get home," He said.

Shocked, I replied, "But Lord, we aren't going home for a year. Christine can't wait that long. She needs treatment now."

"This can't be your voice, Lord," I reasoned. "It must be my subconscious attempting to avoid an uncomfortable trip."

Disregarding the voice, I made my plans according to the need at hand. After packing, I met with the Chief of Transport, who graciously arranged first-class tickets for us. This meant the girls and I could share a bunk bed in a small cabin with several other ladies.

Walter Lupp, a Lutheran missionary, took the three of us down to the port. We struggled through the hundreds of waiting passengers, submitted our tickets and were allowed to board early. We walked across wooden planks onto the boat.

Chickens squawked, children cried, adults elbowed for a place in line, street vendors attempted to shout above the din—*and we were going to try to enjoy this cruise?*

We found our cabin and met the two Asian ladies and an African woman who shared our room. Our roommates were delighted with the little blonde-headed girls. After agreeing on assigned bunks, the ladies turned their attention to mothering the children. Happily, they searched through their well-stocked store of travel supplies and produced home-cooked snacks for the children. The girls enjoyed the attention and the delicious diversity in food. After all of the excitement, we decided to go to bed early. We were tired.

In the moonlight, I watched the children as they slept. My heart was heavy with the pain of my child, but soon, I hoped, she would find relief. Finally, I slept.

About 3:00 A.M., we were awakened by a jolt. People were screaming. Fear, like electricity, surged into our room. What had happened?

Through rapid word of mouth, we learned that the captain had been drinking and had fallen asleep. The boat had drifted thirty kilometers off-course and had hit rocks. We were listing, but were not in immediate danger of sinking. Some of the ladies in our room were panic stricken. "We'll all drown!" they cried. Weeping and wringing their hands, they moaned and bewailed our certain fate.

A cholera epidemic had struck Kalemie before we left. Our roommates logically concluded that it was very possible that someone on board was infected with the disease. In such overcrowded conditions and without proper facilities, the epidemic would spread quickly. Death could only be hours away, they reasoned. If we didn't die of cholera, they were sure it would probably be days before rescuers arrived and we would die from lack of food and water. They were convinced that our end would be tragic.

Quietly, the girls and I prayed together and asked God for mercy. They were looking to me for security and comfort. It was a time to share my faith. We put our trust in God, crawled back into bed, and attempted to sleep.

About 4:00 A.M., a large launch with a Johnson motor pulled alongside. It had the capacity to carry a hundred people. The African man at the helm offered to ferry the people to safety, but the captain and several influential men on board our boat refused.

"Why?" I questioned one African gentleman.

"Because these men are bandits," he replied. "They will put you in their boat, take you out into the darkness, rob you, and throw you overboard."

"Oh," I shuddered, but I was still sorry to see the big boat disappear.

Slowly the sun began to rise over the lake. As the morning's brilliant rays sparkled on the rippling water, our peril didn't seem as great. Then, small dugout canoes began to appear from land. Soon inquisitive paddlers circled our big boat curiously, investigating our situation. Some of the passengers asked the strangers if they would get water for them. They assented. A shower of empty oil jugs and other empty containers descended on the obliging boat-men. Silently, they paddled away, filled the containers, and returned.

Our brawny benefactors, sinewy and muscular from years of work paddling their fishing boats, began the task of throwing the heavy water containers up to the owners. A kind of game ensued. We cheered and applauded as they skillfully tossed the filled containers up to clutching, grateful hands. Then, silently, they disappeared.

Our disappointment didn't last for long. Soon, the canoes came gliding into view again. These were the most opportunistic vendors I had ever seen. Circling our boat, they held up bananas, mangoes, cigarettes, dried fish, candy, beer, and soda pop. Shouting, they stated their price. It was like a circus.

Thankful passengers didn't dicker. Deftly, they tossed coins to our outboard merchants and positioned themselves to catch the flying merchandise. It was quite a feat for the canoe vendors to stand up and throw the purchases without falling overboard. Some of the goods fell into the lake, and I found it interesting that they didn't bemoan the loss. Instead, they laughed with glee and continued to carry on business.

Grateful to be able to get my girls something to drink, I joined in. *Could I catch my purchases?* I wondered. Amidst this group of more than 300 passengers and crew, I was the only white woman on board, and I didn't want to disgrace the race.

Our mutual dilemma produced a helpful camaraderie. Eager hands were ready to assist, in case the anemic-looking white woman with a sick child was unable to meet the challenge. *Success.* The girls and I sampled our catch of orange pop gratefully.

I wiped a few drops from Christine's mouth. She wasn't strong, and I held her most of the time. Our unusual surroundings, no doubt, helped to divert her attention, and she wasn't complaining.

The girls drank a few more sips of pop. We would need to ration the rest of our drink, because no one knew how long we would be stranded.

Lake Tanganyika is the world's longest freshwater lake and the second deepest. It is 420 miles long, and its greatest depth is 4,708 feet. The shores of the lake are mountainous.[11] Now as we tilted precariously, I noticed the sheer cliffs that lined the banks of the lake. Miraculously, we had drifted near a cove along the shores of Zaire with a small, sandy beach.

"I could probably easily swim to the beach," I reasoned, "surely there would be a friendly village nearby. Runners could take the news of our misfortune to missionaries at Baraka, and they would send help."

When I shared my thoughts with one of the crew members, he was instantly alarmed.

"This is a very dangerous area," he said. "Rebels are hiding all through these mountains. You would be killed." Comfortingly, he added, "We have a shortwave radio on board and have contacted the port in Uvira. They are sending help."

Very aware that they knew more about their own people and customs than I did, I followed their lead.

I prayed, "Lord, if you do want me to make an effort to save the girls, please, just put in my heart what you want me to do, and I will do it. Lord, please guide me." We waited. Hours passed. Pumps ran all day pumping water out of the boat. Finally, the fuel was almost gone and the boat was listing badly on the side where we were.

Then, about 4:00 P.M., we spotted our rescue boat, the *Zongwe*. They blew their horn, and our ship answered in return as the weary, frightened passengers shouted a great shout of thanksgiving and joy. Slowly, it drew alongside and was barely secured when patience and courtesy evaporated. The rescue boat was mobbed by desperate humanity fleeing the doomed boat. Angry crew members attempted to arrange an orderly transfer as the boat tipped dangerously, but it was impossible. All of the pent-up fear and distress exploded as people frantically scrambled for safety. Bethanie and I were temporarily separated by the pushing, shoving mob, but some compassionate fellow passengers brought her to me. Somehow we all survived the rescue.

About 12:30 that night, we arrived in Uvira. The port offices were closed, but we were allowed to disembark. Following the lead of the other passengers, the girls and I searched for a flat piece of ground, spread out a piece of cloth, and lay down to get some rest.

The sun baked earth wasn't a very comfortable mattress, and small stones added to our discomfort. We were surrounded by sleeping figures covered by pieces of brightly-colored material called kikwembes. Close by us, a little boy and his pet monkey quietly played while several hens scratched for food. The moonlight cast a kind of eerie glow over the whole scene. The children fell asleep, but I found it impossible. Someone warned me to keep an eye on my belongings.

In my solitude, I had time to reflect. *That must have been God speaking to me when the little voice I heard in the pantry said, "Wait."* How hard it is to obey, when conditions indicate an obviously contrary response. *Would I ever learn? What will happen now that I am in the midst of a huge mistake? Will God be merciful?*

About 3:00 A.M., a young man approached me.

"Come with me," he said, "I will take you to the missionary's house."

How did I know if he was honest and if we would be safe with him?

Breathing a prayer for mercy, I took the girls, gathered up our belongings and followed the man to his vehicle. Panic threatened to engulf me as we drove through the darkness into the unknown.

Oh God, help!

It wasn't long before we arrived at the Swedish mission house. Our benefactor explained our situation to the guard at the gate, and we were admitted. Mrs. Johanson, the resident missionary, gave us a warm welcome with instructions to make ourselves at home.

Oh, blessed relief! It was sheer joy to have toilets, a shower, snack foods, and cold, safe drinking water. "Thank you, God. Oh, thank you."

Finally, we were tucked between clean sheets, reveling in the blissful luxury of comfortable mattresses and safety.

For two days, the girls and I enjoyed the comfort of the mission house. The third night, the girls were asleep when I heard someone knocking on the window. I crept to the window in the darkness and cautiously peered out. It was Charles with Ralph Hagemeier and their interpreter! Quickly, I unlocked the door, and the men came in. Charles grabbed me and hugged me, thanking God that we were all alive and safe.

After the conference in Uvira finished, Charles had been on his way to Uvira, where he planned to catch the boat for Kalemie. En route he and his travel companions had met some travelers who told them that the boat from Kalemie to Uvira had had an accident and had sunk. "A white woman and two girls were among the passengers," they said. Word travels incredibly quickly through the African news and communications system—by word of mouth.

Could it possibly have been Fern and the girls? Charles wondered.

Anxiously, he and his companions continued on to Uvira. When they arrived at the port late at night, they were told that the passengers had been rescued and the white lady and her children had been taken to the Swedish mission compound. The little group hurried on to the mission and knocked tentatively on the window. Sure enough, we were there. After a joyful reunion, I explained our reason for the trip and described our adventure, thankful to be alive. What a blessing to have Charles as leader of this safari now! His innate, God-given traveling skills had brought us through many a seemingly impossible situation, and this safari needed help.

We finally reached Bujumbura safely, and the Johnsons made an appointment for us with a highly recommended, English-speaking dentist. When we entered the modern office building and met the white-coated doctor, poor little Christine was terrified. She was afraid of the strange white man, the sterling instruments, and the modern surroundings. No one could calm her. Finally, the frustrated dentist suggested that we come another time.

Silently, we picked Christine up, thanked the dentist for his efforts, and left.

After making some emergency purchases, we returned to the home of our beloved friends. Visiting with veteran missionaries Carl and Eleanor Johnson, their son Harry, and daughter-in-law Ruth and family was always a treat. It was an honor just to know them. They were loved and respected in the country of Burundi.

Later, we discovered that there would be a flight to Kalemie, and we were able to purchase tickets.

"Perhaps this unusual trip would end comfortably after all," I mused. We were all encouraged.

The twenty-four-seater lifted off the Bujumbura airport runway. We thought we were safely on our way but, about forty-five minutes into our trip, something went wrong. Weather conditions had created a huge water funnel rising from the lake high into the sky. The pilot circled for almost half an hour, hoping the funnel would disintegrate or move away, but it didn't. He didn't dare try to go around it. Finally, he spoke over the intercom.

"It doesn't look like weather conditions are going to change, and I don't have enough fuel to circle any longer," he said. "We'll have to go back."

Several ladies behind me began to wail, "We're all going to die."

Lord, have mercy, I thought. *This is one lesson God is going to make sure that I never forget—if we ever get home alive.*

By now I was very sure that the word I had received in the pantry was indeed the voice of the Lord. It was becoming evident that God wanted me to learn to know His voice better.

My son, despise not thou the chastening of the Lord, nor faint when thou art rebuked of him: for whom the Lord loveth he chasteneth, and scourgeth every son whom he receiveth.
–Hebrews 12:5b,6

"You must learn to listen and obey," I remembered telling my children. "Your lives could depend on your obedience."

My Heavenly Father was obviously giving me the same message.

Suddenly, the pilot spoke over the intercom again. "We'll try a different route," he said. "I'm going overland. It will be a bit rough, but be patient, we should make it."

He changed course, and soon we were looking down on elephant grass and mud huts. He correctly predicted that our detour might be bumpy, and our fearful lady passengers provided suitable background wailing for the tense detour. Finally, we approached the little Kalemie airstrip. The plane made a final lurch, and with our stomachs in our throats, we landed safely. When we arrived at the compound, everyone was ecstatic. When they heard the girls and I had drowned, they felt so bad, they couldn't eat, they said. They all met together and sang hymns and prayed, but the presence of the Lord was so real, they decided we must be all right. Later that day, they heard that everyone on board had been rescued, but the ship had sunk with thirteen crew members and the pilot who was at fault.

Throughout the day, visitors came to greet us and to thank God for our safe return. I invited everyone to a praise meeting at 8:00 P.M. in the evening, and they came. We sang and prayed, I described our ordeal, and then together we praised God for His protection. Afterward, I served tea and muffins to everyone.

Several days later as I stood on our front verandah overlooking Lake Tanganyika, the Lord reminded me of Lamentations 3:22,23: "It is of the Lord's mercies that we are not consumed, because his compassions fail not. They are new every morning: great is thy faithfulness."

Strangely, this was not a word of rebuke, but a word of understanding. I felt that God was saying, "Fern, don't be discouraged or embarrassed about receiving my mercy. I have provided new mercies for you because I knew that you would need them. Receive them. Grow and learn and live. I love you! Remember, 'A just man falleth seven times, and riseth up again' (Proverbs 24:16). The proud stay down, but the humble rise."

"Lord," I prayed, "please forgive me. Help me learn to be obedient."

There on the verandah, I felt the gentle, patient love of God. It was humbling. I felt I deserved to be punished for my mistake, but God apparently didn't think so. He saw my heart, and gave me grace instead. Evidently, God didn't want me to use up precious time walking in sorrow or with a sense of failure.

Several weeks later, rebels invaded Kalemie, and we evacuated. When we arrived in London, Ontario, Canada, we discovered that the University of Western Ontario housed an excellent children's dental clinic. Christine's abscess had healed, but her little black teeth needed to be extracted. Fortunately, they were her baby teeth, and beautiful new ones eventually grew in their place.

Psalm 111:10 tells us that, "The fear of the Lord is the beginning of wisdom." My wisdom was based on circumstances that I could see, but God's wisdom included data from the future which could not be humanly seen. God had attempted to spare my little girls and me a very traumatic trip, but the word "wait" didn't figure into my formula for solving the problem. The result was that I sacrificed obedience on the altar of common sense, and it profited me nothing.

It is human to be tempted to trust our own understanding more than the leading of the Holy Spirit. But, "walking by faith, not by sight" (2 Corinthians 5:7) does not mean taking a step of foolishness into the darkness. No, it is taking a step of confidence onto the Solid Rock.

Several weeks later, rebels invaded Kalemie, and we evacuated, a story I tell in the next chapter. When we arrived in London, Ontario, Canada, we discovered that the University of Western Ontario housed an excellent children's dental clinic. Christine's abscess had healed, but her little black teeth needed to be extracted. Fortunately, they were her baby teeth, and beautiful new ones eventually grew in their place.

Faith Requires Daily Guidance
From the Father

"By faith Noah,
being warned of God of things not seen as yet,
moved with fear, prepared an ark
to the saving of his house;
by the which he condemned the world,
and became heir of the righteousness
which is by faith."
Hebrews 11:7

*Ignorance is not characteristic
of the man or woman of faith.*

29

"Honey, The Rebels Are Coming!"

For I will surely deliver thee, and thou shalt
not fall by the sword, but thy life shall be for a prey unto thee:
because thou hast put thy trust in me, saith the Lord.
—Jeremiah 39:18

"He wakeneth morning by morning,
he wakeneth mine ear to hear as the learned."
—Isaiah 50:4b

As the days and years passed, we became more comfortable in our acculturated lifestyle. Bathing in a bucket, boiling drinking water nightly, using an outhouse, sleeping under a mosquito net, and eating foods like *lengalenga*, *ugali* and *ugi*, no longer seemed so strange and unusual.

Many of the other families with whom we shared the compound had become cherished friends, and with their help and family language study, our children now spoke Swahili fluently. We planned to continue living in Kalemie for another year or two.

It was April, and the spring rains had begun. Normally, by 7:00 P.M. the compound was quiet. Our neighbor's wooden window shutters would be closed to keep out mosquitoes, and their children would be asleep on their bamboo mats. But tonight was different.

After dark, neighboring children came to our back door in a flurry of excitement. Flying termites were emerging from their holes in the ground, and the neighborhood children invited our children to join them in the festivities. Our children hurried to gather all of the available containers they could find and fill them with water. Then, armed with flashlights, they set off for the hunt. It was a seasonal highlight.

As termites swarmed from their holes, the children caught the wriggling insects and plunged them into the containers of water. Once immersed, the wings fell off, and the bugs were ready to fry. Meat is not readily available in these villages far away from well-stocked grocery stores, so the termite catch provided a much-appreciated protein feast.

Our children had learned from eager teachers how the cooking was done. The stove consisted of three stones with charcoal or wood used for fuel. Then, they placed a well-used aluminum pot atop the three stones to complete the native kitchen!

It was dark as insects sizzled in palm nut oil and hungry children watched, squatting around the glowing embers in eager anticipation. Finally, the "delectable" morsels were ready.

"Mom, try them," my children begged. "They kind of taste like bacon."

Gingerly, I tasted one, but even after all of these years, I hadn't yet acquired an appetite for the little insects. Amused parents watched, and in a comfortable bond of familiarity, they laughed knowingly at my squeamish response.

Then one night, I had an unusual dream. I dreamed that our family was in our red Lada traveling together to minister in a local village. After leaving the town of Kalemie, we continued to drive carefully over the rutted, dirt roads when I suddenly spotted a large group of rebel soldiers on my right. They were partly hidden beneath a canopy of trees, but I could see them vigorously engaged in bodybuilding calisthenics.

The dream was in full color. The men were all dressed in green camouflage suits, and I noted that some of the rebels were black-skinned and some were white. I knew intuitively that some of them were Cuban and that the group was preparing for an attack. As we drew closer to the area, I became alarmed. We would be in grave danger if they became aware that we had discovered them. Quietly, I prayed an urgent prayer for protection. As I did, a heavy, white mist fell and covered the car. They could not see the car, and for some reason, they did not seem to hear it. We passed safely.

When I awoke, I described the dream to Charles.

"Honey," I said, "I don't know where, or how, or when, but the rebels are coming."

Is it time to leave? Charles wondered. He was more acquainted with Zaire's history than I was. He knew about the Simba rebellion of the sixties. He knew of the house arrests, the raping of white women, the massacre of missionaries, and the brutality of tribal cleansing.

We had been told that rebels were still hiding in the mountains and that we must be careful about traveling through certain areas. These warnings didn't seem relevant to our mission work and, generally, we didn't worry about them. We even wondered if they were just built on superstition and residual fear.

Now God was letting us know that, indeed, there were rebels and that we needed divine guidance. We didn't want to be like the hireling that Jesus talked about in John 10:12,13, who fled when danger came, but neither did we want to stay beyond God's planned time for us and endanger the lives of our family.

We accepted the dream as a warning and decided to wait on the Lord for further direction. We would keep working, and God would show us when or if He wanted us to go home.

Months went by, and there was no indication that trouble was brewing. Then, in August, we had a breathless visit from one of the Bible school students.

"Baba," he panted, "on our way back from a youth convention we attended up the coast, our boat was seized by rebels. We were taken captive and forced to climb up the cliff path to their hideout. They took our shoes and everything of value, but I hid my money in a crack in the boat. They planned to kill us. All night, I wondered what it would be like to die. We prayed and sang.

"In the morning, for some reason, the rebels decided to let us go. They made us promise not to tell where the camp was located and told us that no prisoner had ever been allowed to leave their camp alive before. God did a miracle.

"They took our gasoline and our motor, and we had to paddle with our hands. Baba, I should have been happy when they told us they were going to kill us. That would mean that we were going to heaven. But I was scared. I was never so scared in my life. When we got back to the boat, I found my money still in the crack, but they took my shoes. I was lucky."

Kalemie had no working telephone system, but we learned to respect the "word-of-mouth" communications network. Information about other planned rebel activities trickled in. One of the young men on our own compound was almost captured by one of the groups when he and a friend went into a mining area to dig for gold. He escaped, but his friend was shot.

As incidents of rebel activity escalated, fear gripped the hearts of the people. Where could they go? One group of people packed their belongings and fled. They fled right into the path of rebel soldiers and were shot. No one knew where to go to find safety.

Then we received word that a Methodist pilot had been killed by rebels in Moba. Government troops were sent in to investigate, but the undisciplined troops looted and burned much of the city.

When the president began to send government troops into our city, I was glad that our girls were away. Veteran missionaries, Ralph and Shirley Hagemeier, had spent several wonderful weeks with us that summer. That fall they had decided to sponsor William, Ruth and Mina in boarding school at Rift Valley Academy (RVA) in Kenya.

We were amazed at God's foresight of protection as undisciplined and underpaid soldiers harassed the local people. Raids were made on local homes in the middle of the night. Meager funds and carefully guarded food stores were stolen. Some of our elderly friends were falsely accused and cruelly beaten. Tensions grew.

The approaching Christmas vacation was a concern. In spite of our desire to be with the children over the holidays, we knew it was unsafe for them to come home. Since we had no way of contacting school officials at RVA to inform them of the danger in our area, we prayed for God's will to be done.

One day as I was making bread, I heard a plane overhead. Running outside, I looked up to see a Missionary Aviation Fellowship (MAF) plane circling our house.

"Charlie, there's a MAF plane overhead," I called.

"Let's go," he shouted. "The kids are here."

Excitedly, we ran to the car and headed for the little airport as fast as bumpy, dirt roads would allow. When we arrived, we made our way past soldiers on guard and into the arms of our happy, tearful offspring. The pilot greeted us warmly, and then made a hasty exit.

On our way home, the children told us their side of the story. When news of rebel activity in the Kalemie area reached the school, the school administrators decided that it was unsafe for the children to go home. The children were informed of the situation and told that they would have to remain at school over the Christmas holidays.

About 4:00 A.M., on the morning that they originally were to have left, the children were awakened.

"Get your things together, you are going home," they were told.

Hurriedly, they packed and were taken to the waiting plane. MAF pilots have a special awareness of the needs of missionary kids. During the flight, chocolate bars, chips and special treats were passed around, accompanied by encouragement and good humor.

As they approached Kalemie, the pilot cautioned, "If there are too many soldiers down there, I won't land. It would be unsafe."

Undaunted, 16-year-old Jeff exclaimed, "If you decide not to land, fly low over the lake so I can jump out, because I am going home!"

Even though troops were guarding the airport, the sympathetic pilot decided to give Jeff, William, Ruth, and Mina the gift of Christmas at home if he could make it possible.

He landed, took enough time to see his little charges safely enveloped in joyous hugs, and quickly returned to the sky.

What a reunion!

Though it was early in December, because of our uncertain future, we decided to celebrate Christmas prematurely. Jeff had taken time to bring along some gifts he had saved, including coveted chocolate bars that he bought for us in Nairobi. The rest of us shared homemade presents or gifts we had bought in our little town. But the most wonderful part was the gift of being together.

In spite of our continued attempts to live with a sense of normalcy, disturbing bits of information kept us uneasy. Then one morning, we awoke to the ominous sound of gunfire and shelling. Rebels had taken control of the airport.

Fear was electric. Groups of people sat huddled on the grass outside and talked in whispers as impending danger sapped their strength. From our compound on the hill, which overlooked the lake and the main road through town, we watched frantic men, women, and children fleeing from the rebel menace. Driven by panic, to the tune of cracking gunfire, they ran, carrying a few treasured possessions in baskets or in basins on their heads.

Fear was so stifling, we wondered how the sun could shine, how nature could display its gorgeous greenery, or how the birds could sing. Even a note of feathered joy seemed sacrilegious in this setting. *How could the world go on?* Yet, it did.

One day, the local church elders came and warned us, "If Baba wants to stay, he can, but you must not stay, Mama. It is very dangerous for you."

Then the ladies on the compound confronted me.

"Mama, go home," they begged. "If the rebels get you, they will make you suffer."

I knew what they were referring to, but I sincerely did not want to be a 'hireling.' If the Lord spoke to me, then I knew I could go home with confidence. I would never look back with guilt and wonder if I had done the right thing.

We met weekly with the Lutheran missionaries for prayer and Bible study. During the evening, we also made time to exchange updated information and discuss possible evacuation plans. Most of our belongings were packed, in case of an emergency.

In the evenings, we gathered in our little living room to gain security and strength from family devotions. We sang choruses to the accompaniment of the accordion; Charles read a selected Scripture, and we took turns praying.

Charles had asked me weeks ago if I would be willing to take the children and go home alone. But there were just too many difficulties to face alone. Our own home had been sold before we left to help pay for our tickets. To add to our dilemma, we did not have winter clothes, and Missouri would be a lot colder than Africa was in December. Friends and family would be glad to help prepare something for us if they knew we were coming, but there was no way to inform them of our needs.

No, I decided. It would be better to wait until Charles and I could face the challenges of relocating our family together or until we had received definite instructions from the Lord about what He wanted us to do.

Isaiah 33:6 tells us, "And wisdom and knowledge shall be the stability of thy times, and strength of salvation: the fear of the LORD is his treasure." As difficult as it was to retain a sense of normalcy in the midst of the confusion and fear, it was imperative to hold onto our trust in God, believing that He would speak at the right time. Our treasure in the midst of the darkness was our fear of the Lord. God is greater. God could be trusted. He would not leave us in darkness or to our own devices. He would give us wisdom and knowledge, and that alone would be the stability of our times.

Three Hebrew men faced a fiery furnace, but they were convinced that the God they served had more authority than the king's decree. Their fate did not lie in the hands of an earthly king but in the hands of a heavenly Father. Daniel 3:17, 18 records their response to the king's command: "If it be so, our God whom we serve is able to deliver us from the burning fiery furnace, and he will deliver us out of thine hand, O king. But if not, be it known unto thee, O king, that we will not serve thy gods, nor worship the golden image which thou hast set up."

They would not presume to dictate the outcome of their situation, and neither could we, but they knew one thing—God was their deliverer, and they would trust Him. When all of those around us were tossed to and fro by the actions of wicked men and the corruption of society, there remained a place of stability. That stability is found in a living, loving God who rules in the affairs of men and who gives divine direction to those who put their faith in Him.

Faith Transforms
Weakness Into Strength

"Through faith
also Sara herself received strength
to conceive seed, and was delivered of a child
when she was past age, because she
judged him faithful who had promised."
Hebrews 11:11

The substance of faith is
inherent in the Word of God.
When we choose to believe the Word,
we choose to receive its faith.

30

"Take the Young Child and Flee"

"So then faith cometh by hearing, and hearing by the word of God."
—Romans 10:17

One evening, Charles decided to reread the Christmas story. As we listened to the familiar passage, part of a phrase suddenly became a message that spoke clearly to my heart: "Take the young child and flee."

After Charles and I had tucked the children in bed, we met back in the living room to share our own thoughts.

"Did the Lord speak anything to you while you were reading that Scripture tonight?" I questioned.

"No," he replied, "I just felt led to read it. Did He speak to you?"

"When you read, 'Take the young child and flee,' it was like the Lord was talking directly to me," I replied. "I feel that God is telling me to pack and leave with the children in the morning."

Charles agreed but still felt that he personally needed to stay and try to help the Bible school students complete their semester. He didn't want them to lose several months of work.

"Suppose there is no flight in the morning?" Charles questioned. The scheduled weekly flights from Bujumbura, Burundi to Kalemie had been discontinued for weeks.

"If this is a word from God, there will be a plane," I assured him.

Morning came. We completed our packing and held a hurried family conference. All of the children would go with me, except Jeff. He wanted to spend the rest of December with Charles, then return to Rift Valley Academy to complete his semester and graduate with his class in the spring.

After calling our workers and friends who lived on the compound, we shared our plans. We were all packed. This was good-bye. We didn't know when, if ever, we would see them again. They approved of our decision, but as we drove out of the driveway, some of them ran alongside the car weeping. It was a difficult good-bye.

We approached the airport. *Would there be a plane?* Our eyes scanned the strip. *There it was, a plane from Bujumbura, Burundi parked on the little tarmac runway.* We finally cleared local customs and boarded the small plane. With our faces pasted to the oval windows, we waved vigorous good-byes to Charles and Jeff as we taxied down the airstrip.

In circumstances like this, I couldn't help but wonder if I would ever see my husband and son again. As the plane lifted off the runway and rose to clear the lake, tears were wrenched from the depths of my heart. My flesh hurt, but my spirit still wasn't afraid. It was amazing. I faced the same difficulties of relocation and need, all alone, but now I had a word from God. Obviously, embedded in the word I received was a measure of faith, which was producing the confidence to perform it.

In Bujumbura, Mr. Johnson, whose years of service had given him a personal acquaintance with many of the local officials, was an invaluable help in updating passports and purchasing airline tickets.

Our first stop en route home was an overnight layover in Paris. What a change of surroundings from our native town! We watched from controlled access areas as filmmakers shot scenes right in the lobby of our hotel for an upcoming movie. Then, from our window, we continued watching the drama as cameras followed the fleeing stars outside and shot street scenes of a dramatic escape. The children were in awe.

That night, Bethanie came to me.

"Mama, can I have a drink?" she asked.

"Of course, Honey," I replied. "Just take a glass and get a drink from the faucet in the bathroom."

She hesitated, then asked, "But Mama, is the water boiled?"

In our hasty departure, I had not had time to think about the culture shock my children would experience. As I anticipated seeing familiar scenes and family, I now realized that the world we were entering was not home to some of my children. It was as foreign now to them, as Africa had been to me. I was going home, but they were not. They were already enveloped in culture shock.

That night, we called our pastor in Missouri to let them know we were coming. When we arrived in Springfield the next evening, we had a surprise. He had informed Deborah, now a student at Evangel College, of our unexpected arrival, and as we walked through the doors of the airport, she came running into our arms. *What a wonderful reunion.*

Quickly, we were bundled into warm cars and taken to the church, where a service was in progress. Our excited church family gave us a warm welcome.

The Assemblies of God had a vacant rental house situated just behind their headquarters building, which they rented to us. When one of the staff came to make sure everything was in good working order, he saw our sparse living conditions. He asked for permission to lend us some furniture that Headquarters had in storage and personally brought it to us. I'll never forget the look of joy on his face as he hauled the furniture through the front door.

It wasn't long after we moved into our new quarters, however, that we discovered all was not well. Fragile Christine was running a fever. All attempts to control it proved futile. Without medical insurance, we couldn't afford professional care, but finally, in desperation, I took her to the local hospital emergency room. Dr. Holland was on call. Alarmed, he did a spinal tap. "With a fever that high, she must have spinal meningitis," he reasoned. The test was negative. He did blood tests. When the results of the blood tests returned, we discovered that Christine had a serious case of malaria.

"She must be admitted into the hospital immediately," Dr. Holland said gravely.

"Dr. Holland, I must be honest with you," I replied. "We do not have medical insurance, and I cannot pay for a hospital stay. I'm very sorry."

Dr. Holland's response was compassionate. "I won't charge you for my services," he said, "and I think the hospital will work out a payment plan."

Christine was admitted, and we worked around the clock to save her life. As I sat beside her hospital bed, I began to understand. When God spoke to me that night in our African living room, we did not know that a deadly parasite had already invaded Christine's body. Neither did we know that she would need plasma, intravenous feeding, and excellent medical care to save her life, but God knew.

We thought God was saving us from the rebels. He was, but He was also fulfilling the word He gave me in that little mud church: "And I will sow them among the people: and they shall remember me in far countries: and they shall live with their children, and turn again" (Zechariah 10:9).

While the rebels planned an invasion, God arranged an escape. Dr. Holland never charged us a cent for the hours of compassionate, professional care he gave our baby, and the hospital helped by working out a payment plan. Two weeks later, Charles came home.

The unrest had made it impossible to hold classes, so he returned to care for his family.

Eleven years later, when Christine and I were visiting Springfield, we decided to try to locate Dr. Holland. *Would he still be there?* We made a series of phone calls and located him still working in pediatrics.

"I'll make you an appointment," his secretary said. Then she added excitedly, "I won't tell him who you are. We'll make it a surprise."

As Christine and I sat in the examination room, I wondered if he would remember me. He walked in, stopped, and said, "Don't I know you from somewhere?" I told him our story and introduced him to Christine, now tall and blonde. She presented him with a thank you card and gratefully thanked the doctor personally for helping save her life.

Later, as we were leaving, Dr. Holland said, "This can be hard work, but it's people like you that make it all worthwhile. Please stay in touch."

When God directs our lives, we never know how far the consequences of our obedience will extend. We, whose eyes are limited to the human facet of sight, cannot possibly comprehend the omniscient wisdom of God. How pleased He is when we receive His word in faith and, in so doing, also receive its imparted strength to live it out.

The journey of trusting obedience is never the way we thought it would be, but in spite of the twists and turns of life, goodness and mercy do follow us every day of our lives. God does hear our call; God does know where we live; God will send His Holy Spirit to blow upon the Red Seas of our lives and make a way for us where there seems to be no way. God will send His manna of divine provision in ways that exceed human expectations and rival comprehension. And yes, God does expect us to conquer difficulties many times greater than our strength, simply because He told us to do it. Why? Because, God wants us to know who He really is and what He can do. He wants us to know that we can walk in heavenly places even though we live on earth.

David knew what it was to be touched by heaven's help when he declared, "For by thee I have run through a troop: by my God have I leaped over a wall" (2 Samuel 22:30). What is more awesome than faith in action as Heaven stoops to lend a hand and earth bows in submission to divine intervention!

Faith Can be Strengthened?
or Defeated by Our Actions

"Seest thou how faith
wrought with his works,
and by works was
faith made perfect?"
James 2:22

*You can't reach a positive goal
by taking negative steps.*

31

"Get Thee Out of Thy Country"

O LORD, I know that the way of man is not in himself:
it is not in man that walketh to direct his steps.
—Jeremiah 10:23

It was the fall of 1985, less than a year after our return from Kalemie, Zaire, where we had lived and worked for four years. We were living in Springfield, Missouri, after a brief stay in London, Ontario. The children were attending the House of Prayer Christian School and I was enrolled at Evangel College, working to complete a Bachelor of Arts degree. We lived within easy walking distance of my elderly mother, and she and I reveled in our daily visits. It was a wonderful privilege to have time together after spending so many years apart.

Our rental property was definitely a divine provision. This property had been someone's pride and joy. Brightly colored flowers, lovely shrubs, and decorative vines flourished all around us. The day we discovered a large strawberry patch, we were so excited, I wonder if even the angels enjoyed the scene.

Our home was a wonder to us in other ways too. We had hot and cold water and security. After hauling water from our backyard cistern for four years, the convenience of hot and cold water at our fingertips made washing dishes, cleaning and bathing, pure luxury.

The first night Charles slept through the night, he panicked.

"Oh no, Fern," he exclaimed, "I slept all night." He grinned sheepishly as he realized that he no longer needed to be on guard for thieves.

Several months passed. It was a Sunday morning. Charles was again away on a missions trip to Africa, and the children and I were attending church at the House of Prayer, where the Sunday morning service was in progress.

The church had grown and changed during the time we were gone, and there were many unfamiliar faces in the congregation. But even our friends had no idea of the culture shock we experienced or the mixture of enjoyment and loss we felt as we learned new choruses and adjusted to church services without such familiar native accompaniments as drums, shakers made of tin oil cans punched full of holes and filled with beans, dried gourd rattles, or metal tire rims clanged vigorously with iron rods. It was wonderful to be home, *but would it ever be truly home again?* Probably not. We had left a part of our hearts in Africa.

As the praise and worship service ended and lingering strains of the organ and piano died away, Brother C.L. Moore, the guest speaker, stood to minister. Brother Moore had traveled in ministry for several decades and was no novice to the gifts of the Spirit or to the voice of the Lord. His prophetic ministry had inspired, encouraged, exhorted, and comforted congregations and individuals in many nations.

As this tenderhearted, old, gray-haired giant of a man stalked back and forth across the platform, he was vibrant with the anointing of the word he spoke. I don't remember his text now, but suddenly, in the midst of his sermon, he put his hand to his ear and cupped it as if hearing a voice. He turned, and with the piercing eyes of a prophet and the voice of thunder, he spoke directly to me.

"Fern," he thundered, "you are going to Canada sooner than you think."

The words confirmed a prophetic message that had been given to us several months earlier. We would go to Canada to open a Bible school where God would use us to help train men and women for the ministry. The word would be an encouragement to Charles, I knew, who carried a burden for his Canadian homeland, but for me, at this moment, it was not a message of joy.

After Brother Moore returned to his sermon, I quietly slid out of my seat and onto my knees. I buried my head in my arms and noiselessly wept out my disappointment to God. With all my heart, I wanted to serve the Lord, but I didn't feel ready to leave my American homeland and to sever the recently renewed ties with my aging mother, nor was I prepared to uproot our family again and expose them to another unknown so soon. Where would we go in the large country of Canada?

"Lord," I prayed, "do we really have to go so soon?"

Before five o'clock the next morning, I was awake thinking about the prophecy. It was hard to pray, "Not my will but thine be done," when I didn't really mean it. *Did I have a choice?* Yes, but not really. What good would a choice be, made within the limitations of my own human nearsightedness. *Whatever it involved*, I decided, *we would obey*, but I still needed further instructions. Though we had a word to go to Canada, we still did not know the precise location in Canada.

"God," I prayed, "if you want us to move to Canada, where do you want us to go? When do you want us to go? Please show me what to do."

Suddenly, in the midst of my predawn plea to God, the phone rang. Who could be calling at this unearthly hour?

"Fern, when are you coming to Canada?" said the voice on the other end of the line. It was Sheila Gale in London, Ontario, Canada.

Incredulously, I replied, "You won't believe this, but I was lying here praying about that very thing. A prophet ministered at the church yesterday and prophesied that we would be going to Canada sooner than we expected."

"Well, that's no problem," she exclaimed. "We have a real estate agent who is an elder in our church. We'll get him busy looking for a house for you right away. In the meantime, you and the children come ahead. You can stay with us until you find a place."

That day, I arranged a meeting with the church elders and relayed the message I had received from Canada. Since I was scheduled to drive to Toronto to pick up Charles in a week, I suggested that I take the children and move to Canada now. That would save us making a second trip. It would also allow us time to find a place to live and enroll the children in school at the beginning of the school year. We prayed together, and the elders gave their approval of the move.

It was a busy week. We had a yard sale, disconnected telephone services, gave away our dog, and packed our Toyota minivan to the brim. At the Friday night church service, the elders announced our departure and asked us to come forward. They, and many members of the congregation, gathered around us and prayed for us. Further prophetic words were given confirming the move and blessing our step into the unknown.

Deborah and I had been attending Evangel College together. It was an unusual occurrence, and our mother/daughter attendance was featured in an article in the school paper. It was difficult to leave, but Deb helped with the move, packing her little Chevy full of family household goods as well. We studied the map and traveled in convoy.

When we arrived in London, Ontario, Harold and Sheila Gale and their family gave us an enthusiastic reception. We needed it. The church elder/real estate agent had not yet located a home for us, but Harold and Sheila welcomed the opportunity to extend their gift of hospitality to us and to demonstrate their assurance that our move to London was of the Lord.

We unloaded the vehicles and were welcomed into their loving home.

The following day, Harold took me to the Toronto airport to meet Charles. Imagine his surprise when Charles discovered that his family had moved to Canada. His dream of serving the Lord in Canada was being fulfilled sooner than he expected.

The prophetic words had been powerful and inspiring at the time of their delivery. Now, those words, spoken by anointed ministers under the unction of the Holy Ghost and witnessed by the church congregation, were about to be tested.

Charles and I began our search for a home. Day after day we bought newspapers, called leads, viewed homes and apartments. *Nothing!* The days stretched into weeks and the weeks to a month. *No success.* I was devastated. *How could we continue to impose on this gracious family?* We tried to help in every way possible, but I still felt terribly guilty about our extended stay. My pride was wounded, for instead of giving, I was doing most of the receiving. It was a very uncomfortable position to be in.

In the midst of this emotional trauma, I began to have physical difficulties. My scalp itched mercilessly. I couldn't sleep. One of my brothers had an inherited scalp condition, normally passed on genetically only to the males. In desperation, I called him to find out the name of the medication that he used to relieve the discomfort it caused. But getting help was not as easy as I thought it would be. The medication was only available by prescription.

In the meantime, someone gave me a bit of money and I decided that a trip to the beauty salon might help my scalp and my morale. Off I went. When I entered the salon, I observed a number of elderly patrons stylishly dressed, and for a moment, I envied their comfortable lifestyle.

The nicely groomed cosmetologist smiled cordially and led me to a seat in front of the sink. She began washing my hair, then she paused, and I saw her beckoning for the owner. A strange sense of impending doom descended on me.

Her gracious attitude suddenly turned to cool distaste as they examined my hair.

"You have lice," the owner tersely informed me. "We cannot serve you. You must leave immediately."

The two of them stepped back away from me in a gesture of quiet abhorrence. What could I say? I looked at them mutely. My hair was soaking wet, but they offered me no towel. Their smiles and my welcome were gone. Instead of leaving the salon well coiffured in the latest hair style, I left in disgrace. *Oh to be a bug and creep out of that place unseen!*

Now what? It was an exercise in self-discipline to be sure, but with my hair wet and tangled and water dripping down the back of my neck, I marched into the nearby K-Mart store and spent my personal gift on lice shampoo.

When Charles came to the shopping center to pick me up, he wasn't impressed with my au naturel hair style. Worse yet, when I told him about my disaster in the salon, he insisted that we tell our hostess of my condition. It was bad enough to be an imposing guest, but an imposing guest with lice was too much. *Oh, God! What were those words about going to Canada to be a blessing?*

We arrived at the house, and I went in to face the music. After sharing my humbling experience, it was concluded that everyone should have a head check. To my surprise, everyone had lice. Sheila, a true teacher and quick to spot a lesson, found a lesson in this.

As individuals in the Body of Christ, we may feel alone or condemned in the tests and difficulties that we go through. Instead of sharing our need and receiving ministry from one another, we often allow ourselves to be segregated instead by pride or inferiority. Generally, however, when experiences are shared, we find that others in the Body are experiencing trials similar to ours.

Our lice episode didn't end here. To our dismay, it was discovered that little Jeremy Gale had unknowingly spread the villain insects to their extended family during a weekend visit. Several of the little boy's cousins were found to have the most astonishingly large head lice that their parents had ever seen. That is when we decided that Charles, recently returned from Africa, must have been the carrier.

Africa is a land of contrasts. Everything is either larger or deadlier or more beautiful, and in this case, more uncomfortable. We bought bottles of lice shampoo and shampooed every head in the house. We washed all the linen, shampooed the living room furniture, cleaned the rugs and scrubbed the pets. We had the shiniest hair, the cleanest house, and the most embarrassed missionaries in town.

Charles and I continued our search. We left early in the morning and came home exhausted at night. No home. Although we all enjoyed each other's company, I was desperate about imposing on the Gales. One evening, I concluded that the children and I could stay no longer.

"I will take the children and return to Springfield," I silently decided. "We will return to Canada when a home becomes available for us."

Exhausted and discouraged, I crawled into bed and fell asleep. About 2:00 A.M., I suddenly awoke, sat up in bed, and heard the words, "You can't reach a positive goal by taking negative steps."

Charles was sound asleep beside me, and the houseful of family and friends were quiet. Someone had purposefully awakened me. Silently, I pondered the unusual message. *I must be careful. I must be patient. God had spoken.*

In the slumbering stillness, I made my apology to God. Taking rash steps in the heat of my own discomfort and indignity would not solve my problems or bring glory to God. Whether or not I understood His way of doing things, and whether or not I liked it, I must trust Him.

A short time later, we found an affordable town house and moved in. A local church, Faith Tabernacle, offered us the use of their church's education wing to begin the Bible school. Anointed men and women volunteered to assist, and Open Word Bible College was born.

Blessing needs a positive path. If we give in to wrong feelings, we can waylay our own victory.

Faith Will Affect
Future Generations

"When I call to remembrance
the unfeigned faith that is in thee,
which dwelt first in thy grandmother Lois,
and thy mother Eunice; and
I am persuaded that in thee also."
2 Timothy 1:5

The greatest gift a child can have
is a heritage of faith.

32

"Mom, There Are Thieves In the Area"

*For I will contend with him that contendeth
with thee, and I will save thy children.*
—Isaiah 49:25b

Rich, lavender bougainvillea cascaded over the kitchen window, bright red amaryllis trumpets lined the gravel driveway, and vivid blue and red-purple morning glories intertwined with pink climbing roses draped one section of fence that surrounded our rental property in Meru, Kenya. After working with the Bible school in London, Ontario, for six years, the Lord directed us to come back to Africa for a couple of years. The school in London continued under the capable leadership of Mr. Gerald Kelsey.

Joseph Mugo, an African pastor and leader of a group of churches that we had worked with for over 20 years, was excited about our arrival in Meru. After considerable searching, he had selected this rental house for us, located in one of the more secure sectors of town. Decorative wrought iron bars covered the windows, and dead bolts were installed on the doors. Large stone pillars secured a protective gate which was kept locked.

After we arrived, we were further instructed to hire a full-time guard. When we found a man who gladly included casual yard maintenance and washing clothes in his job description, we were ready to focus on our work.

On this particular day, Charles was out of town. Sixteen-year-old Bethanie, 10-year-old Christine, and I were alone. It was Saturday, the guard's day off. The mid-morning sun beamed a friendly invitation to come outside and enjoy the tropical surroundings. I readily agreed when Christine asked if I would take her for a walk to meet the Church of Christ missionaries who had a daughter her age. Bethanie had things at home that she wanted to do, so with instructions to lock the door behind us, we left.

Though located right on the equator, Meru is nestled amongst the high hills of the mountainous area of Mt. Kenya, at an elevation of more than 10,000 feet above sea level. Huge evergreens and tropical foliage lined the red dirt roads and shaded us as we walked. When we arrived at the missionary compound, we discovered that they not only had a guard, but two guard dogs. Our approach was greeted by the vigorous barking of two enormous, black rottweilers. Just the sight of them was enough to frighten anyone away. Once the guard let us inside the gate, however, the dogs became animated friends.

The family was delighted to meet us and we adults exchanged information on cooking, shopping, ministry, family, and pertinent news, as the children played. After tea and a snack, we walked home.

When we arrived at our house, we found a note taped to the living room door. "Mom, be careful," it read. "There are thieves in the area. I've gone to Peggy's."

Peggy was a Peace Corps worker who lived a short distance from us. Creative and effervescent, she was inspirational company for our girls. Christine and I locked the house and hurried over. Bethanie was there. Peggy introduced us to her visiting Peace Corps friends and together we returned to the house.

We went from room to room to survey the damage. The girls' tennis shoes, sunglasses and jean jacket were taken. Our bedroom was in a shambles. The thieves had ransacked our room in their search for money, but only our cassette tapes and minor items were stolen.

"What happened, Bethanie?" I asked.

After locking the door behind us, Bethanie said that she busied herself in the house. Suddenly, she heard a noise from the direction of the living room and went to investigate. A man had managed to squeeze through one of the squares in the protective window grating. Before she could get away, he grabbed her. As he did, she saw another man waiting outside.

"Where is your money?" the man demanded.

"We don't have any," Bethanie answered.

Grabbing his knife, he put it to her throat and rudely escorted her from room to room insisting that she show him where our money was hidden.

Bethanie was firm.

"We don't have any money," she stated.

In frustration, he shoved her into the bathroom and closed the door. She stayed there quietly while they searched the house. Finally, when all was quiet, she slipped out and ran for safety.

"Bethanie, how did you feel when they put a knife to your throat?" I asked.

"Mom," she replied confidently, "I just knew that it wasn't my time to die."

That night, some of our new Peace Corps friends spent the night with us. We were grateful for the company and enjoyed the camaraderie as we arranged sleeping places on the living room floor so we could all be together.

We were accustomed to hearing of such invasions in undeveloped countries. Meru town was full of reports of murder and theft. In some cases, the desperate populace hanged and burned the thieves when they caught them. Our home in Zaire had been robbed several times and we were in constant danger of thieves. Just a few years earlier, the Christian world was saddened by the brutal murder and robbery of YWAM workers Mike and Janice Shelling in their home in Baguio, Philippines. Such heartless thievery is not uncommon in areas of joblessness and poverty.

What caused the thieves to spare our daughter? We may never really know, but I believe that the quiet, God-given confidence that surrounded Bethanie as she was taken from room to room was like a cloak of protection. Confidence has its own atmosphere.

The prophet Isaiah must have discovered this when he tells us, "in quietness and in confidence shall be your strength" (Isaiah 30:15b). David, the man who had endured many a nerve-wracking dilemma, knew the power of confidence when he declared, "The LORD is on my side; I will not fear: what can man do unto me?" (Psalm 118:6). King Solomon stood in unshakable confidence and recorded, "Be not afraid of sudden fear, neither of the desolation of the wicked, when it cometh. For the LORD shall be thy confidence, and shall keep thy foot from being taken" (Proverbs 3:25,26).

I did not know to what degree we would need a place of refuge that day as we began our morning with Bible reading and prayer. I did not know that God would be faithful to keep a promise to me even when I was unaware of the danger and wasn't actively claiming it at the moment of need.

"In the fear of the LORD is strong confidence: and his children shall have a place of refuge" (Proverbs 14:26). As we walk in a righteous fear of the Lord, recognizing who He is and acknowledging His mighty power and sovereignty, we can experience a confidence that is beyond imagination, and at the same time, provide a place of refuge for our children. That sense of confidence may be attacked with thoughts like, *You're not being a good parent if you don't worry,* and *What right do you have to be at peace when everyone else is so upset? They'll think you don't care.*

But faith cannot afford to give place to fear. The dwelling place of a righteous man at peace with God is greater than any form of security on earth. The Apostle Paul explains that our confidence in God should never, never, never, be set aside. No matter what kind of conditions we encounter in life, we can live in the ever present atmosphere of confidence that surrounds those who are at peace with the plan of God.

"Cast not away therefore your confidence, which hath great recompense of reward," Hebrews 10:35 urges. The Hebrews account of faith informs us that it is worse to lose our confidence than it is to lose our life. Confidence in God has a sure reward both in this life and in the life to come. For if we continue in confidence, even during periods of loss on earth, God guarantees we will be rewarded in heaven. Confidence shields us from depression, it keeps us from yielding to sin, it nurtures faithfulness, it surrounds us with peace, it keeps us focused on the goal of our high calling in God, and it inspires others to have faith too.

When a man's ways please the LORD, he maketh even his enemies to be at peace with him.
—Proverbs 16:7

Thou wilt keep him in perfect peace, whose mind is stayed on thee: because he trusteth in thee.
—Isaiah 26:3

And all thy children shall be taught of the LORD; and great shall be the peace of thy children.
—Isaiah 54:13

For to be carnally minded is death; but to be spiritually minded is life and peace.
—Romans 8:6

Faith is Substance and Evidence of the Unseen

"Now faith is the substance
of things hoped for,
the evidence of things not seen."
Hebrews 11:1

*Faith is a gift God gives to every man.
But what man does with his faith
is his gift to God.*

33

A Tea Party and an Unwelcome Guest

*For I say, through the grace given unto me, to every man
that is among you, not to think of himself more highly
than he ought to think; but to think soberly according as
God hath dealt to every man the measure of faith.*
–Romans 12:3

Our days in Kenya were numbered because Charles felt a strong
call to go on to Zaire. When we heard rumors of political unrest
there, I was afraid to take our girls into greater peril. We packed,
but the imminent prospects of danger kept me desperately seeking
God. One Sunday, just before we left, we had lunch with a veteran
Norwegian missionary.

"I've been praying for you, Fern," he said. Before we left, he gave
me a Scripture that God had given him to share with me. My heart
was touched and strengthened by his words of encouragement.

The day after we arrived in Bukavu, Zaire, 250 miles north of
our former home in Kalemie, the French Ambassador was shot.
Rumors of retaliation by the French government indicated that we
had indeed landed in an African hot spot. *Now what?* Some missionaries talked about evacuating. The town lived with an ear to its
battery-operated and short-wave radios, scared, waiting.

Then Charles met a young missionary in town, Dan Koehler. Dan knew of several rental houses and offered to help us find a home. It was the beginning of our acquaintance with a wonderful missionary community that loved one another and the people they were there to serve.

This letter to my mother describes some everyday scenes of those first getting acquainted days:

Dear Mom,

Loving greetings from Bukavu, Zaire. Thank you so much for your prayers. It sounds like you have been getting almost as much moisture as we have, only in another form. At least we don't have to shovel after a tropical rainstorm.

It's been raining every morning in tropical deluges. One day, Bethanie and Christine went outside on the verandah in the downpour and danced around until they were soaking wet. Adding to the noise of the rain on our tin roof are white vested crows that tromp around up there. These birds must have a two-foot wing span and when they come in for a landing on the metal roof and race down their runway, it makes no small commotion.

Our house here is just minutes from the Rwanda border, by car. We are told that Bukavu used to be a beautiful town, but with the exit of business men and missionaries, the town is a sad reminder of what it used to be. Bukavu is located beside Lake Kivu and has several small peninsulas extending out into the lake. We live on one of those peninsulas. The land rises quite high out of the water, giving us a lovely view of the lake.

The old house we live in is made of cement block and stuccoed white. It has a red tin roof and a wide verandah across the front and part way around both sides of the house. It is situated on a large lot surrounded by a tall cedar hedge, and whoever lived here before us planted quite a few flowers! Again, I am delighted that the Lord has been so generous and has let me have some beautiful flowers. A section of the roof leaks, and the aged, malfunctioning toilets have defied the repair efforts of our local plumbers.

One morning, I got up while it was dark to go to the bathroom. Alas, I found myself walking in water. Tracing the river to its source, I found that one of our faulty toilets had produced a sizable waterfall. The water ran down the hall, across the living room, out the front door, and cascaded down the steps in a grand finale. This was one time I was very grateful that we didn't have wall to wall carpeting. Charles and I mopped the cement floors and swept water out through the front door for about an hour. After Charles had crept back into bed, I re-mopped with disinfectant. It's one thing to get a case of hepatitis while ministering heroically amongst the needy, but not nearly so noble to get it in your own malfunctioning home. That would be too much!

A week ago Tuesday night, Maleeya Postma picked me up to go with her to the Elizabeth Group, a bi-monthly ladies prayer group. Maleeya is a MAF pilot's wife, and a dear. The ladies take turns meeting in each other's homes and also take turns leading the devotional and prayer time. The prayer time has been a blessing. Last Tuesday there were 11 ladies there. After sharing prayer needs and praise reports, I had more insight into the missionary community here.

It would be nice to get to know the women individually, I thought. Since most women love a tea party, I decided to arrange one. Debbie Parker was my first guest. First I baked some raisin squares with the last of my Kenyan brown sugar. Next I made cauliflower soup from some cauliflower that I bought from a lady who came to our back door selling vegetables. Then I set up a little table outside, cut some flowers for our table centerpiece, and brewed some tea. Everything was ready.

When Debbie Parker arrived, we seated ourselves out on the verandah under the palm trees overlooking the lake. It was delightful. Women's talk flowed back and forth as we enjoyed lunch when suddenly, the tranquility was broken by a frightened cry. It was Debbie scrambling for safety as she pointed to a very unwanted visitor. A bright, jade green snake had climbed the verandah wall right beside us and sat quietly investigating our party. He appeared intrigued by our presence.

Evidently, he would have loved to sample us or some of our goodies but sensed that his company was not welcome. Quietly he slithered away. Debbie was sure that it was a green mamba, although she had never seen one before. She proceeded to tell me how deadly they are.

"When they bite you," she told me, "the poison affects your respiratory system and you die in minutes. There is no cure!"

Although the reptile looked quite harmless in his coat of vivid green, I must confess that her warning left me quite sure that I did not want to meet our visitor again. Hopefully my next tea party will be more peaceful.

With so much energy expended trying to keep body and soul together, it is amazing to see what people do for a living. Not long ago Charlie and I were in one little store paying for some cheese and local butter. There was a young woman there with a bag of used shoes that she had washed and cleaned. The matron of the shop continued counting her money as she held out her foot to the lady who was attempting to fit her with a pair of shoes.

We also see men and women walking up and down the sidewalk carrying racks of shirts or dresses. *How conve-*

nient, to have the store come to your door. Some sell locally-made jewelry, fruits or vegetables, or woven hot mats. Some just beg.

Since we don't have a car yet, we use local "taxis," but it always makes me feel uncomfortable when I use the term taxi in our letters. The concept of a taxi in the U.S. and what we use here in Africa is altogether different. Here, a taxi is any vehicle with a "TAXI" sign posted in the front window. Often the door knobs are broken and the driver has to let you in and out. As many people as possible are packed into the car unless you want to pay for the unused seat. Rarely do they have a starter motor and so the drivers have to make sure they stop on a hill so they can roll to get started, or hope that nearby observers will lend a hand to help push-start the vehicle. Although most taxis are in a desperate state of ill repair and you can't help but wonder how much longer they can possibly run, riding still beats walking.

Yesterday we ministered in a church here in town. They have two services in the morning. Charlie preached in the first service and I was invited to speak in the second. I had been thinking about the fact that each one of us is a king, in a sense. We each have an area of life that we rule over, first of all our own hearts, then our home and our business. Because in this sense we are kings, I decided to search the Scriptures and see what kind of instruction God gives to kings. In Proverbs, I found a number of Scriptures addressed especially to kings. From these, I made a list of things that God wants kings to observe:

1. Live righteously—*It is an abomination to kings to commit wickedness: for the throne is established by righteousness.* —Proverbs 16:7

2. Follow mercy and truth—*Mercy and truth preserve the king: and his throne is upholden by mercy.* —*Proverbs 20:28*

3. Take good counsel and choose your friends wisely—
Take away the wicked from before the king, and his throne shall be established in righteousness.
—Proverbs 25:5

4. Refuse bribes—*The king by judgment establisheth the land: but he that receiveth gifts overthroweth it.*
—Proverbs 29:4

5. Be sexually pure—*Give not thy strength unto women, nor thy ways to that which destroyeth kings.*
—Proverbs 31:3

6. Avoid wine and strong drink—*It is not for kings, O Lemuel, it is not for kings to drink wine: nor for princes strong drink: Lest they drink, and forget the law, and pervert the judgment of any of the afflicted.*
—Proverbs 31:3

After sharing, I invited those who would like to have God's help to live according to His guidelines, and to rule the kingdoms in their lives righteously, to come forward for prayer. It was wonderful to see about twenty men respond to the Word and come forward.

Thanks again for your prayers.

Lovingly,
Fern

The political climate continued to deteriorate. The currency was devalued and for a while no bills less than 50 zaires were available. If a purchase amounted to less than 50 zaires, we couldn't get change. So, although food was available in the stores, there wasn't money to purchase it. Schools closed because the children were too weak from hunger to walk to school.

When there is no substance in government, when there is no substance in the educational system, when there is no substance in the marketplace, where do you turn? The Bible says that faith is substance. As systems failed and unrest grew, we clung to God more closely.

Mike Murdock has written a song that says, "When you've got nothing left but God, you've got enough to start again." Some of the greatest challenges of our lives are the empty days we face when hope has been stolen from us. It may be caused by our own mistakes or by the actions of other people. But, although the indomitable faith that is given to us by the hand of a loving God is our only resource, it is enough.

In the days ahead, life challenged the faith that God had invested in us, but we found that there is no greater strength on earth than when the God-invested faith in a human heart unites with the Spirit of the God of all faith. By His grace we can receive strength to rule our own hearts diligently, to enter into the promises made to those who trust in Him, and to assist Him in bringing beauty from the ashes of hopelessness. Walking on the substance of faith, as evidence of the unseen, is a tribute to the supernatural power of the Word.

Faith Multiplies the
Gifts of the Poor

"Hearken, my beloved brethren,
Hath not God chosen the poor of this world
rich in faith, and heirs of the kingdom
which he hath promised to them that love him?"
James 2:5

*A single act of faith
may yield perennial fruit.*

34

Planting Perennial Perfume

Give, and it shall be given unto you; good measure,
pressed down, and shaken together, and running over,
shall men give into your bosom. For with the same measure
that ye mete withal it shall be measured to you again.
—Luke 6:38

Celebrating birthdays, anniversaries, Christmas, or any other holiday calls for creativity on the mission field. It was Christine's birthday. How could we make it special? I found a pretty piece of material that we had brought with us from Canada. Maybe I could make something nice out of that. When she was safely asleep, I cut and sewed it into a new dress for her. We needed a card but Hallmark hadn't supplied our little shops with greeting cards. My handmade card would need an original verse. Hmmmm. . ..

Happy Birthday, Christine!

I know of a girl named Christine,
A 12-year-old African Queen;
Was born in Zaire,
Ate bugs without fear,
With monkeys she often was seen.

Now she is grown up, and quite staid,
Of bugs she is sorely afraid;
When given a treat,
Like termites to eat,
Our Christine is awfully dismayed.

Her birthday, you see, is this month,
And I've a particular hunch;
No longer she'll view,
Fish eyes in her stew,
As normal cuisine for her lunch.

Christine is now busy with school,
Learns Scripture to use as a tool;
She studies each night,
To get her tests right,
She thinks getting A's is real cool.

Piano she plays with some skill,
And practices it with a will,
Like Dino, some day,
She hopes she will play,
I pray God her wish to fulfill.

Christine, in the coming New Year,
May God give you joy and good cheer;
May angels each day,
Watch over your way,
And grant you God's blessings, my dear.

Earlier that morning while having devotions, I was challenged by the thought of creative provision. I wrote down my thoughts.

POOR CAN BE MORE

Our understanding of mathematics does not consider the power of God, His divine multiplication, and His mercy toward the poor. When we experience a financial shortfall, one of the dilemmas that often confronts us is the difficulty of giving. How can we give when we don't have enough for ourselves? Shouldn't we postpone tithing, save our meager supply, and allow those with the means of philanthropy to exercise their gift?

When there isn't enough to eat, the rent is due, the children need new shoes, and the power company is threatening to disconnect services, that seems like a good reason to start scraping and hoarding until we are in financial good-standing again. That is also the time when the devil tells us that we should skip paying our tithes for a while, and forget about doing any good deeds. Perhaps, if we really try, we might be able to scrape together a dollar to give, but what difference can a dollar make? Besides, it would be embarrassing to give so little. What good is a dollar when the missionary needs so much more than that? Poor is definitely less for everyone, right?

No! The Bible says that poor can be more. Mark 12:43 says, "Verily I say unto you, That this poor widow hath cast more in, than all they which have cast into the treasury."

Just because we can only afford to give a small amount does not mean that that little bit is ineffective. God has always specialized in "little is much." He delights in taking what we have and enlarging it, multiplying it, stretching it, blessing it, and confounding the enemy with it! God does not look at the dollar in view of its physical worth. God looks at the heart of the giver and the depth of their faith as they apply the little that they have toward the need. It is not the greatness of one's financial ability that determines the measure of effectiveness in giving. It is the amount of faith exhibited by the giver.

When God, in His heavenly domain, analyzes all of the ingredients in the heart of the giver, like faith, love toward the brethren, and faithfulness, and applies them toward the object in need, somehow the littlest gift becomes an enormous blessing. And through the years, that gift may continue to give as God multiplies it.

* * *

One of the greatest incidents of giving in my own life took place several years ago on a Monday morning. It dawned, warm, brilliant with sunshine—twenty-four hours waiting to be filled with something. With Charles far away ministering in Africa and four small children to care for, it wouldn't be hard to find something to do.

Sunday had been a good day. A guest minister had visited our church and blessed us with a wealth of inspiration and insight into God's Word. I still felt the effects of that anointing. It was life-giving. The divine inspiration that came as our guest taught the Word of God was like opening a door and giving us opportunity to reach into the supernatural realm to take a wonderful treasure.

My heart was stirred in gratitude, not only for the obedience of a man dedicated to serving God in ministry, but for the wife back home who had sacrificed her own needs so that we could be blessed. Something should be done for her.

The Lord had provided for the financial necessities of Charles' trip, and we had agreed to trust God to provide for the family's needs while he was gone. That meant living one day at a time. We put our hope in God, knowing that He knew where we lived, and what the needs were for me and our family of four, soon to be five, children.

We needed groceries that Monday morning, but the desire to honor the sacrifice of that other wife challenged me. I counted my little stash of grocery money again. It wasn't much, but I decided we would share it. The children and I went to a large department store. What should we get? We decided on a bottle of Chanel No. 5 perfume. Carefully, we wrapped it, and I wrote a note of thanks to the faraway wife for sharing her husband with us. Then we took the gift to our pastor's house and sent it home to her via her husband.

It seemed like a foolish thing to do, to take the food from our mouths and buy Chanel No. 5 for a stranger. But the joy of that moment will never be forgotten.

Many years went by. Then one day the Lord spoke to me.

"Fern, have you ever noticed that since the day you gave that sacrifice of perfume you have never had to buy perfume? And you have never been without perfume, nice perfume?"

Amazed, I realized it was true. Curiously, I also noted that at the same time He spoke to me, my perfume was almost gone. God had my attention. We were scheduled to leave for Africa the next day. *Did God think it was necessary for me to have nice perfume during my next two years of ministry in Africa?* Certainly God had already rewarded me exceedingly and abundantly above the merit of that single sacrifice. *Did He plan to supply me with quality perfume for the rest of my life?* I was awed.

Our last minute preparations were almost complete. The children were all at the house with us, helping pack and repack as boxes and suitcases were weighed and total kilos calculated to meet our luggage restrictions. Suddenly, amid the excitement, the doorbell rang.

Ida Hall, a dear friend, stood there looking very apologetic.

"I won't come in," she hurried to say. "I know you're busy getting ready to leave tomorrow, but my daughter and daughter-in-law and I want to give you this good-bye gift."

Quickly she hugged me, handed me a lovely gift bag and was gone.

The family all gathered around and watched as I opened my gift. Carefully, I opened the beautiful gift bag, removed the bright yellow tissue paper and found a large bottle of Liz Claiborne perfume. *My favorite.* But God wasn't finished affirming my act of giving and His appreciation of it, for in the bag was also a large, matching jar of Liz Claiborne body lotion.

This act amazed me, especially since my friend and her girls did not know that Liz Claiborne was my favorite perfume, nor did they have any idea of their part in this miracle of provision. After our return from Africa, I shared this story with her.

But, there is still another facet to my story of giving. While writing this story, I realized something I had never noticed before. The day that I purchased that bottle of Chanel No. 5, our four older children were with me, but our fifth, unborn Mina, was being carried close to my heart. Through the years, our family has become aware of Mina's exceptional generosity. Family and friends all continually benefit from her intuitive giving. Interestingly, God not only blessed me with an unending supply of lovely perfume, but He gave a gift to our unborn baby as well—the gift of a generous heart.

Through the years of ministry, we have humbly received many a widow's mite. Occasionally, people told us that they thought about giving to missions but their gift didn't seem significant, so they didn't give at all. We learned that God has many ways of blessing the gifts of the poor that are given in love. True value is hidden in the heart of the giver and rewarded or multiplied accordingly. First Corinthians 1:27–29 says this:

> But God hath chosen the foolish things of the world to confound the wise; and God hath chosen the weak things of the world to confound the things which are mighty; And base things of the world, and things which are despised, hath God chosen, yea, and things which are not, to bring to nought things that are: That no flesh should glory in his presence.

Jesus makes a remarkable statement in Luke 18:24b: "How hardly shall they that have riches enter into the kingdom of God!" Neither poverty nor wealth in itself is commendable to God. The crucial point is whether or not we can let our possessions go when God asks for them. When He does, the little we give may become the greatest of all.

Faith Increases When We Know That God Sees Us

"Jesus saw Nathanael coming to him,
and saith of him, Behold an Israelite
indeed,in whom is no guile!
Nathanael saith unto him,
Whence knowest thou me?
Jesus answered and said unto him,
Before that Philip called thee,
when thou wast under the fig tree,
I saw thee. Nathanael answered
and saith unto him, Rabbi,
thou art the Son of God;
thou art the King of Israel."
John 1:47–49

*Every human being wants to be truly
known and truly loved.*

35

"Thou God Seest Me"

*"And she called the name of the LORD that
spake unto her, Thou God seest me: for she said,
Have I also here looked after him that seeth me?"*
—Genesis 16:13

"Mama, will you come and speak to our widows and single lady's group?" Mrs. London asked.

Rev. London was the assistant pastor of a large Swedish Pentecostal church and his capable wife was a busy organizer and leader of various church activities. Their sanctuary was built high on the side of a large hill overlooking a densely populated area of Bukavu, Zaire. It seated more than two thousand people. Now his wife was asking me to speak to the widows and single ladies of this church.

The rutted road leading to the church was also a lifeline of industrious entrepreneurs conducting business. Setting up shop looked easy. Find a spot beside the road, lay out a gunny sack, and arrange your wares on top of it. People could shop as they walked along. There were used blankets, used clothes, used eye glasses, fruits, vegetables, chickens, housewares, soda pop, deep-fried dough balls and goats.

Hundreds of bodies moved about, engulfed in the general din. Hawkers shouted, attempting to attract customers. Impatient drivers vented their feelings with the horns of their slowly moving vehicles. Blaring radios played the syncopated beat of local musicians. Confined animals expressed their pent-up frustrations. Some men, customarily holding hands in friendship, carried on animated conversations as they hurried along together. Women passed, carrying heavy loads on their heads and babies on their backs.

Most of the homes here did not have the convenience of inhouse bathrooms or running water. I observed many of the local women with admiration. Their posture was faultless, gained from years of carrying things on their heads. They did not possess closets full of clothing, but they dressed attractively in brightly colored, cotton, wrap-around skirts called *kikwembes*, with matching blouses and headpieces. Their hair was sometimes decoratively braided by relatives or friends. Golden brown complexions were oiled, sometimes simply with cooking oil. Beauty emerged without the help of modern cosmetics.

As I watched, a poem came to my heart.

Others toiled slowly by,
In their souls, hid a cry,
Wounded, bending 'neath a heavy load.

Leathered feet, gnarled and bare,
Found no rest, only wear,
Stumbling o'er life's rough and rocky road.

Threadbare clothes, wrinkled, torn,
Bodies weak, future gone,
Youthful visions vanished, tarnished, dead.

Where is God, does He see?
Will He come, set them free?
Give new hope, new life, and living bread?

During our stay in Kalemie, we had four years to learn how to live with the basics. We experimented to find the best way to bathe out of a bucket. We tried pouring and dipping. Then we pounded holes in the bottom of the bucket, filled it with water, hung it from a nail and hurried to stand under it before the water all dripped out. Yet I felt that our experiences had not adequately prepared me to speak words of encouragement and instruction to these women. I had never really walked where they walked, though my girls and I had tried unsuccessfully to carry basins on our heads. How could I hope to minister cross-culturally into these differences?

The day of the meeting arrived. Kneeling beside my office chair, I prayed. "God, I yield myself to You. Only You know the needs in the hearts of these women. Only You can heal their wounds, understand the intricacies of their lives, and give guidance, deliverance, and hope. Here is my life. Take me. Use me for Your glory, in Jesus' name."

When I arrived at the church, I was amazed to find about 100 women in attendance. Mrs. London served as my interpreter, and as we chatted before the meeting, she explained that some of the single women were women who had been displaced when their husbands took a second wife.

As I sat on the platform, I observed the congregation. There were older women, gnarled and bent from years of heavy labor. Others were young and attractive. *How were they coping? What stories of the past lay silently enshrined in their hearts? How do single moms manage to survive and rear families here, where the challenges of living without welfare systems or social services seem incomprehensible?*

My hostess introduced me and I stood to speak. My text was Genesis 16:13: "And she called the name of the LORD that spake unto her, Thou God seest me: for she said, Have I also here looked after him that seeth me?"

The passage is about Sarah's maid, Hagar. Sarah decided that she was too old to have a child, so she talked Abraham into having a child by her maid. Hagar, the maid, reacted to the resulting conception with arrogance and pride. Sarah responded with abuse. The situation became so difficult, Hagar ran away.

But Hagar discovered that she wasn't hidden from God. As she sat by a fountain of water in the wilderness, she was visited by the angel of the Lord. The angel instructed her to return to her mistress and submit to her. He also informed her that she would have a son and her seed would be multiplied exceedingly, so that it could not be numbered for multitude (Genesis 16:9,10).

Hagar was in awe. God saw her. He saw her past with its mistakes. He saw the present with its bitterness and hurt. He saw the future with its infinite promise. Nothing, absolutely nothing was hidden from God, and He loved her. The angelic sympathy and promise didn't change her circumstances, but it changed her heart. She knew then that God loved her and cared for her personally. She wasn't alone. She could make it. God told her so.

As I described Hagar's desert encounter, I was engulfed by a deep compassion for the women before me.

"Jesus sees you, too," I said. "He sees your circumstances. He understands your needs. He knows your desires. He loves you. He cares about you today.

"Where did God tell Elisha to go when he needed provision?" I asked them. "He sent him to the widow's house. God expected the impoverished, struggling widow to meet the needs of the man of God. God wasn't hindered by the widow's poverty. His plan was to release divine provision, but He needed her willing obedience first. When she responded, God took the little that she gave and multiplied it.

"God is still looking for women today who are willing to trust Him. Whether you are widowed or single, abandoned, rejected or abused, God sees you. He knows where you are and He wants to meet your need. He wants to bless you and make you to be a blessing to others. Turn to Him with all of your heart. He cares."

Stepping from the platform, I began to walk amongst the women. A powerful compassion gripped my heart. Reaching out, I placed my hands on individual heads, praying and crying aloud to God to heal them and meet their needs. Something happened. We felt the heart of God as healing waves of the Holy Spirit swept over us. God's love released the stored up emotions of courageous women struggling to keep control. And they wept. Burden-weary shoulders shook with sobs as God poured His love over us like healing oil.

Then, in the back of the room, an attractive young woman stood up weeping. Mrs. London translated as she began to speak.

"My husband rejected me and took a second wife," she said. "I was hurt and alone and had no income. I turned my back on God and, to support myself, I went into prostitution. Today I know that God sees me and I want to come back to God."

It was a wonderful welcome.

When the truth that God is a personal God, that He knows us, that He sees us, that He cares for us, breaks like the dawn in our hearts, something happens. We are changed. Faith is born, trust in God's power and authority emerges, and hope for the future arises.

Nathaniel experienced this when he met Jesus for the first time. He had seen enough in his lifetime to make him seriously doubt Philip's declaration that he had found the Christ. Reluctantly, he went to meet this supposed fulfillment of Scripture. But when Jesus saw him coming, He didn't address Nathaniel's doubt or his unbelief. He said, "Behold an Israelite indeed, in whom is no guile!"

Wow! That took Nathaniel by surprise.

"Whence knowest thou me?" he asked Jesus.

"Before that Philip called thee, when thou wast under the fig tree, I saw thee," Jesus responded.

God saw him? God knew him? God knew his thoughts and desires as he sat praying and hoping and meditating under the fig tree?

Something happened in Nathaniel's heart. He felt a sudden bonding in that heart-to-heart encounter.

"Rabbi, thou art the Son of God, thou art the King of Israel," he declared.

Similarly, we are changed when we have that knowing, seeing encounter with God. Faith is born. It causes us to repent of our sin, receive His grace and accept Him as the absolute authority in our life. We rise to a new dimension of living, where we expect the power of the supernatural to have greater authority than the natural conditions that surround us. Why? Because the fragmented pieces of our lives have come into order with the amazing God of truth who saw us and cared enough to pay the price for our restoration.

Faith is Not Passive

"And from the days of
John the Baptist until now
the kingdom of heaven
suffereth violence, and
the violent take it by force."
Matthew 11:12

Although we have been apprehended
we still must contend for the faith.

36

Invaded By Flying Termites

*Beloved, when I gave all diligence to write unto you of the
common salvation, it was needful for me to write unto you,
and exhort you that ye should earnestly contend for
the faith which was once delivered unto the saints.*
–Jude 1:3

One rainy night when I opened the front doors of our Bukavu home to put the padlock on the iron grillwork that protected our front entrance, I was instantly surrounded by a host of flying visitors. They were winged but they certainly weren't celestial. They were flying termites swarming toward our light, dry haven. In those few moments when the door was open, they invaded our home by the thousands.

The clouds of creatures inside flitted about happily as millions of their friends lined up outside and made subtle, determined efforts to share our residence. They crept through crawl spaces under the doors, and sneaked through every unseen air-vent or hole. We scrambled to plug up all possible entrances then tried to determine what to do with the aggressive trespassers we now unwillingly sheltered.

We couldn't open the doors and shoo them back outside, and there were far too many to kill. At first I attempted to continue washing the dishes and making dinner, but they drowned themselves in my dishwater, plugged up the sink drain, sizzled themselves to death on the stove, wandered hopelessly around inside the teacups, coated themselves a bright red in the juice of the pickled beets I had planned to serve, and created general havoc.

Finally, I abandoned my post, climbed on a table in a secluded corner of the kitchen and settled down to watch the unwelcome invaders. Silently, I observed their strange antics, thankful that they didn't bite or sting. They flew around for a while, then, one by one they dropped to the floor and began vigorously walking about. Some of them made frantic efforts to knock off their large, filmy wings. Once freed of the filmy appendages, they scurried off in search of a mate. Romances were quick, and soon dozens of the bugs hurried off in tandem twos, in search of a honeymoon suite . . .

Two bugs in particular caught my attention. One wandered around on the floor flapping his filmy wings as if to say, "I sure wish these things would come off" (flap, flap); "It really would be nice if these wings would come off" (flap, flap); "I just know in my heart that these wings are going to come off" (flap, flap). But he wasn't making any great effort to displace the now unnecessary appendages. Perhaps he figured that nature would eventually take its course, and the predestined changes would automatically take place.

As I watched him, I noticed another bug nearby. This Mr. Bug had a totally different attitude. Obviously he had a purpose, and he intended to achieve it. He flapped vigorously against the cement floor trying to dislodge the cumbersome wings. That didn't work, so he flipped over on his back and did some back stroke whacks on the floor. Still no luck, so he curled up on his side and performed a series of jerking contortions. This little insect was determined to be rid of his wings and get on with his life. It wasn't long before his efforts paid off. The cumbersome wings fell off, and he gleefully scurried away in search of Miss Right.

I looked for the other bug. There he was, still wandering in circles.

What was he thinking? I wondered. *Was he frustrated because his wings hadn't come off yet? Was he jealous because the other bug progressed in life so much faster than he did?*

These bugs are just like some people I know, I mused. *They just wander around, wondering why God doesn't do something special in their lives. Years pass by as they wait for divine calls to be fulfilled. But, in the meantime, they busily kill time with their lack of self-discipline as they wander about, dabbling in activities of no lasting value, and spending time and energy on projects totally unrelated to their God-given call. Then when a door of opportunity does open, they are unprepared.*

Sometimes they simply sit for hours reviewing their problems, sipping the tea of discontent at self-made pity parties. The atmosphere gets even worse when they invite guests to their parties, and exchange bitter memories of failure and criticisms of others who get all the breaks.

Other people rise early to pray, they diligently study the Word, they share their faith with others, and they brighten the atmosphere with their positive attitude. They are willing to serve. They are not too proud to start with a lower position and work. They choose their way wisely and don't kill time wandering down the side roads of life. The Apostle Paul said in Philippians 3:14, "I press toward the mark for the prize of the high calling of God in Christ Jesus." And Jude writes, " . . . it was needful for me to write unto you, and exhort you that ye should earnestly contend for the faith which was once delivered unto the saints" (Jude 1:3).

Those bugs challenged my faith and my walk with God. There in my corner I prayed. "Lord, make me a contender of the faith. Let me spare no effort, like Mr. Bug, to apprehend all for which you have apprehended me."

Faith Does Not Divide.
It Links Believers Together

"Till we all come in the unity of the faith,
and of the knowledge of the Son of God,
unto a perfect man, unto the measure
of the stature of the fulness of Christ."
Ephesians 4:13

*When believers are linked together
in active faith, they form
achain of deliverance.*

37

"Prepare to Leave and Don't Tarry"

Make a chain: for the land is full of
bloody crimes, and the city is full of violence.
—Ezekiel 7:23

Charles was teaching and helping in the administration of a local Bible school in Bukava. I was homeschooling Christine, speaking at ladies' meetings, and on weekends, Charles and I shared speaking engagements in local and village congregations. One Sunday morning, he awoke desperately ill with malaria.

"Fern," he said, "I'm just too sick to speak this morning. I need you to go and speak at the Swedish Pentecostal church in my place." It was that enormous church on the hill.

"What if they don't approve of women preachers?" I asked. The idea of trying to dicker for a suitable taxi, walking alone through the rushing mob of people going up the steep hill, or sitting on the big platform with the church fathers—all these were more than a bit daunting. But I remembered my promise to God. "God, if You want me to preach, I will walk through any doors You open." The promise must be kept.

Upon arrival, the leaders greeted me graciously. We prayed together, then walked out and took our seats in the specially assigned chairs on the platform. After the preliminaries and introduction, I stood up behind the enormous pulpit and opened my Bible to read my text. As hundreds of black faces watched expectantly, a sudden, electric sense of divine destiny enveloped me. The prophetic dream of my youth was in the process of being fulfilled. Yes, I would preach to a thousand people.

In the midst of national crisis and need, in a church on foreign soil, God scheduled a divine appointment. Problems cannot hinder God from helping us achieve our divine destiny. In fact, it seems that God often chooses to bless us at the most inconvenient, impossible times. Jeremiah tells us that God thinks about us and makes plans for us. "For I know the thoughts that I think toward you, saith the Lord, thoughts of peace, and not of evil, to give you an expected end" (Jeremiah 29:11).

Although God does have wonderful plans for us, He needs our cooperation. Paul says, "We are workers together with him" (2 Corinthians 6:1). It would have been so easy for me to have missed this moment of destiny, to have chosen to stay in my safety zone at home with Charles.

Our continued rewards of ministry in Bukavu didn't come without difficulty. One night I stood by the window alone, listening to the crack of gun fire.

"I wonder if the other missionaries are safe," I thought as I hurried to see if they were taking roll call.

We didn't have telephone service, but the missionary community was able to maintain communications via CB radios. When danger threatened, we did a roll call to make sure everyone was safe.

I listened. One family cautiously reported that soldiers were approaching their house. They would stay on the air for a few more minutes, they said, and then they were going to the basement to lock themselves in. That wasn't too reassuring when we knew how vulnerable locks were to a soldier with a gun.

"Lord Jesus, please keep them safe," I prayed as I recalled precious promises.

"The name of the LORD is a strong tower: the righteous runneth into it, and is safe" (Proverbs 18:10).

"I will say of the LORD, He is my refuge and my fortress: my God; in him will I trust" (Psalm 91:2).

As tensions between the Hutu and Tutsi tribes escalated, the ground borders between Rwanda and Zaire were closed. We could no longer send or receive mail from the Rwandan post office just across the river. Then they closed the air borders. It took wisdom for the missionaries to obey government restrictions and yet stay in contact with neighboring missionary bases and the outside world.

One morning, I noticed an interesting verse in Jeremiah: "notwithstanding I have spoken unto you, rising early and speaking; but ye hearkened not unto me" (Jeremiah 35:14a). In further study, I found the same call to morning fellowship with God in Isaiah 50:4, "he wakeneth morning by morning, he wakeneth mine ear to hear as the learned."

That verse challenged me. God says that He comes to us to speak to us. No doubt He wants to give us direction and guidance, but sometimes when He comes to visit He finds us asleep with weariness, slothfulness, ignorance, or unbelief.

Wow! If God comes by my house morning by morning with news for me, I want to be there to listen. Maybe He will have a word of guidance during this time of danger and need, I thought. If I am diligent to be there waiting for him, will He speak to me? What will He say?

I began a serious early morning schedule to meet with God. Morning after morning, I went alone to the living room to read and to pray and to walk around and around the room listening for God to speak. Days went by, then weeks. The air tingled with tension. Some missionaries left, others packed ready for evacuation. Food became scarcer. We were truly willing to stay, but what about Christine? Did God want her to experience the kind of trauma that appeared to be imminent?

Then one morning, it happened. I got up as usual and went to the living room. Around and around the room I walked, quietly praying and praising and focusing on Him. Then, just as I was sitting down to read my Bible, the Holy Spirit spoke clearly to my heart and said, "Prepare to leave and don't tarry."

His quiet, powerful presence accompanied His words. It didn't matter whether He wanted us to stay or to go, it just mattered that He was leading, that we were being given the security of His will.

When Charles and Christine came in for breakfast, I told them what the Lord had said.

"But we don't have any money and the borders are closed," Charles questioned cautiously.

Four days later there was a knock on our door. It was another missionary who had just returned from a business trip to Rwanda. On his way back through Cyangugu, he stopped to check the mail. Typical of our caring missionary community, he checked ours too and found a fax addressed to us. When he reached the border, God gave him favor. He passed safely into Zaire and brought the fax right to our door. It was from our son Jeff.

Jeff explained that the Canadian Open Word Ministries board had met that week, and after praying together, they had a sense of urgency that we should come home right away. He went on to say that a church in London, Ontario had sent $1,500 and another church in Rockport, Illinois had sent $500 marked "transportation." We were amazed.

"You and Christine go ahead home," Charles said, "but I need to stay here and finish up some things."

Charles applied to the governor for permission to cross the border. When it was granted, he made a trip to Kigali to get tickets and make sure our documents were in order. Another missionary offered to drive us and our luggage over to Cyangugu. Charles was our guide as we boarded the country bus and rode through Rwandan mountains and forests. The scenery was breathtaking, and exciting when we spotted groups of black and white colobus monkeys.

When we arrived in Kigali and saw sandbags stacked on the street corners and soldiers driving UN trucks around the city, we were especially grateful for Charles' protective presence. *What was going on?* There was news of tribal conflict but this looked like war. Soldiers stood guard in front of the banks and important buildings. When we arrived at the airport, soldiers were on guard. Some were on the roof. Others patrolled the inside. *Would Charles be all right?* We didn't have long to wonder before our plane was called. We kissed each other good-bye, and Christine and I walked out of sight.

Back in London, Ontario, our daughter Ruth and her husband Andrew welcomed us into their home. News of our arrival spread quickly. One pastor called to welcome us and gave us his mother's car. Another pastor called and offered us a place to live with subsidized rent. New neighbors helped us move and gave unexpected gifts. The acts of love and gifts of provision were too numerous to mention.

Then, two months after we arrived home, the world was rocked by the horror of the massive Hutu/Tutsi massacre that took place in Rwanda. When Charles safely joined us three months later, he told stories of burning homes and fleeing victims.

The same word that God spoke so clearly in my living room had been given to fellow believers across the world at the same time. It linked us together in a common truth, birthed a common goal, and formed a chain of divine provision. Because of it, Christine was spared the trauma of being witness to events surrounding one of the most brutal massacres of this generation.

Other amazing incidents of assistance followed, some demonstrating a divine sense of humor. On the Sundays that we were not traveling in ministry, we attended church at London Gospel Temple in London, Ontario. Pastor Smith was a blessing, often speaking words of impartation, inspiration, encouragement, and deliverance into the lives of his church members. One Sunday as he ministered, he had an unusual moment of inspiration as he deviated from his sermon notes.

"There is help for those who snore," he declared. Our amusement turned to curiosity as he continued. "There is an apparatus that you can wear in your mouth at night that really works. If you're interested, call the office for details."

I was born with sleep apnea and decided to find out about this amazing apparatus that warranted a Sunday morning announcement. After calling the office, I learned that the device could be obtained through a local dentist. An appointment was made and I was introduced to Dr. Richardson. He was concerned when the test he administered revealed that I did have a problem, and he urged me to get the device. But the $700 cost was prohibitive. In the meantime, he had my teeth cleaned and desensitized.

Several months passed, and a longtime facial pain returned with a vengeance. Sleepless nights and grueling pain made ministry an almost impossible effort. "God," I pleaded, "please help. I know You are a healer and You can heal me, or You can lead me to someone You can use to solve this problem. Lord, please have mercy."

One day, while at my desk attempting to prepare for a weekend Women's Aglow conference where I was to speak, the phone rang. It was Dr. Richardson's Public Relations director. Her warm greeting came in the midst of a wave of pain that sent involuntary tears raining down my face.

"How are you?" she inquired lovingly.

"I'm actually in a lot of pain at the moment," I responded with effort. It was not customary for me, a New Englander, to reveal personal problems. In my upbringing, when asked how you were, you always said, "I'm fine." But she caught me at the precise moment the pain was too severe to be hidden.

"The reason I called," she said, "was to tell you that you have been on Dr. Richardson's mind. He and his wife have decided that they want to fit you for the breathing apparatus as a gift, but it sounds like we need to get you in here and see if we can deal with the pain problem first."

Dr. Richardson reviewed my history, did more tests, and we prayed together that God would reveal the problem. Antibiotics were prescribed, one root canal performed, and then a second one. When the second one was completed, he stood up, looked at me with a grin and declared, "Now, in the name of Jesus, may your facial pain be gone forever and ever, amen."

The next morning I woke up to—no pain! Joy. Blessed joy. I felt like running to the dental office and hugging everyone. Oh God, thank you, thank you, thank you. It had been so hard, so long. Years of painful nights of prayer, walking the floor, life an effort, hoping for divine intervention—then lovingly, wonderfully ended! Never did I dream that an unplanned remark about snoring by our minister would pave the way for divine dental deliverance. How amazingly God had orchestrated the pastor's remark, Dr. Richardson's concern, his assistant's call, the intensity of my pain, to form a lifeline of rescue.

IS THY GOD . . . ABLE?
Daniel 6:20

Thou servant of the living God,
Whilst lions round thee roar,
Look up and trust and praise His name,
And all His ways adore;
For even now, in peril dire,
He works to set thee free,
And in a way known but to Him,

Shall thy deliverance be.

Dost wait while lions round thee stand;
Dost wait in gloom, alone,
And looking up above thy head
See but a sealed stone?
Praise in the dark! Yea, praise His Name,
Who trusted thee to see
His mighty power displayed again
For thee, His saint, for thee.

Thou servant of the living God,
Thine but to wait and praise;
The living God, Himself, will work,
To Him thine anthem raise;
Though undelivered thou dost wait,
The God who works for thee,
When His hour strikes, will with a word
*Set thee for ever free.*11

M.E.B.

Although we may have had divine encounters with God that left us changed and healed, there are often areas of our lives that God does not heal nor allow us to conquer ourselves. Why? Is it because He wants us to function as a body, to receive and give ministry for each other's needs, to keep us from becoming independent and self-sufficient?

In John 11:44, the account of the resurrection of Lazarus says, "And he that was dead came forth bound hand and foot with graveclothes: and his face was bound about with a napkin. Jesus saith unto them, Loose him, and let him go."

Lazarus was resurrected bound. Jesus didn't free him and Lazarus could not free himself. Jesus instructed those that stood nearby to "Loose him, and let him go."

Acts 9 relates the story of Saul's conversion. This fearsome persecutor of the church had a divine encounter with Jesus on the road to Damascus and arose a change man. But, he was a blind man. Jesus didn't heal him, and Saul wasn't able to help himself. He was blind for three days. Then Jesus spoke to a man called Ananias and instructed him to go, lay his hands on Saul, and pray for him to receive his sight.

Luke 8 describes the healing of the daughter of Jarius. Jesus took her by the hand, and called, saying, "Maid, arise." Her spirit came again and she arose, but she arose hungry. Jesus then turned to the people of the house and instructed them to feed her.

We would like to "do it ourselves," but God won't let us. He keeps us dependent on Him and dependent on one another. With most of our goal-oriented personalities, we would establish the steps to righteousness, the formula for healing, the ABC's of missions and would attempt to blaze a self-righteous trail of achievement, but God won't allow it. We need the ministry of the other members of the Body of Christ if we are going to walk in freedom. God made the statement at the beginning that it was not good for man to be alone. He hasn't changed His mind.

In whatever walk of life, we need the Ananiases, the Dr. Richardsons, the beloved brothers and sisters that make up the the Body of Christ. We need them to obey the word God has given them, to loose us, to heal us, to feed us, to make us truly whole. Jesus is coming for a body, a many-membered man, a bride, a church without spot or wrinkle. We cannot please God fully, serve God totally, or represent God wholly, until we walk in obedient ministry to one another.

"And above all things, have fervent charity among yourselves."
—1 Peter 4:8

"And this commandment have we from him, That he who loveth God love his brother also."
—1 John 4:21

It is not a shame to have a need. Confessing it is an expression of one's own humility and an acceptance of the good in others. When Jesus hung on the Cross, after being cruelly beaten and inhumanely abused, he turned to the very men that wounded him and said, "I thirst." Jesus refused to be locked in a state of personal pain, misunderstanding, or need. If others did not reach out to Him, He reached out to them. He gave forgiveness to an ignorant world and reached out for their help. He pardoned the penitent thief, then unashamedly cried out Himself for the love of His heavenly Father.

A life of faith may be lived in temporary solitude, but it is not meant to be permanent. Faith gathers, it heals, it gives, it receives, it makes one. Lord, let us be obedient enough to give to our brother's need, and humble enough to receive from others for our own need. May we not hop about in our graveclothes attempting to show everyone how resurrected we are, when in fact we are resurrected helpless until our brethren come to our aid.

> "Confess your faults one to another, and pray one for another, that ye may be healed."
> –James 5:16

> "Finally, be ye all of one mind, having compassion one of another, love as brethren, be pitiful, be courteous."
> –1 Peter 3:8

Is this the reason why the enemy tries so hard to break the links of giving and receiving, of authority and submission, of judgment and righteousness, of truth and mercy, and of love and understanding which are so necessary to the effective joining together of the Body? When we love the Lord of truth with all of our hearts, and love one another with "a pure heart fervently," as described in 1 Peter 1:22, a chain of protection builds a lifeline of hope and life is formed in the midst of our chaotic world.

Faith is Founded on and Maintained by an Intimate Relationship With God

"Looking unto Jesus the author and
finisher of our faith . . .."
Hebrews 12:2a

*Faith is the shield that protects
our bodies, souls and spirits
from unhealable hurt.*

38

An Unexpected Commision

So Daniel was taken up out of the den, and no manner
of hurt was found upon him, because he believed in his God.
—Daniel 6:23

"Father, I thank you for my beloved sister," prayed Roger Pugh. "Lord God, I thank you for your mercy and your grace to my sister. You have shown your provision to her over and over and over again. There have been times when she has been needy, but she put her trust in you."

It was only a few days after Christine and I evacuated from Bukavu, Zaire, and I was attending a convention in Springfield, Missouri, where Roger Pugh was the keynote speaker. Roger had an intimate walk with God which was evidenced by a powerful prophetic ministry. It was the last night of the convention, and he called me from the audience and asked to pray for me. I had never met Roger before that meeting and was amazed at the accuracy of his words.

"I see you clutching the end of a shoestring," he said. "There was nothing left. 'But I have made a way for you again and again when you got to the end of the shoestring,' says the Lord. And the Lord says, 'I've made you a woman with a testimony of faith. And your testimony shall surface,' says the Lord. 'You shall write a book of your testimony, for this is the reason that I've brought you this way. You shall declare what it is that God has done in your life. Daughter, it shall go all over the world. It shall inspire faith in the hearts of people that you will never see. And there will be many women of God that will rise after the example that you shall show to them of God's provision and God's faith, and they shall stand as soldiers in their house.

"'There have been times when you have felt like God has made you like a soldier in your house, where you had to stand guard against the enemy. But daughter, this is the spirit that I've put upon you to raise you up as a standard, not only over your household, to weep and cry and make intercession, but over my people. For daughter, I've seen you weeping and crying over the sons and daughters of God.

"'Daughter, I'm going to cause you to share a testimony through a book, that is going to cause you to impart your very heart and life into others as they read the book, and they shall also become faith's testimony.

"'And I will do a great work through the women that I will raise up from the book that you will write. There will be men that will read it and be blessed, but there will be an anointing on the women. You've had a burden for my body, but you've had a special burden for my daughters, and when they read it, that burden is going to come upon them and their heart is going to be gripped. And they shall stand for their household and become women of God.

"'And in this hour I am going to raise up a multitude of women of God and give them a new release in right order,' says the Lord. 'And daughter, I'm going to give you the ability to share that right order with them which brings release to them, and launches them into powerful ministry,' says the Lord.

"'For I need not half an army in this day, but I need my whole army in this day; both men and women and young and old,' says the Lord. 'And daughter, I will release my daughters in particular, in a special way, through the book that you shall write. And this is confirmation. So get to it,' says the Lord, 'Get to it.'" Roger stopped and looked at me.

"Is that true?" he asked.

"I began writing, but decided that there are already so many books I shouldn't try to write another one," I replied.

"What's the name of it?" Roger asked.

"*When Faith is Enough,*" I answered.

"Ohhhhhhhh! Hallelujah!" hollered Roger as the congregation joined his shout.

Trembling under the power of the imparted word, I made my way back to my seat. The divine command I had just received left no question that God had a purpose for all of the experiences in my life. Private times of fellowship with God had converted the incidences of possible trauma and disaster to profitable learning experiences, and now God wanted to use them to bless others. *What an honor. What a responsibility.*

As I stood there trembling, a pastor's daughter came running from the front of the congregation. She hugged me excitedly and pressed $10 into my hand.

"Sister Willner, I want the first copy of your book," she exclaimed.

A tall, distinguished looking gentleman walked over to me from the center of the audience.

"This is toward your book," he said as he handed me a one-hundred-dollar bill.

A woman came crying, from the other side of the church.

"Sister Willner, I want to give you this toward your book," she said as she gave me more than $200. By the time I left church that night, I held God's seed promise for publishing the book, more than $500.00.

Back in Canada, I sat down to write but inspiration fled in the face of such responsibility.

How do your write a book of such dynamic proportions? I thought. *What style should it have? What should be included, and what should be left out? How deeply should I share personal feelings? Was my heart pure enough to tell my story constructively? Suppose I should inadvertently misrepresent someone?* Worry led to discouragement, fear and inability.

Then, one morning, in my daily devotions I read where Jesus commanded Peter to "launch out into the deep, and let down your nets for a draught."

"We've toiled all night and taken nothing," Peter replied. But, midway through his answer, he suddenly changed his attitude.

"Nevertheless, at thy word I will," he declared (Luke 5:5).

Did Peter hear the same power in Jesus' voice that he heard the day that Jesus spoke to his desperately ill mother-in-law and commanded her to be healed? Did he recall how Jesus' spoken word made her raging fever leave, "and immediately she arose and ministered to them?" (Luke 4:39). I don't know if he recalled that incident, but in a sudden change of heart, he decided to obey Jesus' command. When he did, a miracle followed.

As I read Peter's words, they pierced my heart. "Nevertheless, at thy word I will." I, too, had received a command from God, and like Peter, no matter what my circumstances appeared to be, I, too, would choose to obey it. The issue of importance was not my success but my obedience.

The result of my assent, like Peter's, was miraculous. Former Bible school students, who knew nothing of the prophecy, felt led to buy me a computer. God provided avid, heaven-sent encouragers. Mom presented me with a box of my letters that she had saved, to use as resource material, along with her complete confidence and prayers for the endeavor. Finally, after almost five years of working on the manuscript, I decided I had done my best. It was time to have it published.

In reviewing what God has done, I realize that God wants to take the piercings of our lives and create raiment of 'wrought gold and needlework' (Psalm 45:13,14). He wants to make us 'glorious within,' honorable, and splendid with beauty. But such richness only emerges out of the place of relationship. It doesn't matter if God keeps us in the midst of difficulty or if He delivers us out of it, but the faith to be kept or to be delivered comes from a personal relationship with God.

Daniel is an outstanding example of such a relationship. He was so dedicated to his Jewish faith, so confident of the reality of the God of Israel that he prayed three times a day. He prayed in the morning. He prayed on his lunch hour, and he prayed after work. But Daniel's prayer time wasn't just a fulfillment of a religious obligation that he felt more strongly than most, Daniel's time with God was a lifeline of relationship.

Daniel was a good man. So good that God Himself referred to him as one of the three most righteous men that ever lived (Ezekiel 14:14). Yet, God allowed Daniel, faithful, prayerful, brilliant, righteous Daniel, to have a most unfair experience.

Daniel had already served under King Nebuchadnezzar, King Belshazzar, and now King Darius. His impeccable work ethic, his outstanding ability in the palace, his personal bearing of confidence and grace was an indication of exemplary inner character. It hadn't taken King Darius long to notice Daniel's qualifications. When Daniel was promoted above his aspiring peers, they didn't like it. The air was rank with jealousy as frustrated business associates discussed plans to depose him. When no fault could be found in him, however, they devised a decree that so blinded the king with flattery that he didn't even see its evil intent. No one should be allowed to pray to anyone but the king for thirty days.

Great! the king probably thought. *My subjects are finally recognizing the power of my authority.* In blind pride, he approved the decree and stamped it with his seal.

Daniel didn't know it, but God was preparing an assignment for him of national importance. Could God trust him with such an assignment? Was his relationship strong enough? Would Daniel fight the miserable, scheming members of the monarchy for his legal rights? Would he discontinue his prayer time? Would he panic and look for a place of escape until the thirty days were over?

No! Those daily hours of prayer had established a solid trust, a deep faith in God that remained steadfast even when Daniel did not understand God's ways. Daniel was undaunted. He believed in his God, decree or no decree. He continued his practice of prayer, still kneeling in front of an open window, although he knew the possible results.

He was caught. Couldn't God have allowed a cloud to cover the window so he wouldn't be seen? Yes, but God allowed him to be sentenced to death in the lion's den instead. Couldn't God have shown the repentant king a legal loophole? Couldn't God have created some sort of lion virus to kill all the lions before Daniel got there? Yes. But God didn't. He allowed faithful Daniel to be led to the den and thrown in.

Someone of lesser character might have thought, *Why is God silent when I need him? What went wrong? The lion's den is no place for a faithful man of God. Brother, if that is how God rewards faithfulness, I'm not sure I want to serve him. Proverbs 28:20 says that "a faithful man shall abound with blessings." This sure is a strange case of abundant blessings.*

Perhaps he found a spot on the nearest pile of bones and sat down to see what was next on God's agenda. Those daily prayer vigils that Daniel had been keeping all this time had not been prayers of vain repetition. He had been busy praying for the restoration of his people; he had been confessing the sins of his people as his own sin; he had been receiving creative ideas from God as he executed his position as the highest ranking official in the kingdom (Daniel 6:2). No. It had not been a time of ritualistic recitation of prayers but a bonding time with Divinity, a time of building relationship with almighty God.

Daniel understood that the God who made him a ruler in the kingdom was the same God who allowed him to be put into the den. His change in position didn't change God's character. God was still good, all the time, and Daniel believed that. He would wait. The den didn't smell good and the lions were hungry for a meal. Before the lions could take a bite, though, an angel appeared. What was happening?

God had allowed Daniel to be placed in a position where he could be a living demonstration of faith to the whole kingdom of the Medes and Persians. In the process, the king would become a believer, the entire kingdom would know that the God of Israel still reigned, and God would get rid of Daniel's antagonistic co-workers in the process. Daniel's apparent defeat was actually an appointment with victory.

At daybreak, the king scurried down to the den.

"O Daniel, servant of the living God, is thy God, whom thou servest continually, able to deliver thee from the lions?" (Daniel 6:20).

Daniel was alive and joyful. "My God hath sent his angel, and hath shut the lions' mouth, that they have not hurt me," Daniel replied (Daniel 6:22).

What had Daniel and the angel talked about all night? Or had Daniel talked at all? Perhaps the angel brought such a strong atmosphere of heaven with him, such an anointed peace that Daniel melted in his presence and slept the deep healing, refreshing, rejuvenating sleep of heaven. No one actually knows. But, that night, the den of destruction became a sacred sanctuary.

When Daniel was taken from the den, he was unhurt. I don't believe he ever had nightmares as a result of the incident. I don't believe he needed counseling to help him forgive the selfish act of the self-centered king and the rejection of his peers. I don't believe he needed time off to rest and get over the trauma of the awful night that hungry lions eyed him and he slept with dead men's bones. When Daniel was taken up out of the den, "no manner of hurt was found upon him, because he believed in his God" (Daniel 6:23).

Our own circumstances of life may change dramatically. We may not understand the situations in which we find ourselves. But, like Daniel, there is a divine factor that can protect us from the hurt that the devil means to inflict. It is a living, daily relationship of faith in God.

FAITH IS ENOUGH
by Fern Willner

Faith may not solve all my problems,
Give all the knowledge I seek;
Faith may not give me beforehand,
Answers or words I should speak.
But,

Faith doesn't leave people battered,
Scarred by the problems of life;
Faith doesn't leave people wounded,
Damaged with hurts from the strife.

Yes, I may cry in the night time,
But, there's a God holding me;
Yes, I may doubt where I'm going,
But, there's a God who can see.

Faith is a lifeline to heaven,
As I meet with God in prayer;
Faith calms my storms, stills my thinking,
Tells me that He's always there.

Faith is the strength of believers,
Faith is the pathway secure;
Faith is a hand holding God's hand,
Faith is a heart that is pure.

Like Daniel, God has planned and provided for his children to emerge from the challenges of life unharmed. That isn't possible if we are attempting to live an overcoming life on episodes of faith. It is possible when, like Daniel, we consistently choose a relationship of faith.

Daniel's exploits were not the consequence of positive thinking; they were the fruit of intimate relationship. Nothing is greater. He spoke positively because he was positive, he stayed connected to the source of positive power.

Psalm 34:19 shows us clearly that faith is not an escape from life's challenges. It says, "Many are the afflictions of the righteous: but the LORD delivereth him out of them all." Faith will not keep us from afflictions, but it will keep our souls and spirits from being harmed by those afflictions. Isaiah 26:13,14 describes this miracle of restoration in its song of confidence in God. It says:

> O LORD our God, other lords beside thee have had dominion over us: but by thee only will we make mention of thy name. They are dead, they shall not live; they are deceased, they shall not rise: therefore hast thou visited and destroyed them, and made all their memory to perish.

Those old enemy lords can no longer challenge the present for "they are destroyed." They cannot threaten our future for "they are dead, they shall not live."

Paul was so secure in his freedom from the past that he said, "For I have learned, in whatsoever state I am, therewith to be content" (Philippians 4:11). Adversity, to him, was not a threatening resurrection of the old lords, because old things were dead. So, whether he was shivering in a foreign prison cell as a result of sharing the gospel, or enjoying fine dining as a guest in the king's palace, there was a powerful force which brought all of life's circumstances into a common perspective; it was his daily, living relationship of faith in God.

The enemy of our souls will always see to it that there is something more necessary or enticing than time spent with God. Can we substitute less time for quality time? We can try, but I'm afraid we will find ourselves in the same difficulty that the children of Israel did when they tried to gather manna at their own convenience. When they neglected to gather, they suffered, and when they tried to gather extra, they found it couldn't be preserved.

Faith must be exercised daily. Today's faith is born of today's relationship and will meet today's needs. Tomorrow's needs will be different and the person who tries to make yesterday's faith meet tomorrow's needs will eventually fall into confusion and failure. "Behold, now is the accepted time; Behold, now is the day of salvation," Paul says in 2 Corinthians 6:2. Hebrews also shows us that faith is a "now" experience. "Now faith is," we read in Hebrews 11:1.

At no point in our walk of faith are we able to receive enough enrichment, enlightenment, or deliverance to make a new beginning with God's help and then take over the direction of our own lives. "Are ye so foolish?" Galatians says, "having begun in the Spirit, are ye now made perfect by the flesh?" (Galatians 3:3).

King Solomon is a sad example of such an attempt. The young king had a divine encounter at Gibeon. God met him in a dream and answered the cry of his heart for wisdom (1 Kings 3:11). But Solomon didn't maintain his relationship with God. He let other things take his time and attention. Solomon began his reign as the wisest man who ever lived and ended it in shame.

> For it came to pass, when Solomon was old, that his wives turned away his heart after other gods: and his heart was not perfect with the LORD his God, as was the heart of David his father. For Solomon went after Ashtoreth the goddess of the Zidonians, and after Milcom the abomination of the Ammonites. And Solomon did evil in the sight of the LORD.
> –1 Kings 11:4–6

You don't have to be a missionary, sacrificing all of your personal possessions and living in daily need of God's provision, to live a life of faith. You can be a government official like Daniel, or a national leader like Solomon, both of whom were wealthy and famous. Great faith is not measured by our possessions or the lack of them. It is not measured by our honor or the lack of it. It is measured by relationship. Daniel's faith spun such a cord of communication between him and heaven that he was addressed as "a man greatly beloved." Out of that relationship he was touched and strengthened, and shown "that which is noted in the scripture of truth" (Daniel 10:21).

May our faith lead us into such a relationship. May we become the beloved of God. May we find release from fear. May we receive an impartation of peace and strength from the Lord. Faith in God will deliver us, and faith in God will one day lead us triumphantly into the safe haven of our everlasting reward with God.

In those early days in Quakertown, Connecticut, God and I began a safari designed to teach me principles of faith. He let me make the decision as to whether or not I wanted to continue during the rough times, but I discovered that when I did, we went to incredible places. I also discovered that the enemy often tries to frighten us away from God's intended blessings by posting false road signs. For instance, he may put danger signs where God directs us to proceed to a miracle, or high speed signs where God wants us to proceed with caution. Faith is a gift, but its fruit is no accident. It is the result of a committed, loving relationship with God. That is when faith is enough!

REFERENCES

[1] Amy Carmichael, *Gold Cord* (Fort Washington, PA: Christian Literature Crusade, 1992) p. 190.

[2] Amy Carmichael, *Gold Cord* (Fort Washington, PA: Christian Literature Crusade, 1992) p. 233.

[3] James Strong, S.T.D., 11.D., "kept," *Abdingdon's Strong's Exhaustive Concordance of the Bible*, Forty-third Printing, 1984 ed.: p. 561 (Main Concordance); p. 76 (Greek Dictionary).

[4] *Hymns of the Christian Life* (Harrisburg, Pennsylvania: Christian Publications, Inc., 1962) p. 316.

[5] "Diamonds," *The World Book Encyclopedia*, Vol. 5, 1990 ed.: pp. 186–189.

[6] Mrs. Charles E. Cowan, *Springs in the Valley* (Minneapolis, Minnesota: World Wide Publications, 1980) pp. 186–187.

[7] David Werner, "Where There Is No Doctor: A Village Health Care Handbook. Hesperian Foundation, May 1992.

[8] John W. Kitchens, "George Washington Carver," *The World Book Encyclopedia*, Vol. 3, 1990 ed.: pp. 268–269.

[9] Larry Dossey, M.D., "Does Prayer Heal?" *Reader's Digest*, September 1996: pp. 27–32.

[10] Thomas H. Weller, "Schistosomiasis," *World Book Encyclopedia*, Vol. 17, 1990 ed.: p. 176.

[11] Hartmut Walter, "Lake Tanganyika," *World Book Encyclopedia*, Vol. 12, 1990 ed.: p. 48.

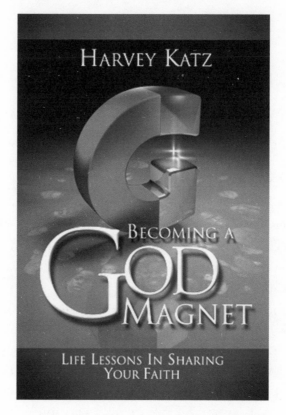

Harvey Katz

BECOMING A GOD MAGNET
Life Lessons In Sharing Your Faith

If you've ever had your heart pound as you opened your mouth to share your faith . . . this book is for you!

Many Christians view evangelism as a chore, a responsibility they dread. Harvey Katz has good news: God wants to attract people to Jesus Christ through your life . . . in a relaxed, natural, joyful way. In this book, Harvey Katz will show you how.

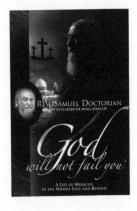